POETIC FORM
AN INTRODUCTION

David Caplan

Ohio Wesleyan University

PEARSON
Longman

New York   San Francisco   Boston
London   Toronto   Sydney   Tokyo   Singapore   Madrid
Mexico City   Munich   Paris   Cape Town   Hong Kong   Montreal

Editor-in-Chief: Joseph Terry
Executive Marketing Manager: Ann Stypuloski
Production Manager: Denise Phillip
Project Coordination, Text Design, and Electronic Page Makeup:
    WestWords, Inc.
Cover Design Manager: Wendy Ann Fredericks
Cover Designer: Kay Petronio
Cover Photo: © Sotiris Blatsis
Manufacturing Manager: Mary Fischer
Printer and Binder: Courier Corporation
Cover Printer: Coral Graphic Services

For permission to use copyrighted material, grateful acknowledgment is made to
the copyright holders on pp. 251–252, which are hereby made part of this
copyright page.

Library of Congress Cataloging-in-Publication Data

Caplan, David
    Poetic form : an introduction / David Caplan.
        p. cm.
    ISBN 0-321-19820-4
    1. Poetry—History and criticism. 2. Poetics. 3. Literary form. I. Title.
PN1300.C37 2006
809.1—dc22

                                                2006018970

Copyright © 2007 by Pearson Education, Inc.

All rights reserved. No part of this publication may be reproduced, stored in a
retrieval system, or transmitted, in any form or by any means, electronic,
mechanical, photocopying, recording, or otherwise, without the prior written
permission of the publisher. Printed in the United States.

Visit us at www.ablongman.com

ISBN 0-321-19820-4

1 2 3 4 5 6 7 8 9 10—CRW—09 08 07 06

CONTENTS

12   CLASSICAL IMITATIONS   185

13   FORMS OF FREE VERSE   195

14   PROSE POETRY   226

15   NEW FORMS AND OLD   237

ACKNOWLEDGMENTS

I want to thank my editor Joe Terry and his editorial assistant Christine Halsey for their aid and counsel, and for Dana Gioia for the suggestion that I attempt this project. Thanks also to Charles Bernstein, Rich Cureton, Dick Davis, R. S. Gwynn, Timothy Steele, William Logan, my colleagues Don Lateiner and Lee Fratantuono, who offered helpful comments that helped me to clarify individual chapters, and Pat McCutcheon, who supervised the copyediting of the manuscript. Amanda French supplied helpful supplementary material for the chapter on the villanelle, based on her considerable research in the form. As always, I appreciate the help that Mara Amster, Kevin Clarke, Ana M. Echevarría-Morales, Mike Esler, Bob Olmstead, John Picker, and Nelson Tarr shared, as I muddled through matters formal and informal.

This book is dedicated to my parents, whose love and support begins with the first example.

INTRODUCTION TO THEORIES OF FORM

When I was a boy, my mother bounced me on her knee and chanted:

> Trot, trot to Boston,
> Trot, trot to Lynn,
> Watch out little David,
> Or else you'll fall in!

For a grand finish she shouted, "Weeee!" and dangled me from her lap.

My mother did not randomly bounce me. She bounced me four times on the odd lines and three on the even ones. She kept to the pattern of the song, which I will reproduce by capitalizing the syllables where I received a bounce and the language a little emphasis:

> TROT, TROT, to BOS-TON,
> TROT, TROT to LYNN,
> Watch OUT LITTle DA-VID,
> Or ELSE you'll FALL IN!

We know a lot more about poetic form than we think we do. We experience it before we can speak; we hear it on commercials, on the playground, and at sporting events. When a crowd chants, they do so in form. In college the basketball player Marcus Camby outplayed his rival Tim Duncan. At every road game that followed, the opposing crowd mocked Duncan with the singsong taunt, "MARcus CAMby!" When New Yorkers turn against a coach, they make their opinion known by chanting words fit into the same pattern: "FIre CHAney!" (and Donald Chaney, the coach in question, was soon unemployed).

Formal elements distinguish poetry from prose. Poetry foregrounds these structures to a greater degree than prose, making form expressive, whether of an emotion, a tone, or an attitude. Form, though, does not exist simply to support an extractable meaning. To see how, read the following poem, a deer song of the Yacqui Indians, silently to yourself:

First you just look,
    later you will find, find.
First you just look,
    later you will find, find.

First you just look,   5
    later you will find, find.
First you just look,
    later you will find, find.

Over there, I, in an opening
    in the flower-covered grove,   10
        I went out,
            then you will find, find.
First you just look,
    later you will find, find.

Now read the poem again, this time aloud.

Like most poems, the deer song demands to be heard so its patterns can be felt, not merely noted. As prose, the poem's circularity might seem maddening. When the poem is read aloud or performed, the form extends an invitation. It asks the reader to enter the poem's rhythms, to delight in the arrangement of language into a pattern. The repetitions gain intensity and interest; the poem's incremental development foregrounds the process of looking, not the thing found. If I were to ask a hunter for advice, I would seek practical information; namely, the most effective way to track and shoot prey. Poetry works differently. Verse form directs the reader's attention to the verbal articulation, not the expressed idea. Demanding a certain mindfulness, it dramatizes the intensity of looking.

Poetic form structures language into a reproducible pattern. A reproducible pattern means that someone else can duplicate it. The resulting poem may strike readers as more or less successful than the original that inspired it; regardless, the two examples share the same form. When the poet Seamus Heaney was a boy in Ireland, he and his classmates "used to fling at one another" a "scurrilous and sectarian" rhyme:

> Up the long ladder and down the short rope
> To hell with King Billy and God bless the Pope.

To which [Heaney adds] the answer was:

> Up with King William and down with the Pope.

As these relatively simple examples suggest, poetic form possesses a remarkable flexibility. The same form can express contradictory emotions and attitudes. One rhyme blesses the Pope and calls for King's death; the response borrows the same form to express the opposite values. It is a mistake, then, to assume that all poems in one form are alike. Instead, they might differ more than they correspond. Almost all parodies, for instance, share the form with the poem they satirize.

This is not to say that any one poetic form can do everything. A group chant would struggle to express a quiet intimacy, just as a limerick would hardly convey most kinds of sincere admiration. Classical rhetoricians linked form to genre, arguing that certain kinds of literature required certain meters. Aristotle asserted that "nature itself," not literary convention, governed the formal choices that poets made. "No one has ever composed a poem on a great scale in any other than heroic verse," he observed. "Nature itself . . . teaches the choice of the proper measure." Poets, though, continually find new uses for forms, adapting them to suit their purposes. History has proven Aristotle wrong: poems on a great scale have employed a number of meters other than heroic. Poets change the forms they discover, especially when claimed from different cultures, languages, and historical periods.

The chapters that follow discuss the language's main forms and their uses. They provide clear, evocative examples to illustrate complex effects. To understand poetic form, we must understand poetic *forms:* the history and features that distinguish a sestina from a ballad, a sonnet from an epigram. This idea organizes this book. Accordingly, the chapters represent how specific forms work.

Virtually all of our language's forms originated outside English. As a form moves from one language to another, it inevitably changes, drawing from new linguistic resources and changed cultural contexts. This extreme example illustrates a general truth. Forms are always in a state of flux, drawing from what has been previously done in the form and adjusting it to a different set of circumstances. A poem presents a snapshot, an image of what the form seems capable of to a certain person living in a particular time and place. Each chapter begins with a poem that raises important issues about the form under discussion. Often I sketch the circumstances surrounding the composition in order to suggest the pressures that inspired the choices the poet made.

As the chapters will suggest, each form offers a shifting range of possibility, not a fixed agenda. Just because the poets have used a form in a particular way, it does not follow that future generations will continue similarly. In fact the opposite is more likely: forms find new inflections and purposes or they retain only an historical appeal.

Form is worth considering from at least two points of view: the author's and the reader's. "[I]f technique is of no interest to the writer," Marianne Moore observed, "I doubt that the writer is an artist." Poets care about technique because it allows them to transform an impulse into a work of art. Yet form does not help poets only to write what they want. It allows them to express ideas and emotions that they could not otherwise imagine. Form, H. L. Hix observes, "enables the poet to defy her own limitations of intelligence, knowledge, and point of view and thus to discover and reveal what she did not already know." A "silly" person (as Auden called Yeats) can write a wise poem because it expresses more than he or she intends. Form can impede the author's usual associations and suggest other options that he or she might pursue. It inspires what Hix calls "alchemy"; it helps the author to create knowledge instead of repeating what he or she "already know[s]."

This process occurs during the innumerable calculations that an author must make. A poet drafts a pleasant but unexceptional start to a rhyming couplet, "License my roving hands, and let them go." The rhyme "go" presents a host of possible pairs, "woe," "show," "although," "foe," and so on. Each suggests certain syntactical, rhetorical, and thematic possibilities. A conjunction such as "although" would raise some kind of qualification. (When "although" appears midway in a sentence, we know that what follows will contradict the sentence's opening.)

"Woe" might introduce an unattractively self-pitying tone. "Foe" would repeat an epithet used a few lines before. The poet tries a few more rhymes. It would be easy to start the next line with "below," "License my roving hands, and let them go / Below your shoulders . . ." but the form requires that the rhyme appear at the line's end. This difficulty suggests an opportunity: to get to the rhyme "below," the line may linger a bit. It could trace and retrace the route the speaker's hands would take across his beloved's body. Addressing a technical challenge, the author discovers an unusual grammatical construction—a string of five prepositions—with an arrestingly sexy rhythm and movement, "License my roving hands, and let them go / Before, behind, between, above, below."

In addition to inspiring individual lines, form helps poets to revise their drafts. Faced with a promising but unsatisfactory start, an author may recast it into a different form. If the draft has nine syllables per line, the revision might have seven. The need to remove two syllables from each line requires numerous alterations to the poem's syntax, imagery, and rhetoric. If successful, this technique might introduce an economy that the earlier version lacks, clarifying the draft's most interesting suggestions. Recognizing that a change in form can inspire a new style, many poets dissatisfied with their careers try different forms, exploring the new opportunities and obstacles they offer. "The only way you can follow a poet's evolution," Joseph Brodsky asserted in a characteristic overstatement, "is by his prosody, his meters."

Because poets choose the forms they use, a poet's choice of form can define his or her enterprise. Invoking the form's masters, a new poem might challenge its predecessors or pay them homage. Or it might do both:

> When I have fears that I may cease to be
> Before my pen has glean'd my teeming brain,
> Before high-piled books, in charact'ry,
> Hold like rich garners the full-ripen'd grain;
> When I behold, upon the night's starr'd face,   5
> Huge cloudy symbols of a high romance,
> And think that I may never live to trace
> Their shadows, with the magic hand of chance;
> And when I feel, fair creature of an hour!
> That I shall never look upon thee more,   10
> Never have relish in the faery power
> Of unreflecting love!—then on the shore
> Of the wide world I stand alone, and think
> Till love and fame to nothingness do sink.

In chapter four I will discuss sonnets at greater length. For now it is important to note that Keats rather self-consciously shares the form with Shakespeare, a poet whose work he greatly admired. In one of his most celebrated sonnets, Shakespeare declares, "Not marble, nor the gilded monuments / Of princes, shall outlive this powerful rhyme." Keats does not prophesize his poetry's immortality. He expresses a fear that he may write little of lasting value. The borrowed form mitigates this despair, invoking Shakespeare's authority as well as his intimidating example. The form places Keats in the company of those authors whose ranks he yearns to join, suggesting that the young poet has started to achieve his ambition.

As Keats's invocation of Shakespeare suggests, poetic forms carry affinities and expectations. "By the act of writing in verse," William Wordsworth maintained, "an Author makes a formal engagement that he will gratify certain habits of associations." According to Wordsworth, a form makes a "promise" that it will fulfill the expectations it raises. Reading a sequence of four-line stanzas, readers assume that the next stanza will repeat this pattern. If it doesn't, they will wonder why. If the elegy rhymes its first and fourth lines and its second and third, the form introduces Tennyson's "In Memoriam" as a point of comparison and departure. The study of poetic form makes readers more alert to the expectations that a poem raises; it clarifies the process by which a poem fulfills or frustrates the desires it arouses.

Only dull poetry, though, precisely meets its readers' expectations. Just as groundbreaking poems create new associations, forms fall in and out of fashion as taste changes. All poems are written in some form. The form may be hard to classify because we lack a good critical terminology or because its elements are difficult to identify. Just as poets who claim to be "for form" generally mean that they favor certain forms and dislike others, poets who stand "against form" typically reject currently fashionable kinds of form. A writer who hates sonnets, for instance, may live in a sonnet-crazy era. One option would be to invent new forms or to import them from other arts, discourses, and cultures. Poets have composed poems in the form of the menus or based on musical progressions, computer programs, and mathematical formulae. Such forms structure language into reproducible patterns; such forms are poetic when used in poems.

Form might be thought of as the poem's architecture, presenting the most visible structures of support. By necessity the same kind of building inspires a host of architectural styles. A house designed by Frank Gehry hardly looks like Thomas Jefferson's Monticello or Frank Lloyd Wright's

Falling Water. Similarly, the same form invites different poetic styles. Hardy and Milton shared certain meters, but few readers would confuse their poems. Hardy modeled his style after the gothic churches he loved, full of pleasant irregularities, while Milton's verse shares affinities with the Italian baroque. When the two poets employed the same form, the shared structures clarify their differences. In this way, form's impersonal demands can reveal a writer's personality. The apparently humble effort to find an interesting rhyme or a graceful end to a stanza has inspired singular works. America's most arrestingly odd poet, Emily Dickinson, wrote in hymn meters, a form that encouraged her idiosyncrasy, her profound weirdness.

The more familiar a form's conventions grow, the more they can be played with, frustrated and varied for expressive effect. In the mid-eighteenth century an anonymous poet published an untitled poem:

> Dear Phoebus, hear my only vow;
> If e'er you loved me, hear me now.
> That charming youth—but idle fame
> Is ever so inclined to blame—
> These men will turn it into a jest;   5
> I'll tell the rhymes and drop the rest:
> ——— ——— ——— desire,
> ——— ——— ——— fire,
> ——— ——— ——— lie,
> ——— ——— ——— thigh,   10
> ——— ——— ——— wide,
> ——— ——— ——— ride,
> ——— ——— ——— night,
> ——— ——— ——— delight.

"I'll tell the rhymes and drop the rest," the poem mischievously declares. As it slyly implies, these rhymes "tell" nearly the whole story; not only the depicted affair but also the kind of poet who would use such trite language to describe it. The anonymous poet uses these stupid rhymes smartly, quoting rather than singing the clichés (unlike certain postmillennial pop stars who unblushingly rhyme "fire" with "desire"). Just as the poem can play with these bad rhymes because they are so familiar, it departs from the opening lines' form, substituting typographical lines for words, because the reader knows the conventions they replace.

This technique establishes a visual pattern. Existing on the page, it needs to be *seen*. The rhyme my mother sang to me needed to be *heard*

and *felt*. The bounces she gave me marked the form. As with many childhood encounters of poetry, the rhyme presented a physical, bodily pleasure. Form need not emphasize either the visual or the auditory; instead
it might explore the interplay between them:

> Fair daffodils, we weep to see
> You haste away so very soon;
> As yet the early-rising sun
> Has not attain'd another noon.
> Stay, stay, until the hasting day   5
> Has run but to the evensong;
> And, having prayed together, we
> Will happily go with you along.

This is dull verse, plodding and not very inventive. The poem I have
weakened, Robert Herrick's "To Daffodils," is much more interesting,
though I have made only a few small revisions:

> Fair daffodils, we weep to see
>   You haste away so soon;
> As yet the early-rising sun
>   Has not attained his noon.
>   Stay, stay   5
> Until the hasting day
>   Has run
>   But to the evensong;
> And, having prayed together, we
>   Will go with you along.   10
>
> We have short time to stay as you,
>   We have as short a spring;
> As quick a growth to meet decay,
>   As you, or anything.
>   We die   15
> As your hours do, and dry
>   Away
>   Like to the summer's rain;
> Or as the pearls of morning's dew,
>   Ne'er to be found again.   20

Rearranged into a simpler form, the words lose intensity and interest. The familiar argument remains largely the same, but the poem's limber, agile lines grow sluggish. Herrick's poem offers a very different experience. Regarding it on the page, we see a striking pattern of shorter and longer lines. Reading it aloud, we encounter a voice as it moves through these elaborate stanzas. Rhymes fall in consecutive lines and in nearly the greatest distance that the stanza allows, the opening and the penultimate lines. The first kind of rhyme, a couplet, is easily heard; a rhyme that takes nine lines to repeat must be seen on the page. Consisting of one sentence, the first stanza is especially acrobatic, pausing at the end of some lines and racing through others.

"Art to disguise art" is not Herrick's motto. A show off, he introduces conspicuous difficulties so he might overcome them. Elaborate restrictions inspire skillful displays; the freedom needs restraint. Describing playground basketball, the novelist John Edgar Wideman calls it "an imaginary labyrinth testing how ingeniously, elegantly players can actually work their way out." The poem's movements evoke the bodily pleasure of graceful movement, of a diver spinning in the air three times before tucking into the water or a schoolyard player smoothly whipping a pass around her back.

Whether Herrick's poem delights or annoys you might suggest your assumptions about form. Those who view it as a game generally favor elaborate forms whose elaborate restrictions inspire virtuoso flourishes. No one wants to watch a game of tic-tac-toe, no matter how talented the players; chess aficionados travel continents to watch grand masters compete. Other theories argue that form arises from a compulsion to arrange disparate experience into a shapely pattern, "a rage for blessed order" (in Wallace Stevens's phrase). This approach often emphasizes the psychological effects that an impersonal form achieves; it "gives," I. A. Richards writes, "both poet and reader a firm support, a fixed point of orientation in the indefinitely vast world of possible rhythms; it has . . . [the] virtues of a psychological order." If form provides "a fixed point of orientation," a clearly defined kind might seem appealing.

A poem's form, though, need not stay constant. It might expand or contract, shifting from line to line or stanza to stanza. Some poems suggest clear connections between their arguments and forms, while others use form to exert a counter force to the argument, a point of tension.

Writing around 400 A.D., St. Augustine asserted a classically stern conception of form. "The very art by which I composed poems," he maintained, "did not have different laws in different places but was always the same." From its start poetry in English has lacked this certainty; it generated a host of theories and forms. (One of the language's very first treatises on form opens with the observation, "Quot homines, tot Sententiae," meaning, "There are as many opinions as people.") To understand our subject, form in English, we must remain open to its many arts. To speak of "laws" or "rules" implies that form has regulations that cannot be broken except under threat of penalty. Poems in English have strategies, tactics that they employ and, in some happy cases, invent.

2

METER

Descending from the Greek word for measure, a "meter" measures a poetic line; it counts certain elements. To do so, a meter draws from spoken language but should not be confused with it. Speakers in casual conversation employ some of the techniques this chapter will discuss, but no one truly talks or thinks in meter. Meter manipulates the resources that a language provides, transforming them into a stylized performance.

Speakers of English stress certain syllables and not others; they emphasize certain syllables more than others. My name, "David Caplan," receives a stress in the first syllable of each word and not on the second. A non-native speaker, say, a Frenchman, might shift the stress to the second syllable of my first name, saying something akin to "DavEED." The name of the poet "Emily Dickinson" also receives a stress on the first syllable of each word, but two unstressed syllables follow, not one as in my name. Other names are less rigidly pronounced. The author Henry David Thoreau most likely pronounced his last name with an accent on the first syllable, as in the adjective "thorough." Most contemporary readers of his work shift the accent to the second syllable, saying "ThoROW."

Stress also distinguishes some words that share the same spelling. When stressed on the first syllable, "reject" can be a noun, as in the insult, "You are such a reject!" When stressed on the second syllable, "reject" is a verb: "We must reject this application." The poet Wendy Cope has a little fun with this quirk of language:

> He would refuse to put the refuse out.
> The contents of the bin would start to smell.
> How could she be content?

With the stress falling on its second syllable, "refuse" is a verb, meaning to decline or refuse; when the stress moves to its first syllable, it changes into a noun, a synonym for garbage. Similarly, in the phrase "[t]he contents of the bin," "contents" is a noun, with the first syllable stressed. In the question, "How could she be content?" content is an adjective, receiving a stress on its second syllable.

The stresses that words receive also change according to the rhetorical situation. Consider the seemingly simple statement, "Don't go there." An irate speaker might stress all three words, bellowing: "*Don't go there!*" An angry but self-possessed speaker might say the same words more sharply, pointedly interrupting, "*Don't* go there." Other situations would suggest different emphases. "Don't go *there*," one might say of a particularly sensitive subject, "*That's* off limits."

Background and Structure of *Accentual Meter*

The oldest of English's three main meters, *accentual meter* regulates the number of accents per line. Each line, in other words, has the same number of accents. Old and Middle English verse typically contains four stresses in each line; it also features a mid-line pause and a pattern of alliteration. A modern translation of "Beowulf" approximates this meter's effect:

> Now the hard helmet,   hammered with gold,
> Must be stripped of its plating;   the polishers sleep.

Accentual verse has only one requirement, though: each line must keep to the same number of accents. When scanning lines of accentual verse, the most common method is to place the mark " ´ " above stressed syllables and " ˘ " above unstressed. Using this method we might scan a child's irreverent grace:

Bless the meat,

Damn the skin.

Open your mouth

And cram it in.

As this scansion shows, each line has two stresses. The stresses appear in different places and the number of unstressed syllables changes, but only slightly. Each of the first two lines has three syllables while each of the last two lines has four.

An accentual poem might include a greater range of unaccented syllables. Introducing his poem "Christabel," Samuel Coleridge observes that it relies on "[c]ounting in each line the accents, not the syllables. Though the latter vary from seven to twelve, yet in each line the accents will be found to be only four." The poem opens:

Tis the middle of night by the castle clock,

And the owls have awakened the crowing cock;

Tu—whit!—Tu—whoo!

"Christabel" sometimes violates the "new principle" that Coleridge impudently claims he invented. (Accentual meter, as we have seen, enjoys a long history.) More interestingly Coleridge argues that that "Christabel" introduces different numbers of syllables neither randomly nor for "convenience, but in correspondence with some transition in the nature of the imagery or passion." Especially if the reader allows the poem a little leeway, this passage includes a rare construction: four consecutive stresses. In a short line punctuated with two exclamation points, the meter adds the equivalent of two more, amplifying an animal-like noise, a cacophony of owls and cocks.

Confirming the meter's rarity in the modern age, accentual verse's next master also claimed to have rediscovered the form after centuries of disuse. Writing of accentual verse—or, as he called it, "sprung rhythm," Gerald Manley Hopkins maintained: "it has ceased to be used since the Elizabethan age." Hopkins found many precedents in popular verse, "hints of it in music, in nursery rhymes, and popular jingles."

The meter that poets choose suggest their notion of how their work should be performed, how readers should hear and pronounce the lines and imagine the speakers. "Prosody," Ezra Pound observed, "is the articulation of the total sound of the poem." Just as a meter can emphasize certain words, it can suggest the sound—and sounds—a poem makes. Hopkins wanted "not reading with the eye but loud, leisurely, poetical (not rhetorical) recitation, with long rests, long dwells on the rhyme and other marked syllables and so on." In short, the god-haunted Jesuit wanted the kind of performance that contemporary rappers might best give.

Such artists favor four-stress lines because the form's relative looseness gives them the ability to compress certain syllables and elongate others, as when a member of The Roots brags in lines that echo the nursery rhymes that Hopkins loved:

Yo, one, two, one-two one-two

That's how we usually start, once again it's the Thought

The Dalai Lama of the mic, the prime minister Thought.

MORE WORKS IN *ACCENTUAL METER*

WILLIAM BUTLER YEATS
Easter, 1916

I have met them at close of day
Coming with vivid faces
From counter or desk among grey
Eighteenth-century houses.
I have passed with a nod of the head   5
Or polite meaningless words,

Or have lingered awhile and said
Polite meaningless words,
And thought before I had done
Of a mocking tale or a gibe   10
To please a companion
Around the fire at the club,
Being certain that they and I
But lived where motley is worn:
All changed, changed utterly: 15
A terrible beauty is born.

That woman's days were spent
In ignorant good-will,
Her nights in argument
Until her voice grew shrill.   20
What voice more sweet than hers
When, young and beautiful,
She rode to harriers?
This man had kept a school
And rode our wingèd horse;   25
This other his helper and friend
Was coming into his force;
He might have won fame in the end,
So sensitive his nature seemed,
So daring and sweet his thought.   30
This other man I had dreamed
A drunken, vainglorious lout.
He had done most bitter wrong
To some who are near my heart,
Yet I number him in the song;   35
He, too, has resigned his part
In the casual comedy;
He, too, has been changed in his turn,
Transformed utterly:
A terrible beauty is born.   40

Hearts with one purpose alone
Through summer and winter seem
Enchanted to a stone

To trouble the living stream.
The horse that comes from the road   45
The rider, the birds that range
From cloud to tumbling cloud,
Minute by minute they change;
A shadow of cloud on the stream
Changes minute by minute;   50
A horse-hoof slides on the brim,
And a horse plashes within it;
The long-legged moor-hens dive,
And hens to moor-cocks call;
Minute by minute they live: 55
The stone's in the midst of all.

Too long a sacrifice
Can make a stone of the heart.
O when may it suffice?
That is Heaven's part, our part   60
To murmur name upon name,
As a mother names her child
When sleep at last has come
On limbs that had run wild.
What is it but nightfall?   65
No, no, not night but death;
Was it needless death after all?
For England may keep faith
For all that is done and said.
We know their dream; enough   70
To know they dreamed and are dead;
And what if excess of love
Bewildered them till they died?
I write it out in a verse—
MacDonagh and MacBride   75
And Connolly and Pearse
Now and in time to be,
Wherever green is worn,
Are changed, changed utterly:
A terrible beauty is born.   80

Background and Structure of *Accentual-Syllabic Meter*

Accentual syllabic is the language's principle meter, both the most common and the most flexible. Until recently it has dominated the poetry, showing a great range of effects and accommodating nearly every major poet in the language. Accentual-syllabic counts the number of both the accented and unaccented syllables. In the second half of the sixteenth century, Chidiock Tichborne was sentenced to death because he participated in a plot to murder Queen Elizabeth. Awaiting execution, he wrote the one poem that he is known for. Untitled, it starts:

My prime | of youth | is but | a frost | of cares,

My feast | of joy | is but | a dish | of pain,

My crop | of corn | is but | a field | of tares,

And all | my good | is but | vain hope | of gain

The day | is past, | and yet | I saw | no sun,   5

And now | I live, | and now | my life | is done.

To scan this accentual-syllabic poem, I have marked the unaccented syllables as " ˘ " and the accented ones as " ´ ." Both elements are marked because both define accentual-syllabic meter. These lines are iambic pentameter, which means they adhere to a pattern of an unstressed syllable followed by an stressed syllable (iambic) five times in each line (pentameter). The term, "foot," refers to the smallest metrical unit; an iambic foot (also called an iamb) consists of an unstressed syllable followed by a stressed one. Following convention, I have used the mark, " | " to separate each foot. The first foot of the fifth line, for instance, consists of the words, "The day," with "The" unstressed and "day" stressed.

Tichborne's gloomy, fatalistic self-elegy sticks to this pattern with dogged persistence. Syntax and phrasing aligns with meter; no word extends from one metrical foot into the next. None can, because the poem employs only monosyllabic words. "My prime of youth is but a frost of cares," Tichborne writes, not, say:

My yo**u**th | f**u**l pr**i**me is but a frost of cares.

A series of grammatical parallelisms (adjective, noun, preposition, object of preposition) and mid-line pauses further accentuate the meter, snapping each syllable into its metrical position.

A remarkable poem but a poor model, Tichborne's elegy represents the best instance of a limited practice. Tichborne's self-elegy makes meter and rhythm coincide. Rhythm, in the sense that I mean, refers to the patterns that occur in spoken language, culture, and in bodies. To master a new language, one must learn its particular rhythms, not just the meaning of its words. Meter refers to an abstract pattern of (in the case of accentual-syllabic poetry) accent and unaccented syllables. As much as possible, Tichborne's verse heightens the difference between a stressed and unstressed syllable. He made it difficult to place *any* emphasis on an unstressed syllable without sounding foolish.

The poets who developed iambic pentameter trusted the meter's suppleness; it need not be rigidly propped up with syntax, grammar, and a mid-line pause. The meter instead might play with these elements. Such work had already been undertaken by the time of Tichborne's elegy, as, most notably, Surrey, Sidney, and Spenser, explored the meter's flexibility. Building on their accomplishment, Shakespeare demonstrated the connection between meter and rhythm, with lines that have grown so familiar we might overlook their daring:

To be, | or not | to be, | that is | the question:

Whether | 'tis nob | ler in | the mind | to suffer

The slings | and ar | rows of | outrag | eous fortune,

Or to | take arms | against | a sea | of troubles,

And by | oppos | ing end | them. To die, | to sleep—   5

Performing the monologue's first line, some actors emphasize "that," not "is":

> To be, or not to be, | thát ĭs | the question

Hamlet, though, does not suddenly realize the nature of his dilemma; he names an already-defined "question." Read this way, the first line resembles Tichborne's verse as each phrase coincides with a metrical foot:

> Tŏ bé, | ŏr nót | tŏ bé, | thăt iś | thĕ quéstĭon:

> Thĕ dáy | ĭs pást, | ănd yét | Ĭ sáw | nŏ sún,

There is one subtle difference. While Tichborne ends every line with a stressed syllable, Shakespeare adds an extra unstressed syllable, an adjustment so subtle that a reader might not notice it. Generalizing about this technique, George Puttenham observes that the accent "doth so drowne the last [syllable], as he seemeth to passe away in maner unpronounced." Other Tudor poets, though, neglected this technique; Surrey and Gasciogne, for instance, "rarely used" the extra-metrical ending. The extra syllable softens the end of Shakespeare's line; it rounds it into the next.

The passage's next lines play with degrees of stress. That is, they follow the same abstract pattern but show an understanding that, to count as unstressed, syllables need not be wholly unstressed, they need only to receive less emphasis than the surrounding syllables. To count as stressed, syllables likewise need only receive more stress than the surrounding syllables. Exploiting this principle, the meter approaches the rhythms of spoken language. Consider the line:

> Whether | 'tĭs nóbl | ĕr ín | thĕ mĭnd to suffer

Surrounded by two very weak syllables—namely, the second syllable in "nobler" and "the"—"in" counts as stressed, even though it receives less stress than "'tis," which counts as unstressed because it precedes the harder stress of the first syllable of "nobler." A word's placement, then, influences its metrical status; the same word placed differently might receive a different stress.

An art often mistaken for a science, scansion marks a certain way of hearing a line: an interpretation, not an objective fact. Controversies arise because, instead of simple binaries, metrical poetry generally presents a range of stresses. To account for this complexity, we might rank the levels of stress from one to four, with four as the highest:

3 1   2   3   1 2   1   3   1 3 1
Whether | 'tis nobl | er in | the mind | to suffer

Some feet assert a more emphatic contrast. The first, fourth, and fifth feet, for instance, seem stronger than the second and third. To account for this range, some prosodists use the term "secondary stress" to describe a syllable between accented and unaccented. Regardless of the terminology we use, the crucial point is to recognize that a meter offers an abstract paradigm; individual lines approach this paradigm differently, moving toward and away from it.

The other crucial innovation occurred when poets discovered the second half of this idea, what George Saintsbury called "the secret" of "poetic melody": variation. Iambic pentameter gains rhythmic richness when certain variations are introduced. Instead of causing a metrical collapse, this apparent irregularity enriches the pattern, offering a relief from monotony and a greater expressiveness. The variations *belong* to the pattern, so long as it can still be heard. They do not break the melody; they complicate and deepen it.

In the four lines that follow, Shakespeare uses three of the five most common substitutions. The opening line uses the most popular substitution, reversing the normal order of the first foot. Instead of an iambic pattern, an unaccented syllable followed by an accented one, the line presents what is called a trochaic substitution:

Whéthĕr | 'tis nobler in the mind to suffer

And not:

Íf ĭt | is nobler in the mind to suffer

Trochaic substitutions appear most frequently at the start of the line, sometimes in a verb that opens the line with a metrical burst:

Dó ăs | the heavens have done, forget your evil

Second only to the first foot, substitutions frequently occur around a mid-line pause:

> But if you hold it fit, | áftĕr | the play

> —Béttĕr | than born, | báptĭzed | and hid away

There are four other kinds common metrical substitutions.

1. An anapest adds an extra unstressed syllable to the start of an iambic foot:

> And by opposing, end | thĕm. Tŏ díe, | to sleep—

> And know | ĭng thăt whát | is not about to be

> Ĭ ceăsed máking journal entries, so what follows

2. A dactyl adds an extra unstressed syllable to the end of a trochaic foot:

> Wínnŏwĭng | the lightsome air with languid plumes

> His children are his pictures, oh they be

> Píctŭrĕs ŏf | him dead . . .

3. A spondee increases the stress of the first syllable in a foot so the two syllables receive approximately the same stress;

> When he | stóod néar | the Russian partisan

> If flattering language all the passions rule

> Than sense, I fear, will be a mere | dúll fóol.

4. A pyrrhic decreases the stress of the stressed syllable so that neither syllable receives a stress. A pyrrhic followed by a spondee is called an ionic foot:

Ŏr tŏ táke arḿs | against a sea of trouble

Let those that merely talk, and never think,

That live | ĭn thĕ wíld án | archy of drink

Certain periods favor some of these substitutions and ignore others. Keeping to a strict syllable count, Augustan poets rarely used the trisyllabic substitutions. Milton liked to elide extra syllables, counting two consecutive open vowels as one because speakers typically slur them together:

As lords, a spacious world, | to our na | tive heaven

More adventurously, Milton exploited a possibility that early English writers largely ignored: that the transitions between lines might enhance the poem's expressive possibilities, instead of simply existing to mark the end of one line unit. Milton's line breaks stage dramas of anticipation and revelation or, as he called it, "the sense variously drawn out from one verse into another, not in the jingling sound of like endings."

Especially in his blank verse, Milton uses line breaks to play with the reader's expectations, as in a scene in *Paradise Lost* when Satan finishes a defiant speech to his comrades in hell:

So having said, a while he stood, expecting
Their universal shout and high applause
To fill his ear, when contrary he hears
On all sides, from innumerable tongues
A dismal universal hiss, the sound   5
Of public scorn . . .

The awfulness of the punishment largely occurs between the lines, where the horrific scene unfolds. The reader discovers along with Satan that God has transformed him and the devils into serpents. The last two lines employ one of Milton's favorite constructions, a noun followed by a line break then a preposition and the object of the preposition: "the sound / Of public scorn." In this peripeteia, the seemingly incomprehensibly bizarre moment reveals divine justice.

Milton's blank verse explores the different ways that sentence patterns can exploit line breaks. Countering syntax and meter, the first sentence of *Paradise Lost* takes 16 verse lines, twice using this grammatical construction. Tichborne's elegy repeats the same grammatical and syntactical arrangement from line to line. Milton's grand sentences wind through lines; the attentive reader witnesses different units—grammatical, rhythmic, syntactic, and metrical—playing with and against each other.

Meter, then, does not exist in isolation but intertwines with the poem's other elements. Instead of using Milton's high Latinate diction, other poets counterpoint meter with more vernacular language. "Poetry," Robert Frost maintained, "plays the rhythms of dramatic speech on the grid of meter." One of his poems starts:

I met a lady from the South who said

The arrangement of words, not the word themselves, define the metrical grid: in this case, iambic pentameter. The first of the following alterations roughens the meter; the second ruins it:

The lady from the South I met said
The lady I met from the South

Poets interested in writing verse that uses "the rhythms of dramatic speech" gravitate to iambic pentameter because it offers the most speechlike meter. Consider these lines from Marilyn Nelson Waniek's "Balance":

She think she something, stuck-up island bitch.
That hoe Diverne think she Marse Tyler's wife

The other slaves insult Diverne because she has attracted the slave master's attention. The slave's dramatic speech, the particular vernacular they use to belittle the "island bitch," animates and strains the abstract iambic pentameter pattern, with the explosive slurs introducing a distinctive rhythm.

While Waniek's lines adhere strictly the iambic pentameter patterns, other contemporary writers substitute with an abandon that would have surprised not just Pope but also Shakespeare and Milton, two more permissive metricists. Poets such as Seamus Heaney and Derek Walcott test the iambic pentameter line, seeing how much tension it can take before it breaks. Their most daring lines exploit two facts. First, once a poem establishes a pattern, readers compulsively fit subsequent lines into it, if possible. The context influences readers to hear lines as iambic that might seem unmetrical when read in isolation. Second, to count as accentual syllabic a line must pass a qualitative test; it must sound like words set in that meter. The test is not mathematical: no set number of feet qualifies or disqualifies a line as metrical. Walcott in particular pushes this notion to an extreme, crafting lines of iambic pentameter that do not include a simple iambic foot.

While iambic remains the most popular accentual-syllabic meter, it is certainly not the only one. A host of others exist, including anapest, dactylic, and trochaics, all which can be used as meters, as well as substitutions. The first two are sometimes called triple meters because the foot consists of three syllables, not two as in iambic or trochaic poetry. Some of the nineteenth century's most popular poems were written in these meters. Generations of schoolchildren memorized Longfellow's rather thumping invocation:

> This is the forest primeval. The murmuring pines and the hemlocks,
> Bearded with moss, and in garments green, indistinct in the
>   twilight . . .

Triple meters have yet to regain their popularity, though they have attracted the attention of contemporary poets interested in promoting what Annie Finch calls "metrical diversity." Most commonly used as substitutions, not as a metrical base, anapests have been used to evoke a sense of swift movement:

> With a leap and a bound the swift Anapests throng.

Spondees typically achieve the opposite effect. Because it is difficult to say two consecutive stresses quickly, writers who want a line to move slowly sometimes introduce this foot, a technique that Keats favored:

> Thou foster child of silence and slów tíme

Pope uses the same technique more playfully:

When Ajax strives some rock's vást weíght to throw,

The line tóo labóurs, and the words móve slów

These examples make witty teaching aids (both the first and third appear in poems about prosody). As models, though, they seem nearly as limited as Tichborne's elegy, especially when compared to Sylvia Plath's more complicated use of triple meter substitutions:

> There's a stake in your fat black heart
> And the villagers never liked you.
> They are dancing and stamping on you.

Addressed to the speaker's father, these lines unsettlingly echo nursery rhymes. Written in tri-syllabic feet, they depict a grotesque ritual, an intensification of the fancifully child-like violence that many nursery rhymes describe. Accusatory and gleeful, the passage moves with violent propulsion; "They are dancing and stamping on you" could be said of both the villagers and the poem's heavy accents.

MORE WORKS IN *ACCENTUAL-SYLLABIC METER*

JOHN MILTON
From *Paradise Lost,* Book I

Of man's first disobedience, and the fruit
Of that forbidden tree, whose mortal taste
Brought death into the world, and all our woe,
With loss of Eden, till one greater Man
Restore us, and regain the blissful seat,   5
Sing Heav'nly Muse, that on the secret top
Of Oreb, or of Sinai, didst inspire
That shepherd, who first taught the chosen seed,
In the beginning how the heav'ns and earth
Rose out of chaos: Or if Sion hill   10

Delight thee more, and Siloa's brook that flowed
Fast by the oracle of God; I thence
Invoke thy aid to my advent'rous Song,
That with no middle flight intends to soar
Above th' Aonian mount, while it pursues   15
Things unattempted yet in prose or rhyme.
And chiefly thou O Spirit, that dost prefer
Before all temples th' upright heart and pure,
Instruct me, for thou know'st; thou from the first
Wast present, and with mighty wings outspread   20
Dove-like sat'st brooding on the vast Abyss
And mad'st it pregnant: What in me is dark
Illumine, what is low raise and support;
That to the height of this great argument
I may assert Eternal Providence,   25
And justify the ways of God to men.

WILLIAM WORDSWORTH
**Lines, Composed a Few Miles Above Tintern Abbey,
On Revisiting the Banks of the Wye During a Tour,
July 13, 1798**

Five years have passed; five summers, with the length
Of five long winters! and again I hear
These waters, rolling from their mountain-springs
With a sweet inland murmur.—Once again
Do I behold these steep and lofty cliffs,   5
Which on a wild secluded scene impress
Thoughts of more deep seclusion; and connect
The landscape with the quiet of the sky.
The day is come when I again repose
Here, under this dark sycamore, and view   10
These plots of cottage-ground, these orchard-tufts,
Which, at this season, with their unripe fruits,
Among the woods and copses lose themselves,
Nor, with their green and simple hue, disturb
The wild green landscape. Once again I see   15
These hedge-rows, hardly hedge-rows, little lines
Of sportive wood run wild: these pastoral farms
Green to the very door; and wreathes of smoke

Sent up, in silence, from among the trees.
With some uncertain notice, as might seem,   20
Of vagrant dwellers in the houseless woods,
Or of some hermit's cave, where by his fire
The hermit sits alone.

          Though absent long,
These forms of beauty have not been to me,   25
As is a landscape to a blind man's eye:
But oft, in lonely rooms, and mid the din
Of towns and cities, I have owed to them,
In hours of weariness, sensations sweet,
Felt in the blood, and felt along the heart,   30
And passing even into my purer mind,
With tranquil restoration:—feelings too
Of unremembered pleasure: such, perhaps,
As may have had no trivial influence
On that best portion of a good man's life;   35
His little, nameless, unremembered acts
Of kindness and of love. Nor less, I trust,
To them I may have owed another gift,
Of aspect more sublime; that blessed mood,
In which the burthen of the mystery,   40
In which the heavy and the weary weight
Of all this unintelligible world
Is lighten'd:—that serene and blessed mood,
In which the affections gently lead us on,
Until, the breath of this corporeal frame   45
And even the motion of our human blood
Almost suspended, we are laid asleep
In body, and become a living soul:
While with an eye made quiet by the power
Of harmony, and the deep power of joy,   50
We see into the life of things.

        If this
Be but a vain belief, yet, oh! how oft,
In darkness, and amid the many shapes
Of joyless day-light; when the fretful stir   55
Unprofitable, and the fever of the world,

Have hung upon the beatings of my heart,
How oft, in spirit, have I turned to thee,
O sylvan Wye! Thou wanderer through the woods,
How often has my spirit turned to thee!   60

And now, with gleams of half-extinguish'd thought,
With many recognitions dim and faint,
And somewhat of a sad perplexity,
The picture of the mind revives again:
While here I stand, not only with the sense   65
Of present pleasure, but with pleasing thoughts
That in this moment there is life and food
For future years. And so I dare to hope,
Though changed, no doubt, from what I was, when first
I came among these hills; when like a roe   70
I bounded o'er the mountains, by the sides
Of the deep rivers, and the lonely streams,
Wherever nature led: more like a man
Flying from something that he dreads, than one
Who sought the thing he loved. For nature then   75
(The coarser pleasures of my boyish days,
And their glad animal movements all gone by,)
To me was all in all.—I cannot paint
What then I was. The sounding cataract
Haunted me like a passion: the tall rock,   80
The mountain, and the deep and gloomy wood,
Their colours and their forms, were then to me
An appetite: a feeling and a love,
That had no need of a remoter charm,
By thought supplied, or any interest   85
Unborrowed from the eye.—That time is past,
And all its aching joys are now no more,
And all its dizzy raptures. Not for this
Faint I, nor mourn nor murmur: other gifts
Have followed, for such loss, I would believe,   90
Abundant recompence. For I have learned
To look on nature, not as in the hour
Of thoughtless youth, but hearing oftentimes
The still, sad music of humanity,
Nor harsh nor grating, though of ample power   95

To chasten and subdue. And I have felt
A presence that disturbs me with the joy
Of elevated thoughts; a sense sublime
Of something far more deeply interfused,
Whose dwelling is the light of setting suns,   100
And the round ocean, and the living air,
And the blue sky, and in the mind of man,
A motion and a spirit, that impels
All thinking things, all objects of all thought,
And rolls through all things. Therefore am I still   105
A lover of the meadows and the woods,
And mountains; and of all that we behold
From this green earth; of all the mighty world
Of eye and ear, both what they half create,
And what perceive; well pleased to recognize   110
In nature and the language of the sense,
The anchor of my purest thoughts, the nurse,
The guide, the guardian of my heart, and soul
Of all my moral being.

       Nor, perchance,   115
If I were not thus taught, should I the more
Suffer my genial spirits to decay:
For thou art with me, here, upon the banks
Of this fair river; thou my dearest Friend,
My dear, dear Friend, and in thy voice I catch   120
The language of my former heart, and read
My former pleasures in the shooting lights
Of thy wild eyes. Oh! yet a little while
May I behold in thee what I was once,
My dear, dear Sister! and this prayer I make,   125
Knowing that Nature never did betray
The heart that loved her; 'tis her privilege,
Through all the years of this our life, to lead
From joy to joy: for she can so inform
The mind that is within us, so impress   130
With quietness and beauty, and so feed
With lofty thoughts, that neither evil tongues,
Rash judgments, nor the sneers of selfish men,
Nor greetings where no kindness is, nor all

The dreary intercourse of daily life,   135
Shall e'er prevail against us, or disturb
Our chearful faith that all which we behold
Is full of blessings. Therefore let the moon
Shine on thee in thy solitary walk;
And let the misty mountain winds be free   140
To blow against thee: and, in after years,
When these wild ecstasies shall be matured
Into a sober pleasure, when thy mind
Shall be a mansion for all lovely forms,
Thy memory be as a dwelling-place   145
For all sweet sounds and harmonies; Oh! then,
If solitude, or fear, or pain, or grief,
Should be thy portion, with what healing thoughts
Of tender joy wilt thou remember me,
And these my exhortations! Nor perchance,   150
If I should be where I no more can hear
Thy voice, nor catch from thy wild eyes these gleams
Of past existence, wilt thou then forget
That on the banks of this delightful stream
We stood together; and that I, so long   155
A worshipper of Nature, hither came,
Unwearied in that service: rather say
With warmer love, oh! with far deeper zeal
Of holier love. Nor wilt thou then forget,
That after many wanderings, many years   160
Of absence, these steep woods and lofty cliffs,
And this green pastoral landscape, were to me
More dear, both for themselves, and for thy sake.

ROBERT FROST
Home Burial

He saw her from the bottom of the stairs
Before she saw him. She was starting down,
Looking back over her shoulder at some fear.
She took a doubtful step and then undid it
To raise herself and look again. He spoke   5
Advancing toward her: 'What is it you see

From up there always?—for I want to know.'
She turned and sank upon her skirts at that,
And her face changed from terrified to dull.
He said to gain time: 'What is it you see?'   10
Mounting until she cowered under him.
'I will find out now—you must tell me, dear.'
She, in her place, refused him any help
With the least stiffening of her neck and silence.
She let him look, sure that he wouldn't see,   15
Blind creature; and a while he didn't see.
But at last he murmured, 'Oh,' and again, 'Oh.'

'What is it—what?' she said.

                     'Just that I see.'

'You don't,' she challenged. 'Tell me what it is.'   20

'The wonder is I didn't see at once.
I never noticed it from here before.
I must be wonted to it —that's the reason.
The little graveyard where my people are!
So small the window frames the whole of it.   25
Not so much larger than a bedroom, is it?
There are three stones of slate and one of marble,
Broad-shouldered little slabs there in the sunlight
On the sidehill. We haven't to mind *those*.
But I understand: it is not the stones,   30
But the child's mound—'

           'Don't, don't, don't, don't,' she cried.

She withdrew shrinking from beneath his arm
That rested on the banister, and slid downstairs;
And turned on him with such a daunting look,   35
He said twice over before he knew himself:
'Can't a man speak of his own child he's lost?'
'Not you! Oh, where's my hat? Oh, I don't need it!
I must get out of here. I must get air.
I don't know rightly whether any man can.'   40

'Amy! Don't go to someone else this time.
Listen to me. I won't come down the stairs.'
He sat and fixed his chin between his fists.
'There's something I should like to ask you, dear.'

'You don't know how to ask it.'   45

                    'Help me, then.'

Her fingers moved the latch for all reply.

'My words are nearly always an offence.
I don't know how to speak of anything
So as to please you. But I might be taught   50
I should suppose. I can't say I see how.
A man must partly give up being a man
With women-folk. We cold have some arrangement
By which I'd bind myself to keep hands off
Anything special you're a-mind to name.   55
Though I don't like such things 'twixt those that love.
Two that don't love can't live together without them.
But two that do can't live together with them.'
She moved the latch a little. 'Don't—don't go.
Don't carry it to someone else this time.   60
Tell me about it if it's something human.
Let me into your grief. I'm not so much
Unlike other folks as your standing there
Apart would make me out. Give me my chance.
I do think, though, you overdo it a little.   65
What was it brought you up to think it the thing
To take your mother-loss of a first child
So inconsolably—in the face of love.
You'd think his memory might be satisfied—'

'There you go sneering now!'   70

                    'I'm not, I'm not!
You make me angry. I'll come down to you.
God, what a woman! And it's come to this,
A man can't speak of his own child that's dead.'

'You can't because you don't know how to speak.   75
If you had any feelings, you that dug
With your own hand—how could you?—his little grave;
I saw you from that very window there,
Making the gravel leap and leap in air,
Leap up, like that, like that, and land so lightly   80
And roll back down the mound beside the hole.
I thought, Who is that man? I didn't know you.
And I crept down the stairs and up the stairs
To look again, and still your spade kept lifting.
Then you came in. I heard your rumbling voice   85
Out in the kitchen, and I don't know why,
But I went near to see with my own eyes.
You could sit there with the stains on your shoes
Of the fresh earth from your own baby's grave
And talk about your everyday concerns.   90
You had stood the spade up against the wall
Outside there in the entry, for I saw it.'

'I shall laugh the worst laugh I ever laughed.
I'm cursed. God, if I don't believe I'm cursed.'

'I can repeat the very words you were saying.   95
'Three foggy mornings and one rainy day
Will rot the best birch fence a man can build.'
Think of it, talk like that at such a time!
What had how long it takes a birch to rot
To do with what was in the darkened parlour.   100
You *couldn't* care! The nearest friends can go
With anyone to death, comes so far short
They might as well not try to go at all.
No, from the time when one is sick to death,
One is alone, and he dies more alone.   105
Friends make pretense of following to the grave,
But before one is in it, their minds are turned
And making the best of their way back to life
And living people, and things they understand.
But the world's evil. I won't have grief so   110
If I can change it. Oh, I won't, I won't!'

'There, you have said it all and you feel better.
You won't go now. You're crying. Close the door.
The heart's gone out of it: why keep it up.
Amy! There's someone coming down the road!'   115

'*You*—oh, you think the talk is all. I must go—
Somewhere out of this house. How can I make you—'

'If—you—do?' She was opening the door wider.
'Where do you mean to go? First tell me that.
I'll follow and bring you back by force. I *will!*—'   120

Background and Structure of *Syllabic Meter*

Syllabic meter is the rarest of the three main meters, far less popular in
English than in Romance languages and in Japanese. A syllabic poem
counts the number of syllables: for the purposes of the meter, whether the
syllables are accented or unaccented does not matter. In one kind of syllabic verse, each line might have different numbers, but the pattern
remains constant from stanza to stanza. Employing an intricate pattern,
each stanza of Marianne Moore's "The Fish" follows a pattern of 1/ 3/ 8/
1/ 6/ 8 syllables per line. (Moore counts "iron" as one syllable and "opening" as two.)

   In the least complicated kind of syllabic verse, each line shares the
same number of syllables, as in this passage Thom Gunn's "The Goddess":

When eyeless fish meet her on
her way upward, they gently
turn together in the dark
brooks. But naked and searching
as a wind, she will allow   5
no hindrance, none, and bursts up . . .

   Gunn recalled that he wrote syllabics as "a way of getting iambics out
of my ears." Each line consists of seven syllables. They are enjambed: that
is, they run to the next without terminal punctuation. This technique
makes the lines hard to hear as units when read aloud. Despite his efforts,
iambic pentameter still haunts Gunn's ear. Rearranged, the last phrase in

the second line and the third line makes a rather graceful line of iambic pentameter, "They gently turn together in the dark." Other writers of syllabics have resisted accentual and accentual-syllabic meters less successfully. Poets who want their poems to be recognized as syllabics must make sure that an accentual or accentual-syllabic base does not take over.

Of the three main meters, syllabic verse is the least aural, adhering to a pattern that approaches a mathematical formula. For this reason, readers treat variations in syllabic verse more harshly than in accentual or accentual-syllabic poems. David Baker's "Works and Days" starts by stressing the importance of counting. In a long sentence that comprises fourteen lines, the poem describes the birds' return:

> More in number, five
> or six at a time
> perched atop stiff cat-
>
> tail tufts or calling
> from lush caverns in   5
> the willow limbs—more
>
> on the wing, more flash
> and blood, more wild song,
> who seldom travel
>
> in numbers bigger   10
> than a pair—the red-
> wings returning this
>
> spring to the park pond
> have surprised us all.
> It's supposed to be   15
>
> a bad time for birds.
> El Niño has smeared
> California
>
> for months, spreading east
> and windward its strain   20
> of killer drought, of

> greenhouse-effect storms.
> A few blocks away
> the factory mill
>
>   dusts our own fields with   25
> a mineral mist . . .
> pesticide spills from
>
>   the well-water taps.
> The honeybees are
> dying out and what-   30
>
>   ever food these birds
> are used to has thinned
> next to nothing: yet
>
>   here they are, bright as
> bobbers, floating the   35
> rich, brown surfaces.
>
>   It's a windless day
> of someone's childhood.
> Small wonder so many
>
>   of us have come   40
> to sun with the red-
> wings on the flat bank.
>
>   The birds, to see us,
> must think all is well,
> to see so many   45
>
>   so happy to be
> here—, to see so many
> more gathering now.

Baker crafts a complicated syntax onto a simple form, syllabics. As a consequence it takes nearly a dozen lines to discover that the opening phrase ("More in number, five / or six at a time") modifies "the redwings." Exploiting this ambiguity, the punning opening enjambment, "five," names the number of birds that the speaker counts as well as the number of syllables placed in each line. The poem describes these acts as roughly analogous; just as the speaker counts the redwings he sees, the poet counts syllables. Emphasizing these activities, the opening sentence mentions "number" and "numbers," and aggressive, hyphenated enjambments such as "cat / tails" and "red / wings," show the significant pains the poem takes to maintain the syllable count.

The poem's conclusion employs a different strategy. It departs from the five syllable count, including two, six-syllable lines ("Small wonder so many" and "here—,to see so many") and one, four-syllable line ("of us have come"). Such lines demonstrate how the experience of variation differs in accentual-syllabic and syllabic verse.

To discover the variations in Baker's lines, I counted the syllables on my fingers, even though the lines conspicuously suggest their metrical irregularity. The five-syllable line, "to see so many," highlights the extra syllable placed two lines later, "here—, to see so many." Competent readers generally hear variations in accentual syllabic verse. An anapest sounds a departure from a metrical base; an extra foot makes a line drag a bit. As a general rule, variations in syllabic verse are counted; variations in accentual and accentual-syllabic verse are heard. In the case of "Works and Days," the metrical variation seems to exist for its own sake, to introduce a pleasant irregularity. As we have seen, iambic-syllabic verse demands some variation in order to avoid monotony. Syllabic verse does not face this risk because it remains less obvious to the reader in the act of reading. (For this reason, many syllabic poems are mistaken for free verse.) The less insistent form does not demand variations; instead, it makes them seem unnecessary, if not puzzling.

MORE WORKS IN *SYLLABIC METER*

MARIANNE MOORE
The Fish

wade
through black jade.
   Of the crow-blue mussel-shells, one keeps
   adjusting the ash-heaps;
     opening and shutting itself like   5

an
injured fan.
   The barnacles which encrust the side
   of the wave, cannot hide
      there for the submerged shafts of the   10

sun,
split like spun
   glass, move themselves with spotlike swiftness
   into the crevices—
      in and out, illuminating   15

the
turquoise sea
   of bodies. The water drives a wedge
   of iron through the iron edge
      of the cliff; whereupon the stars,   20

pink
rice-grains, ink-
   bespattered jelly-fish, crabs like green
   lilies and submarine
      toadstools, slide each on the other.   25

All
external
   marks of abuse are present on this
   defiant edifice—
      all the physical features of   30

ac-
cident—lack
   of cornice, dynamite grooves, burns, and
   hatchet strokes, these things stand
      out on it; the chasm-side is   35

dead.
Repeated
   evidence has proven that it can live
   on what can not revive
      its youth. The sea grows old in it.   40

3

MUSICAL FORMS:
BALLAD AND THE BLUES

In the eighteenth century literate culture "discovered" ballads, peasant songs performed by farmers, storytellers, and other "folk." When David Herd traveled the Scottish countryside, he transcribed a song that began:

> Hame came our Goodman,
>   and hame came he,
> And then he saw a saddle-horse,
>   where nae horse should be.

Soon after Herb published *Ancient and Modern Scottish Songs*, London merchants printed a broadside version of "Our Goodman." Impressed, others translated the ballad into German, and versions appeared throughout Continental Europe. Wherever the ballad went, local singers changed it. Several versions exist, "some of them unprintably obscene" (according to an editor too timid to publish them). This version of "Our Goodman" appears in an anthology of folksongs from the American South. In the early twentieth century it was heard in West Virginia, passed down from mother to daughter.

Home came the old man,
   Home came he;
He went into the house,
   Strange boots did see.

"My wife, my beloved wife,   5
   O what does all this mean?
Strange boots here,
   Where mine ought to been?"

"You old fool, you blind fool,
   Can you not but see,   10
'Tis nothing but a bootjack,
   That my mother sent to me?"

"Miles have I travelled,
   Five hundred miles or more,
But spurs on a bootjack,   15
   I never saw before."

Home came the old man,
   Home came he;
He went into the kitchen,
   A strange hat did see.   20

"My wife, my beloved wife,
   O what does all this mean?
A strange hat here,
   Where my own ought to been?"

"You old fool, you blind fool,   25
   O can you not but see,
'Tis nothing but a dinner pot,
   That mother sent to me?"

"Miles have I travelled,
   Five hundred miles or more,   30
But crape on a dinner pot,
   I never saw before."

Home came the old man,
    Home came he;
He went into the house,   35
    A strange shirt did see.

"My wife, my beloved wife,
    O what does all this mean?
A strange shirt here,
    Where my own ought to been?"   40

"You old fool, you blind fool,
    Can you not but see,
'Tis nothing but a table cloth,
    My mother sent to me?"

"Miles have I travelled,   45
    Five hundred miles or more,
But sleeves on a table cloth,
    I never saw before."

Home came the old man,
    Home came he;   50
He went into the bed room,
    A strange face did see.

"My wife, my beloved wife,
    O what does all this mean?
A strange face here,   55
    Where mine ought to been?"

"You old fool, you blind fool,
    O can you not but see,
'Tis nothing but a baby,
    My mother sent to me?"   60

"Miles have I travelled,
    Five hundred miles or more,
But whiskers on a baby's face,
    I never saw before."

Background and Structure
of the *Ballad* and the *Blues*

Ballads typically tell melodramatic tales; their characters include witches, demons, outlaws, and wildly unfaithful lovers. Connoisseurs of crude, earthy weirdness, ballad writers love catastrophes: gruesome, disfiguring deaths, strange accidents, and other freakish events. "I must confess my own barbarousness," Sir Philip Sidney said, a little ashamed by the guilty pleasure that a favorite song gave him. Ballads tell stories with great directness; they do not pause to explain the characters' motivations or to add lyrical effusions. "Our Goodman" never says why the husband is so gullible (although another version describes him as drunk); it describes a series of events that reveal his gross inability to see his wife's deceit.

To help a singer remember the words, ballads employ a host of mnemonic devices. "Our Goodman" repeats phrases: "Home came the old man," "My wife, my beloved wife," and "You old fool, you blind fool." Questions are asked, following a predictable development. Scholars argue whether a community or an individual wrote these ballads; regardless, their illiterate authors remain anonymous. The ballads offer few clues about authorship because they stay impersonal. The singer does not describe his or her own experience but sings about other people, slipping into their voices. Like many ballads, "Our Goodman" features stock characters: a bossy, cheating wife and a foolishly trusting older husband, with questionable sexual potency. Adding to the song's impersonality, the singer performs both parts.

"Our Goodman" uses the most common ballad structure. It consists of quatrains, four-line stanzas. The second and fourth lines rhyme. Its lines, though, remain a little shorter than in most ballads, with two or three stresses. Instead, the ballad or hymn meter typically follows either an accentual-syllabic or accentual pattern of 4, 4, 4, 4 (called the long measure) or 4, 3, 4, 3 (called the common measure).

It is often said that there are two kinds of ballads: those made to be sung and those made to be read. True as a generalization, this point needs a little qualification. Anthologists often edited the ballads they found, complicating any claim that these songs remained "pure" or "authentic." Both read and sung, modern ballads enjoy tellingly complicated histories. They cross cultures, nations, and races. German singers encountered "Our Goodman" through a translation of a broadside version of an anthologist's transcription of the Scottish ballad.

I call the ballad, like the blues, a musical form in the sense that a musical tradition stands closely behind poems written for the page. Poetic forms generally arise from music. A musical form stays a little nearer, asking the reader to hear the musical implications of written lines. Borrowing techniques developed for oral transmission, the poems ask readers to perform the lines more robustly, to avoid the gentle, lulling voice that many adopt when reading poetry aloud. The ballad and blues, then, illustrate a larger point. Despite the forbidding terminology and arcane disputes that discussions of versification generate, poetic form did not originate as an academic pursuit. It developed from the needs that performance demands. Its techniques embody this history.

The late eighteenth century marks a crucial point in the form's development. In 1765 Thomas Percy published *Reliques of Ancient English Poetry;* a century later Francis James Child started his massive, five-volume *The English and Scottish Popular Ballads.* Introduced to a literate audience, ballads changed. Fearing that publication would forever ruin the songs she loved, one source regretted the assistance she gave to an anthologist:

> There war never ane o' my sangs prentit till ye prentit them yoursel', an' ye hae spoilt them awthegither. They were made for singing an' no for reading; but ye hae broken the charm now, an' they'll never be sung mair.

Percy's *Reliques* exerted an immediate, notable influence. "I do not think," Wordsworth observed, "there is an able writer in verse of the present day who would not be proud to acknowledge his obligations to the *Reliques.*" Wordsworth, Coleridge, and Keats self-consciously borrowed from this folk tradition, admiring its "simplicity" but adding a modern literary sophistication. As the examples at the end of the chapter suggest, modern literary ballads differ from their anonymous, improvised, and easily changeable oral models. They favor inventive phrasing instead of formulaic repetition and modern authors signed their ballads, eager to claim credit for their work.

It is easy to over-emphasize this distinction. Ballads, like blues songs, are often described as simple, heartfelt utterances, a compliment that slights the performer's artistry and the form's complexity. "The work that seems to us the most natural and simple product of its time," Oscar Wilde cautioned, "is probably the result of the most deliberate and self-conscious effort." To sing or write a ballad or the blues takes training; the

forms' masters create performances as stylized and complete as in any villanelle or sestina.

Publication, though, does significantly change at least one aspect of
balladry. While folk ballads continually change, the page more firmly
establishes print-bound poems. In general publication fixes a ballad; performance generates new versions. A meticulous anthologist, Child
printed alternative versions beside each other, highlighting the alterations each song underwent. In the examples at the end of this section, I
include four versions of "The Unquiet Grave." Each version derives from
different sources: in order of presentation, "as written down from the lips
of a girl in Sussex," "cited" by a correspondent "from memory, after more
than seventy years," "[f]rom a yeoman in Suffolk, who got it from his
nurse," and from another ballad collector's manuscript.

Placed next to the selection from Child's manuscript, Thomas
Hardy's two poems suggest musical technique adapted to the page. Born
after the Romantic revival, Hardy read Wordsworth's and Keats's ballads.
He also heard and performed ballads, singing them at his father's knee
and playing fiddle tunes late into life. An image from one of his poems
captures the era that Hardy witnessed. When a speaker urges, "Sing,
Ballad-singer from your little book," the injunction acknowledges that
the singer needs a book to remember the "country song"; he performs a
transcribed folk tune.

Many of Hardy's poems, though not technically ballads, use ballad
technique, imagery, and stories. With grim humor, "Are You Digging at
My Grave?" reverses the trajectory of "The Unquiet Grave." While the
folk ballad warns against the dangers of excessive mourning, Hardy's
poem shows how quickly the living grow utterly indifferent to the dead,
an inattention that extends even to the family pet. Hardy's greatest
poem, "During Wind and Rain" uses a ballad-like refrain to counterpoint
remembered scenes with a present anguish. Significantly, the poem starts
with a family performance:

> They sing their dearest songs—
> He, she, all of them—yea
> Treble and tenor and bass,
>   And one to play;
> With the candles mooning each face . . .   5
>   Ah, no; the years O!
> How the sick leaves reel down in throngs!

A shocking movement occurs in the ellipses. The opening five lines seem gentle, light and gay, joyful as the music the family performs. In those lines, the ballad-like structure evokes a seemingly pleasant nostalgia. Memory seems to erase the distance of time; the speaker participates in the remembered song, exclaiming "yea" both to himself and the "dearest songs" the family sings. The third line features a skipping rhythm, with several lightly stressed syllables:

Tréble ănd ténŏr ănd báss

When the poem abruptly presents an ominous, inhuman image of decay, a rhythm shift signals this terrible change. In a cry of anguish, four stresses occur in five syllables:

Áh, nó; thĕ yeárs Ó!

As "During Wind and Rain" suggests, many successful poems written for the page borrow from musical forms more by drawing from its conventions than by reproducing them. Hardy's poem evokes the ballad, using its music as a backdrop, an evocation of the past, and a contrast to the present.

Another kind of written ballad stayed close to the folk ballad's anarchic spirit. Broadside ballads reported the tabloid news of murderers about to "pay" for their crimes. Sold at executions, "right under the drop," as one merchant recounted, these poems catered to a bloodthirsty clientele. In a Nova Scotia version of an English ballad, the doomed man warned:

Come all ye royal lovers,
    A warning take by me,
And never treat your own true love
    To any cruelty.

For if you do you'll rue like me   5
    Until the day you die;
You'll hang like me, a murderer,
    All on the gallows high.

Like the speaker, who inexplicably beats his fiancée to death with a fence stake, the ballads claim a questionable moral authority. Perfunctory

and rather forced, the admonition barely disguises the poem's real interest: the crime's violent gory details, which the poem often embellishes.
As in the final minutes of an episode of *The Jerry Springer Show*, when the
host offers his "final thoughts," the poem barely hides how much it enjoys
the voyeuristic spectacle it presents, a senseless murder followed by a
public hanging. Renouncing any self-righteous pretensions, one version
of the American ballad "Frankie and Johnny" concludes:

> This story has no moral,
> This story has no end,
> This story just goes to show
> That there ain't no good in men.

When teaching the ballad, creative writing instructors might emphasize the ballad's status as the tabloid journalism of its day. Assigned to
write a ballad based on an article in the *National Enquirer* or the *Star*, the
students may take liberties with the story (which, given the source, seems
only fair), but cannot editorialize: they must tell the story without
overtly interjecting their views. The resulting poems are often the least
polite and most accomplished of the semester.

Because of its long history in the British Isles, the ballad has been
called the most "English" of all meters, belonging to a "native" tradition.
The ballad, George Saintsbury maintained, constituted "perhaps the
most definitely English—blood and bone, flesh and marrow—of all English metres." Confidently extending this point, Saintsbury maintained
that anyone unmoved by a good ballad "is no Englishman; and if, not
being an Englishman . . . he is either a very cold-blooded person, or no
judge of poetry, or (most probably) both."

Immigration and mass literary, though, carried the ballad across
oceans, cultures, languages, and races. It mingled with other forms,
inspiring ballads that also might be classified as blues. The blues developed out of work songs, hollers, and other musical forms familiar to
black America:

> Layin' in my bed with my face turned to the wall
> Lord, layin' in the bed with my face turned to the wall
> Tryin' to count these blues, so I could sing them all

In a classic, three-line blues stanza, the second repeats the first line, often
with a slight variation, and the third line rhymes with the opening two.

"Ma" Rainey, for instance, changed "My bed" to "the bed" and adds "Lord" to the start of the second.

Such songs treat "the blues" and "heartache" as nearly synonymous. "Good morning, blues," one song begins while another starts, "Good morning, heartache." A more personal form than the ballad, the blues invites the audience to assume that the singer draws from personal experience, that he or she has suffered the emotions the song describes, if not the actual events. Robert Johnson sang so convincingly about selling his soul to the devil that some listeners assumed that he had. While the songs express an existential dread and sadness, the form insists on transcendence. "The blues," Ralph Ellison observed, "is an impulse to keep the painful details and episodes of a brutal experience alive in one's aching consciousness, to finger its jagged grain, and then transcend it, not by the consolation of philosophy but by squeezing from it a near-tragic, near-comic lyricism. As a form, the blues is an autobiographical chronicle of personal catastrophe expressed lyrically."

Restless as its most popular motif, a train about to leave a station, the blues followed the black migration to the Northern cities such as Chicago, where, according to his own account, Muddy Waters switched to an electric guitar because the acoustic guitar he used in the rural South could not compete with the city's loud sounds. Like the ballad, the blues developed along two lines, as "country" and "city" blues considered the two kinds of experience. Like the ballad, another "low culture" form, the blues suffered embarrassing appropriations by "high" culture. In a pervasive exploitation, many white managers repeatedly stole from the black artists they "discovered."

As poets started to write blues poems, they necessarily explored the connection between their lines on the page and musical performance. To suggest how, I include Langston Hughes's blues lyric "Homesick Blues" and "The Weary Blues," which draws from the form. "The Weary Blues" quotes a blues song amidst Hughes's own words, setting a call-and-response between the song and the poem. When the poem interjects, "O Blues!" it is unclear whether Hughes's speaker quotes the singer or adds his own exclamation. For Hughes, "[c]oming from a black man's soul," the blues expresses racial knowledge. Just as Hardy's ballads work best by invoking and departing from their model, Hughes's blues poems confidently stray from the form's structure. Both poets assume that a reader knows the invoked songs, whether Handy's blues or the English folk tunes. If the reader does not, he or she can only partially experience the poem, reading the words but not hearing them.

"Never was white man had the blues," Leadbelly believed, "'cause nothing to worry about." W. H. Auden's "Refugee Blues" suggests otherwise. In 1935 Auden married Erika Mann, daughter of the novelist Thomas Mann, in order to help her escape from Nazi Germany. Four years later he wrote "Refugee Blues" about German Jews unable to secure visas to stay in America. Drawing from the blues' traveling motif, Auden describes a darkly ironic journey, in which only those who wish to annihilate the Jews care about their fate.

MORE WORKS IN THE *BALLAD*

TRADITIONAL
Get Up and Bar the Door

"Get Up and Bar the Door" uses a traditional ballad structure. The second and fourth lines of each stanza rhyme. For instance, the opening stanza rhymes "name" and "fame." The poem follows a loose iambic structure of 4/3/4/3.

Thĕre livéd | ă mán | ăt thĕ foót | ŏf ă hi̇́ll,

    Jŏhn Blúnt | ĭt wás | hĭs námé;   a

Ănd hĕ | sŏld li̇́quor | ănd yi̇́ll | ŏf thĕ bést,

    Whĭch eárned | hĭm wónd | rŏus fáme.   *a*

Now it fell about the Martinmas time   5
    (And a gay time it was than)
That Janet his wife did puddings make
    And boiled them in the pan.

The wind blew cold from north to south,
    It blew across the floor;   10
Quoth old John Blunt to Janet his wife:
    'Rise up and bar the door!'

'My hands are in my housewife keep,
 Good man, as ye may see,
And if ye will not bar it yerself   15
 It will ne'er be barred by me.'

They made a paction 'twixt them twain,
 They made it firm and sure,
That the one that spake the foremost word
 Was to rise and bar the door.   20

Then by there came two gentlemen,
 Were riding over the moor;
And they came unto John Blunt's house
 Just by the light of the door.

Now whether is this a rich man's house,   25
 Or whether is it a poor?
But never a word spake man or wife
 For the barring of the door.

They came within and bade them good e'en,
 And syne bade them good morrow;   30
But never a word spake man or wife,
 For the barring of the door, O.

O, first they ate the white pudding,
 And syne they ate the black;
Though Janet thought muckle to herself,   35
 Yet never a word she spake.

O, syne they drank of the liquor so strong,
 And syne they drank of the yill.
'O, now we have gotten a house of our own
 I'm sure we may take our fill.'   40

Then said one gentleman to his friend:
 'Here, man, take thou my knife,
And thou scrape off this goodman's beard
 While I kiss his goodwife.'

'But there's no water in the house—   45
   How shall I shave him than?'
'What ails thee with the pudding bree
   That boils within the pan?'

O, up then started old John Blunt,
   And an angry man was he: 50
'Will ye kiss my wife before mine eyes
   And scald me with pudding-bree?'

Then up then started Janet his wife,
   Gave three skips upon the floor:
'Goodman, e've spoke the foremost word,   55
   Get up and bar the door!'

The Unquiet Grave

Version one:

'The wind doth blow today, my love,
   And a few small drops of rain;
I never had but one true-love,
   In cold grave she was lain.

'I'll do as much for my true-love   5
   As any young man may;
I'll sit and mourn all at her grave
   For a twelvemonth and a day.'

The twelvemonth and a day being up,
   The dead began to speak: 10
'Oh who sits weeping on my grave,
   And will not let me sleep?'

''Tis I, my love, sits on your grave,
   And will not let you sleep;
For I crave one kiss of your clay-cold lips,   15
   And that is all I seek.'

'You crave one kiss of my clay-cold lips;
    But my breath smells earthy strong;
If you have one kiss of my clay-cold lips,
    Your time will not be long.   20

''Tis down in yonder garden green,
    Love, where we used to walk,
The finest flower that ere was seen
    Is withered to a stalk.

'The stalk is withered dry, my love,   25
    So will our hearts decay;
So make yourself content, my love,
    Till God calls you away.'

Version two:

'How cold the wind do blow, dear love,
    And see the drops of rain!
I never had but one true-love,
    In the green wood he was slain.

'I would do as much for my own true-love   5
    As in my power doth lay;
I would sit and mourn all on his grave
    For a twelvemonth and a day.'

A twelvemonth and a day being past,
    His ghost did rise and speak: 10
'What makes you mourn all on my grave?
    For you will not let me sleep.'

'It is not your gold I want, dear love,
    Nor yet your wealth I crave;
But one kiss from your lily-white lips   15
    Is all I wish to have.

'Your lips are cold as clay, dear love,
    Your breath doth smell so strong;'
'I am afraid, my pretty, pretty maid,
    Your time will not be long.'   20

Version three:

'Cold blows the wind oer my true-love,
  Cold blow the drops of rain;
I never, never had but one sweetheart,
  In the greenwood he was slain.

'I did as much for my true-love   5
  As ever did any maid;
. . . . .
  . . . . .

One kiss from your lily-cold lips, true-love,
  One kiss is all I pray,   10
And I'll sit and weep all over your grave
  For a twelvemonth and a day.'

'My cheek is as cold as the clay, true-love,
  My breath is earthy and strong;
And if I should kiss your lips, true-love,   15
  Your life would not be long.'

Version four:

'Proud Boreas makes a hideous noise,
  Loud roars the fatal fleed;
I loved never a love but one,
  In church-yard she lies dead.

'But I will do for my love's sake   5
  What other young men may;
I'll sit and mourn upon her grave,
  A twelvemonth and a day.'

A twelvemonth and a day being past,
  The ghost began to speak: 10
'Why sit ye here upon my grave,
  And will not let me sleep?'

'One kiss of your lily-white lips
  Is all that I do crave;

And one kiss of your lily-white lips   15
    I would have.'

'Your breath is as the roses sweet,
    Mine as the sulphur strong;
If you get one kiss of my lips,
    Your days would not be long.   20

'Mind not ye the day, Willie,
Sin you and I did walk?
The firstand flower that we did pu
Was witherd on the stalk.'

'Flowers will fade and die, my dear,   25
Aye as the tears will turn;
And since I've lost my own sweet-heart,
I'll never cease but mourn.'

Lament nae mair for me, my love,
    The powers we must obey;   30
But hoist up one sail to the wind,
    Your ship must sail away.'

THOMAS HARDY
"Ah, Are You Digging My Grave?"

"Ah, are you digging on my grave
    My loved one?—planting rue?"
—"No: yesterday he went to wed
One of the brightest wealth has bred.
'It cannot hurt her now,' he said,   5
    'That I should not be true.'"

"Then who is digging on my grave?
    My nearest dearest kin?"
—"Ah, no: they sit and think, 'What use!
What good will planting flowers produce?   10
No tendance of her mound can loose
    Her spirit from Death's gin.'"

"But some one digs upon my grave?
    My enemy?—prodding sly?"
—"Nay: when she heard you had passed the Gate   15
That shuts on all flesh soon or late,
She thought you no more worth her hate,
    And cares not where you lie."

"Then, who is digging on my grave?
    Say—since I have not guessed!"   20
—"O it is I, my mistress dear,
Your little dog, who still lives near,
And much I hope my movements here
    Have not disturbed your rest?"

"Ah, yes! *You* dig upon my grave . . .   25
    Why flashed it not on me
That one true heart was left behind!
What feeling do we ever find
To equal among human kind
    A dog's fidelity!"   30

"Mistress, I dug upon your grave
    To bury a bone, in case
I should be hungry near this spot
When passing on my daily trot.
I am sorry, but I quite forgot   35
    It was your resting-place."

THOMAS HARDY
During Wind and Rain

They sing their dearest songs—
He, she, all of them—yea,
Treble and tenor and bass,
    And one to play;
With the candles mooning each face   5
    Ah, no; the years O!
How the sick leaves reel down in throngs!

They clear the creeping moss—
Elders and juniors—aye,
Making the pathways neat   10
   And the garden gay;
And they build a shady seat . . .
   Ah, no; the years, the years;
See, the white storm-birds wing across!

They are blithely breakfasting all—   15
Men and maidens—yea,
Under the summer tree,
   With a glimpse of the bay,
While pet fowl come to the knee . . .
   Ah, no; the years O!   20
And the rotten rose is ript from the wall.

They change to a high new house,
He, she, all of them—aye,
Clocks and carpets and chairs
On the lawn all day,   25
And brightest things that are theirs . . . .
   Ah, no; the years, the years;
Down their carved names the rain-drop ploughs.

TRADITIONAL
Sir John Barleycorn

There came three men from out of the west
Their victory to try;
And they have ta'en a solemn oath,
Poor Barleycorn should die.

They took a plough and ploughed him in,   5
Clods harrowed on his head;
And then they took a solemn oath
John Barleycorn was dead.

There he lay sleeping in the ground
Till rain on him did fall;   10

Then Barleycorn sprung up his head,
And so amazed them all.

There he remained till Midsummer
And look'd both pale and wan;
Then Barleycorn he got a beard   15
And so became a man.

Then they sent men with scythes so sharp
To cut him off at knee;
And then poor Johny Barleycorn
They served most barbarouslie.   20

Then they sent men with pitchforks strong
To pierce him through the heart;
And like a doleful Tragedy
They bound him in a cart.

And then they brought him to a barn   25
A prisoner to endure;
And so they fetched him out again,
And laid him on the floor.

Then they sent men with holly clubs,
To beat the flesh from th'bones;   30
But the miller served him worse than that,
He ground him 'twixt two stones.

O! Barleycorn is the choicest grain
That e'er was sown on land:
It will do more than any grain   35
By the turning of your hand.

It will make a boy into a man,
A man into an ass:
To silver it will change your gold,
Your silver into brass.   40

It will make the huntsman hunt the fox,
That never wound a horn;

It will bring the tinker to the stocks
That people may him scorn.

O! Barleycorn is the choicest grain   45
That e'er was sown on land.
And it will cause a man to drink
Till he neither can go nor stand.

SAMUEL TAYLOR COLERIDGE
The Rime of the Ancient Mariner, Book IV

The Wedding-Guest feareth that a Spirit is talking to him;

'I fear thee, ancient Mariner!
I fear thy skinny hand!
And thou art long, and lank, and brown,
As is the ribbed sea-sand.

I fear thee and thy glittering eye,   5
And thy skinny hand, so brown.'—
Fear not, fear not, thou Wedding-Guest!
This body dropt not down.

But the ancient Mariner assureth him of his bodily life, and
*   proceedeth to relate his horrible penance.*

Alone, alone, all, all alone,
Alone on a wide wide sea!   10
And never a saint took pity on
My soul in agony.

He despiseth the creatures of the calm,

The many men, so beautiful!
And they all dead did lie:
And a thousand thousand slimy things   15
Lived on; and so did I.

And envieth that they should live, and so many lie dead.

I looked upon the rotting sea,
And drew my eyes away;
I looked upon the rotting deck,
And there the dead men lay.   20

I looked to heaven, and tried to pray;
But or ever a prayer had gusht,
A wicked whisper came, and made
My heart as dry as dust.

I closed my lids, and kept them close,   25
And the balls like pulses beat;
For the sky and the sea, and the sea and the sky
Lay like a load on my weary eye,
And the dead were at my feet.

But the curse liveth for him in the eye of the dead men.

The cold sweat melted from their limbs,   30
Nor rot nor reek did they:
The look with which they looked on me
Had never passed away.

An orphan's curse would drag to hell
A spirit from on high;   35
But oh! more horrible than that
Is the curse in a dead man's eye!
Seven days, seven nights, I saw that curse,
And yet I could not die.

In his loneliness and fixedness he yearneth towards the journeying Moon,
and the stars that still sojourn, yet still move onward; and every where
the blue sky belongs to them, and is their appointed rest, and their native
country and their own natural homes, which they enter unannounced,
as lords that are certainly expected and yet there is a silent joy at their
arrival.

The moving Moon went up the sky.   40
And no where did abide:
Softly she was going up,
And a star or two beside—

Her beams bemocked the sultry main,
Like April hoar-frost spread;   45
But where the ship's huge shadow lay,
The charméd water burnt alway
A still and awful red.

By the light of the Moon he beholdeth God's creatures
  of the great calm.

Beyond the shadow of the ship,
I watched the water-snakes: 50
They moved in tracks of shining white,
And when they reared, the elfish light
Fell off in hoary flakes.

Within the shadow of the ship
I watched their rich attire: 55
Blue, glossy green, and velvet black,
They coiled and swam; and every track
Was a flash of golden fire.

Their beauty and their happiness.

He blessed them in his heart.

O happy living things! no tongue
Their beauty might declare: 60
A spring of love gushed from my heart,
And I blessed them unaware:
Sure my kind saint took pity on me,
And I blessed them unaware.

The spell begins to break

The self-same moment I could pray;   65
And from my neck so free
The Albatross fell off, and sank
Like lead into the sea.

JOHN KEATS
La Belle Dame Sans Merci

O what can ail thee, knight-at-arms,
    Alone and palely loitering?
The sedge has wither'd from the lake,
    And no birds sing.

O what can ail thee, knight-at-arms,   5
    So haggard and so woe-begone?
The squirrel's granary is full,
    And the harvest's done.

I see a lilly on thy brow,
    With anguish moist and fever dew,   10
And on thy cheeks a fading rose
    Fast withereth too.

I met a lady in the meads,
    Full beautiful—a faery's child,
Her hair was long, her foot was light,   15
    And her eyes were wild.

I made a garland for her head,
    And bracelets too, and fragrant zone;
She look'd at me as she did love,
    And made sweet moan.   20

I set her on my pacing steed,
    And nothing else saw all day long,
For sidelong would she bend, and sing
    A faery's song.

She found me roots of relish sweet,   25
    And honey wild, and manna dew,
And sure in language strange she said—
    'I love thee true.'

She took me to her elfin grotto
    And there she wept, and sigh'd full sore,   30
And there I shut her wild wild eyes
    With kisses four.

And there she lulled me asleep,
 And there I dream'd, Ah—woe betide!
The latest dream I ever dream'd   35
 on the cold hill side.

I saw pale kings and princes too,
 Pale warriors, death-pale were they all;
They cried—'La Belle Dame sans Merci
 Hath thee in thrall!'   40

I saw their starved lips in the gloam,
 With horrid warning gaped wide,
And I awoke and found me here,
 On the cold hill's side.

And this is why I sojourn here,   45
 Alone and palely loitering,
Though the sedge is wither'd from the lake,
 And no birds sing.

ANONYMOUS
The Wife of Usher's Well

There lived a wife at Usher's Well,
 And a wealthy wife was she;
She had three stout and stalwart sons,
 And sent them o'er the sea.

They hadna been a week from her,   5
 A week but barely ane,
Whan word cam to the carline wife,
 That her three sons were gane.

They hadna been a week from her,
 A week but barely three,   10
When word came to the carline wife
 That her sons she'd never see.

"I wish the wind may never cease,
 Nor fashes in the flood,
Till my three sons come hame to me,   15
 In earthly flesh and blood!"

It fell about the Martinmas,
    Whan nights are lang and mirk,
The carline wife's three sons cam hame,
    And their hats wer o' the birk.   20

It neither grew in syke nor ditch,
    Nor yet in ony sheugh,
But at the gates o' Paradise,
    That birk grew fair eneugh.

Blow up the fire, now, maidens mine,   25
    Bring water from the well!
For a' my house shall feast this night
    Sin my three sons are well."

And she has made to them a bed,
    She's made it large and wide;   30
And she's happed her mantle them about,
    Sat down at the bed-side.

Up then crew the red red cock
    And up and crew the gray;
The eldest to the youngest said,   35
    "'Tis time we were away."

"The cock doth craw, the day doth daw,
    The channerin' worm doth chide;
Gin we be miss'd out o' our place
    A sair pain we maun bide?   40

"Lie still, lie still a little wee while,
    Lie still but if we may;
Gin my mother should miss us when she wakes,
    She'll go mad ere it be day."

O it's they've ta'en up their mother's mantle,   45
    And they've hangd it on the pin:
"O lang may ye hing, my mother's mantle,
    Ere ye hap us again!

'Fare-ye-weel, my mother dear!
   Fareweel to barn and byre;   50
And fare-ye-weel, the bonny lass
   That kindles my mother's fire."

AMERICAN TRADITIONAL
Frankie and Johnny

Frankie and Johnny were lovers, O, how that couple could love.
Swore to be true to each other, true as the stars above.
He was her man, but he done her wrong.

Frankie she was his woman, everybody knows.
She spent one hundred dollars for a suit of Johnny's clothes.   5
He was her man, but he done her wrong.

Frankie and Johnny went walking, Johnny in his brand new suit.
"Oh good Lawd," says Frankie, "but don't my Johnny look cute?"
He was her man, but he done her wrong.

Frankie went down to Memphis. She went on the evening train.   10
She paid one hundred dollars for Johnny a watch and chain.
He was her man, but he done her wrong.

Frankie went down to the corner to buy a glass of beer.
She says to the fat bartender, "Has my loving man been here?
He was my man, but he done me wrong."   15

"Ain't goin' to tell you no story. Ain't goin' to tell you no lie.
I seen your man 'bout an hour ago with a girl named Alice Fry.
If he's you man, he's doin' you wrong."

Frankie went back to the hotel. She didn't go there for fun.
Under her long red kimono she toted a forty-four gun   20
He was her man, but he done her wrong.

Frankie went down to the hotel, looked in the window so high.
There she saw her lovin' Johnny a-lovin' up Alice Fry.
He was her man, but he done her wrong.

Frankie threw back her kimono, took out that old forty-four.   25
Root-a-toot-toot, three times she shot, right through the
   hotel door.
She shot her man, 'cause he done her wrong.

Johnny grabbed off his Stetson. "O good Lawd, Frankie, don't shoot!"
But Frankie put her finger on the trigger, and the gun went
   root-a-toot-toot.
He was her man, but she shot him down.   30

"Roll me over easy, roll me over slow,
Roll me over easy, boys, 'cause my wounds are hurting me so,
I was her man, but I done her wrong."

With the first shot Johnny staggered; with the second shot he fell;
When the third bullet hit him, there was a new man's
   face in hell.   35
He was her man, and she done him wrong.

Frankie heard a rumbling away down under the ground.
Maybe it was Johnny where she had shot him down.
He was her man, and she done him wrong.

Oh, bring on your rubber-tired hearses. Bring on your
   rubber-tired hacks.   40
"They're takin' Johnny to the buryin' ground but they'll
   never bring him back.
He was my man, but he done me wrong."

The judge said to the jury, "It's as plain as plain can be.
This woman shot her lover, so it's murder in the second degree.
He was her man, though he done her wrong."   45

Now it wasn't murder in the second degree. It wasn't murder
   in the third.
Frankie simply dropped her man like a hunter drops a bird.
He was her man, but done her wrong.

"Oh, put me in that dungeon. Oh, put me in that cell.
Put me where the northeast wind blows from the southeast
   corner of hell,   50
I shot my man 'cause he done me wrong."

Frankie walked up to the scaffold, as calm as a girl could be,
She turned her eyes to heaven and said, "Good Lord, I'm
    coming to thee.
He was my man, and I done him wrong."

MORE WORKS IN THE *BLUES*

LANGSTON HUGHES (?)
Homesick Blues

De railroad bridge's
A sad song in de air.
De railroad bridge's
A sad song in de air.
Ever time de trains pass   5
I wants to go somewhere.

I went down to de station.
Ma heart was in ma mouth.
Went down to de station.
Heart was in ma mouth.   10
Lookin' for a box car
To roll me to de South.

Homesick blues, Lawd,
'S a terrible thing to have.
Homesick blues is   15
A terrible thing to have.
To keep from cryin'
I opens ma mouth an' laughs.

LANGSTON HUGHES
The Weary Blues

Droning a drowsy syncopated tune,
Rocking back and forth to a mellow croon,
    I heard a Negro play.
Down on Lenox Avenue the other night
By the pale dull pallor of an old gas light   5
    He did a lazy sway . . . .

He did a lazy sway . . . .
To the tune o' those Weary Blues.
With his ebony hands on each ivory key
He made that poor piano moan with melody.   10
   O Blues!
Swaying to and fro on his rickety stool
He played that sad raggy tune like a musical fool.
   Sweet Blues!
Coming from a black man's soul.   15
   O Blues!
In a deep song voice with a melancholy tone
I heard that Negro sing, that old piano moan—
   "Ain't got nobody in all this world,
     Ain't got nobody but ma self.   20
     I's gwine to quit ma frownin'
     And put ma troubles on the shelf."

Thump, thump, thump, went his foot on the floor.
He played a few chords then he sang some more—
   "I got the Weary Blues   25
     And I can't be satisfied.
     Got the Weary Blues
     And can't be satisfied—
     I ain't happy no mo'
     And I wish that I had died."   30
And far into the night he crooned that tune.
The stars went out and so did the moon.
The singer stopped playing and went to bed
While the Weary Blues echoed through his head.
He slept like a rock or a man that's dead.   35

W. H. AUDEN
The Refugee Blues

Say this city has ten million souls,
Some are living in mansions, some are living in holes:
Yet there's no place for us, my dear, yet there's no place for us.

Once we had a country and we thought it fair,
Look in the atlas and you'll find it there: 5
We cannot go there now, my dear, we cannot go there now.

In the village churchyard there grows an old yew,
Every spring it blossoms anew:
Old passports can't do that, my dear, old passports can't do that.

The consul banged the table and said,   10
"If you've got no passport you're officially dead":
But we are still alive, my dear, but we are still alive.

Went to a committee; they offered me a chair;
Asked me politely to return next year:
But where shall we go to-day, my dear, but where shall
    we go to-day?   15

Came to a public meeting; the speaker got up and said;
"If we let them in, they will steal our daily bread":
He was talking of you and me, my dear, he was talking of
    you and me.

Thought I heard the thunder rumbling in the sky;
It was Hitler over Europe, saying, "They must die":   20
O we were in his mind, my dear, O we were in his mind.

Saw a poodle in a jacket fastened with a pin,
Saw a door opened and a cat let in:
But they weren't German Jews, my dear, but they
    weren't German Jews.

Went down the harbour and stood upon the quay,   25
Saw the fish swimming as if they were free:
Only ten feet away, my dear, on ten feet away.

Walked through a wood, saw the birds in the trees;
They had no politicians and sang at their ease:
They weren't the human race, my dear, they weren't
    the human race.   30

Dreamed I saw a building with a thousand floors,
A thousand windows and a thousand doors:
Not one of them was ours, my dear, not one of them was ours.

Stood on a great plain in the falling snow;
Ten thousand soldiers marched to and fro: 35
Looking for you and me, my dear, looking for you and me.

AN EXERCISE IN THE *MUSICAL FORMS*

These forms remind us that poetry need not express ideas and depict events thought to be "in good taste." Instead write a ballad based on an article in a tabloid such as the *National Enquirer* or the *Star*. Stick strictly to a ballad stanza, presenting in detail the story that the article presents. You may take liberties with the story, but you cannot editorialize. Tell the story without interjecting your view of it.

4

SONNETS AND THE RONDEAU

Before George Herbert turned seventeen, he sent his mother an intriguing sonnet:

> My God, where is that ancient heat towards thee,
>   Wherewith whole shoals of Martyrs once did burn,
> Besides their other flames? Doth poetry
>   Wear Venus' livery? only serve her turn?
> Why are not sonnets made of thee? and lays   5
>   Upon thine altar burnt? Cannot thy love
> Heighten a spirit to sound out Thy praise
>   As well as any she? Cannot thy Dove
> Outstrip their Cupid easily in flight?
>   Or, since thy ways are deep, and still the same,   10
>   Will not a verse run smooth that bears thy name?
> Why doth that fire, which by thy power and might
>   Each breast does feel, no braver fuel choose
>   Then that which, one day, worms may chance refuse.

As if from a high pulpit, the schoolboy poet sermonizes against poets who direct their attention to women, not God. Represented by pagan figures

69

such as Cupid and Venus, this earthly love remains inferior to the love of the divine. In the poem's most playful image, Herbert asserts that the dove, the symbol of the Holy Spirit, flies faster than Cupid, the Roman god of erotic love.

It was an odd moment for Herbert to criticize secular love. Right around the time he shared the poem with her, Magdelen Herbert, a widow, married Sir John Danvers, a man only a few years older than Herbert and half her age. Addressing "my dear mother," Herbert explained in a letter that the poem testified to his "resolution to be, that my poor abilities in poetry shall be all and ever consecrated to God's glory." As in the poem, it is hard to know why Herbert chose this particular moment to declare his single-minded devotion to God: whether his words express piety or adolescent petulance disguised in religious garb.

Background and Structure of the *Sonnet*

What Herbert meant by "sonnets" also remains a little ambiguous. "Some think," George Gascoigne observed in 1575, "that all Poems (being short) may be called Sonets." *Sonnet* derives from the Italian for little song or sound; it wasn't until the late Renaissance that the word's definition narrowed to define a more particular form, although writers occasionally evoked the older sense of the word as recently as the early nineteenth century.

Despite Herbert's protests, from its start in thirteenth-century Italy the sonnet has mixed earthly and divine love. Early masters such as Petrarch and Dante praised their "angelic" beloved in mystical terms. They addressed their lovers as if they were deities, mixing the erotic and the spiritual. Petrarch's widely influential poems to Laura established a vocabulary for imagining love, in which the poet extravagantly praises a virtuously unattainable lady. The poems chart the experience of endless frustration, love's "icy-fire," as the poet burns for what he cannot have.

Employing the resources of a language rich in rhyme, the Italian or Pertrarchan sonnet opens with eight lines, also called the octave, which rhyme according to this pattern:

a
b
b
a

a
b
b
a

The next six lines, the sestet, rhyme according to several patterns, the most common of which are:

c	c	c	c
d	d	d	d
d	e	e	c
c	d	c	d
d	c	e	c
e	e	d	d

The sonnet entered English in the mid-sixteenth century, after Thomas Wyatt encountered the form while on a diplomatic mission abroad. Wyatt and his fellow courtier Henry Howard, Earl of Surrey translated Petrarch's poetry then composed original verses in the form. In 1557, 15 years after Wyatt's death and ten years after Surrey's, the printer Richard Tottell published an anthology titled *Songs and Sonnets written by the Right Honorable Lord Henry Howard late Earl of Surrey.* More commonly called *Tottell's Miscellany*, the book introduced the sonnet to an English readership. The printer also regularized Wyatt's rough meter, producing smoother but less compelling versions.

When Wyatt translated Petrarch's Rime 140, he wrote:

The long love that in my thought doth harbor,
And in my heart doth keep his residence,
Into my face presseth with bold pretence
And therein campeth, spreading his banner.
She that me learns to love and suffer   5
And wills that my trust and lust's negligence
Be reined by reason, shame, and reverence
With his hardiness taketh displeasure.
Wherewithal unto the heart's forest he fleeth,
Leaving his enterprise with pain and cry,   10
And there him hideth, and not appeareth.
What may I do when my master feareth,

But in the field with him to live and die?
For good is the life ending faithfully.

Surrey translated the same poem as:

Love, that doth reign and live within my thought,
And built his seat within my captive breast,
Clad in the arms wherein with me he fought,
Oft in my face he doth his banner rest.
But she that taught me love and suffer pain,   5
My doubtful hope and eke my hot desire
With shamefast look to shadow and refrain,
Her smiling grace converteth straight to ire.
And coward Love, then, to the heart apace
Taketh his flight, where he doth lurk and plain,   10
His purpose lost, and dare not show his face.
For my lord's guilt thus faultless bide I pain,
Yet from my lord shall not my foot remove:
Sweet is the death that taketh end by love.

   In addition to suggesting the poets' different styles and preoccupations,
the translations show how Wyatt and Surrey adapted the sonnet form to
the English language, which lacks the Italian's density of rhymes. Wyatt's
version stays closest to the rhyme scheme that Petrarch employs, making
only one change. Wyatt's final line rhymes with the penultimate and tenth
lines, while Petrarch's final line rhymes with the ninth, eleventh, and
twelfth lines. Wyatt would have followed the original rhyme scheme
had he rhymed the last line with "pain," not "remove." Wyatt instead
introduces the terminal couple that would characterize many sonnets in
English, a technique that has been praised and criticized for the epigrammatic sense of closure it adds, an element I will discuss shortly.
   Surrey also ends his translation with a couplet, but he adds an alternative rhyme scheme. Except for the rhyme on "pain," which snakes from the
octave to the sestet, his poem anticipates the sonnet structure that would
dominate the language: the English or Shakespearean sonnet, marked by a
terminal couplet and an alternative rhyme. If literary history had been
kinder to Surrey, we would say that Shakespeare uses the Surrey sonnet:

When my love swears that she is made of truth,
I do believe her though I know she lies,

That she might think me some untutored youth,
Unlearnèd in the world's false subtleties.
Thus vainly thinking that she thinks me young,   5
Although she knows my days are past the best,
Simply I credit her false-speaking tongue
On both sides thus is simple truth suppressed.
But wherefore says she not she is unjust?
And wherefore say not I that I am old?   10
O love's best habit is in seeming trust,
And age in love loves not to have years told.
    Therefore I lie with her, and she with me,
    And in our faults by lies we flattered be.

"Therefore," the couplet begins as if ending a logical syllogism. As in this kind of philosophical argument, Shakespeare's sonnets often move toward a structurally neat conclusion, which comments on, analyzes, or summaries the depicted experience. Some readers have criticized Shakespeare's couplets as offering trite aphorisms, although in this sonnet the more proverbial, impersonal lines occur in lines eleven and twelve. The poem's neatness, though, barely disguises the anguish that underpins it, as the speaker's self-justifications seem hopelessly implausible. The great sense of closure that the poem achieves barely disguises the fact that little has been resolved, that the speaker turns to formulas and casuistry for solace.

Poets subsequently invented many variations of these two types. Through the late nineteenth century, the Petrarchan form was considered the "legitimate sonnet" and the Shakespearean sonnet viewed as a departure from this standard model. When Keats tried (in his own words) "to discover a better sonnet stanza than we have," he did so because both models dissatisfied him. "The legitimate," he wrote, "does not suit the language over-well from the pouncing rhymes—the other kind appears too elegiac—and the couplet at the end has seldom a pleasing effect." Keats disliked the Petrarchan sonnet because the first eight lines feature rhymes in quick succession, leading to a "pouncing effect." The Shakespearean model displeased him because it resembled the elegiac stanzas (four-line stanzas that rhyme a b a b) and because the couplet offered a neat resolution.

We no longer call the Petrarchan sonnet "the legitimate" at least partly because the poets have developed countless alternatives and variations, with various rhyme schemes and meters (and some without any meters or rhymes at all). The sonnet is not only English's major form; its influence extends nearly worldwide. During the last decade alone, it has attracted the attention of international poets as different as Charles Baudelaire, Rainer Maria Rilke, and Pablo Neruda, and poets have written sonnets in a great number of languages, including French, Italian, Croatian, and Chinese.

Many observers have puzzled over why this form has achieved such prominence. The sonnet seems rather puny, especially when compared to the form that antiquity placed at the top of its hierarchy, the epic. Some scholars have speculated that the sonnet's proportions echo architectural or philosophical ideals; they have drawn parallels to the symmetries that exist within nature or human physiology. Coleridge, who defined the sonnet as "a small poem, in which some lonely feeling is developed," argued that custom largely dictated the form, although he noted that length places the sonnet between the epigram and the elegy. My view is that the sonnet has gained such popularity because it offers a form attuned to the problem that has obsessed poetry for the last four centuries: how self-consciousness operates, especially when it faces the sharpest and most painful dilemmas.

Background and Structure of the *Rondeau*

A comparison with a similar form clarifies the sonnet's advantages. *Tottel's Miscellany* introduced the rondeau to English. Almost precisely sonnet-length, the thirteen-line form includes several prominent repetitions. The first phrase repeats as a refrain in the other two stanzas. Not counting the refrain, the poem consists of three stanzas of five, three, and five lines, which rhyme a a b b a, a a b, and a a b b a. Wyatt wrote a half-dozen rondeaus that survive, including the following poem, which some editors represents as a single stanza:

> Help me to seek, for I lost it there,
> And if that ye have found it, ye that be here,
> And seek to convey it secretly,
> Handle it soft and treat it tenderly,
> Or else it will plain and then appear: 5
> But rather restore it mannerly,
> Since that I do ask it thus honestly:

For to lose it, it sitteth me too near.
  Help me to seek.
Alas, and is there no remedy?   10
But have I thus lost it wilfully?
I wis it was a thing all too dear
To be bestowed and wist not where—
It was my heart, I pray you heartily,
  Help me to seek.   15

When Tottel published Wyatt's poems, he revised three rondeaus, expanding the initial refrain to a full line and cutting the concluding refrain. Showing how little separated the forms, he changed the rondeaus into sonnets. Yet the two work very differently. A rondeau embodies steadfastness; it begins and ends with the same phrase. Unlike a ballad, narrative development does not complicate the refrain. The form inspires assertive displays of tenacity, whether patriotic (as in John McCrae's "In Flanders Fields") or racial (Paul Laurence Dunbar's "We Wear the Mask"), poems of impressive immobility.

The sonnet demands movement. It might be called the most lyric of the major lyric forms, focused inward, packed with tension and intensity, and inhospitable to asides and extended explanation. A form such as the heroic couplet licenses explication, elaboration, and digression. In theory a poet can go on for however long he or she wants. The sonnet in contrast demands a self-questioning brevity, as a poem contests the idea it just introduced. It excels at representing ambivalent self-reflection.

When addressing the grandest of themes—love, god, and politics—the sonnet requires great compression, a readjustment of scale in which seemingly trivial events grow in stature while great events are reduced to small moments. Ben Jonson "cursed Petrarch for redacting Verses to Sonnets," comparing the sonnet form to a tyrant's bed, in which "some who were too short were racked, others too long cut short." At its most effective, though, the sonnet's brevity inspires a passionate intensity, in which the lover lingers over nearly everything that the beloved does and does not do. As in life, moments of great fervor reconfigure time and distance: an absent lover feels wholly present while a brief meeting inspires decades of longing. While many of the sonnet's well-worn poses seem artificial and hackneyed, the form's defenders protest that its conventions capture the dynamics of passionate love, in particular the bittersweet emotions that desire arouses. "The sense contained in this Sonnet will seem strange," a Renaissance sonneteer explained, "to such as never been acquainted themselves with Love and his Laws, because of the contrarieties mentioned therein. But to such, as Love at any time hath under his banner, all and every part of it will appear to be a familiar truth."

Bursting with such "contrarieties," sonnets express strong emotions; reading a sequence straight through recalls the sensation of drinking shot after shot of espresso. A structural unbalance helps poems to achieve this dizzying effect. Rarely do poets split the fourteen lines into two, seven-line halves. Instead, sonnets typically feature a *volta* or turn at the start of the ninth line, where it shifts its tone or argument. Because sonnets generally turn against themselves, they excel at representing the self in conflict.

William Wordsworth's "Surprised by Joy" offers a good example:

Surprized by joy—impatient as the Wind
I wished to share the transport—Oh! with whom
But Thee, long buried in the silent Tomb,
That spot which no vicissitude can find?
Love, faithful love recalled thee to my mind—   5
But how could I forget thee?—Through what power,
Even for the least division of an hour,
Have I been so beguiled as to be blind
To my most grievous loss?—That thought's return
Was the worst pang that sorrow ever bore,   10
Save one, one only, when I stood forlorn,
Knowing my heart's best treasure was no more;
That neither present time, nor years unborn
Could to my sight that heavenly face restore.

The opening lines seem willfully averse to my analysis of how sonnets work; how can anyone be ambivalent about unexpected pleasure? Yet, as we have seen, sonnets turn against themselves. As in many other sonnets, the speaker is eager to narrate, "to share the transport." (Love sonnets in particular exploit a certain fact: that affairs demand to be recounted, which is why its participants endlessly describe them to anyone who will listen, especially themselves.) Before the speaker can describe his happiness, a greater absence overwhelms him, as he recalls that the person he addresses has passed away. Evoking the absent daughter with language familiar to the Petrarchan tradition, the poem quickly turns self-accusatory, "But how could I forget thee?" then sorrowfully guilt ridden, contemplating "the worst pang that sorrow ever bore." The final rhyme—"no more" and "restore"—addresses the poem's dilemma; no poem can raise the dead. At most it can atone for the speaker's rather understandable mistake, one perhaps necessary for his emotional health: he has momentarily forgotten his child's early death.

A master of the form, Claude McKay exploits the sonnet's doubleness in surprising ways. Like many other sonnets, "To the White Fiends" opens with a series of questions:

> Think you I am not fiend and savage too?
> Think you I could not arm me with a gun
> And shoot down ten of you for every one
> Of my black brothers murdered, burnt by you?
> Be not deceived, for every deed you do   5
> I could match—out-match: am I not Afric's son,
> Black of that black land where black deeds are done?
> But the Almighty from the darkness drew
> My soul and said: Even thou shalt be a light
> Awhile to burn on the benighted earth,   10
> Thy dusky face I set among the white
> For thee to prove thyself of higher worth;
> Before the world is swallowed up in night,
> To show thy little lamp: go forth, go forth!

First published in September 1919, the sonnet describes the tense atmosphere that followed a long summer of race riots, when McKay carried a gun for self-defense. The poem's form enacts the anger the octave expresses and the lofty status the sestet claims. Along with the hard monosyllabic rhymes, the heavy stresses spit out lines as challenges:

> Bláck of that bláck lánd where bláck déeds are dóne?

The octave threatens a modern violence, using a gun to kill ten whites for every one black killed by fire. The octave responds with archaic language that presents the speaker as divinely chosen. McKay did not employ the sonnet haphazardly. Like the other major poets of the Harlem Renaissance (except Hughes), he preferred it to more controversial forms such as the blues and jazz. By skillfully handling a well-established form, he asserted a cultured superiority, recasting the white racist as the "savage."

MORE WORKS IN THE *SONNET*

The sonnet has inspired many variations in English. The most familiar
types are the Shakespearean, which rhymes a b a b c d c d e f e f g g (represented by Shakespeare's "Two loves . . ."), and the Petrarchan, which has
two main rhyme schemes: a b b a a b b a and either c d e c d e or c d c d c d.
Milton's "On His Blindness" uses the first kind of Petrarchan sonnet. The
most common meter is iambic pentameter, though many sonnets use either
other meters or unmetrical lines.

WILLIAM SHAKESPEARE

Two loves I have, of comfort and despair,	*a*	
Which like two spirits do suggest me still:	*b*	
The better angel is a man right faire;	*a*	
The worser spirit a woman coloured ill.	*b*	
To win me soon to hell my female evil	*c*	5
Tempteth my better angel from my side,	*d*	
And would corrupt my saint to be a devil,	*c*	
Wooing his purity with her foul pride.	*d*	
And whether that my angel be turned fiend	*e*	
Suspect I may, yet not directly tell,	*f*	10
But being both from me, both to each friend,	*e*	
I guess one angel in another's hell.	*f*	
Yet this shall I ne'er know, but live in doubt,	*g*	
Till my bad angel fire my good one out.	*g*	

JOHN MILTON

When I consider how my light is spent,	*a*	
Ere half my days in this dark world and wide	*b*	
And that one talent which is death to hide	*b*	
Lodged with me useless, though my soul more bent	*a*	
To serve therewith my Maker, and present	*a*	5
My true account, lest he returning chide,	*b*	
"Doth God exact day-labor, light denied,"	*b*	
I fondly ask. But Patience, to prevent	*a*	
That murmur, soon replies, "God doth not need	*c*	
Either man's work or his own gifts; who best	*d*	10

Bear his mild yoke, they serve him best. His state   *e*
Is kingly. Thousands at his bidding speed,   *c*
And post o're land and ocean without rest;   *d*
They also serve who only stand and wait."   *e*

GEORGE HERBERT

Prayer, the church's banquet, angels' age,
    God's breath in man returning to his birth,
    The soul in paraphrase, heart in pilgrimage,
The Christian plummet sounding heav'n and earth;

Engine against th' Almighty, sinner's tower,   5
    Reversed thunder, Christ-side-piercing spear,
    The six-day's world transposing in an hour,
A kind of tune, which all things hear and fear;
Softness, and peace, and joy, and love, and bliss,
    Exalted manna, gladness of the best,   10
    Heaven in ordinary, man well dressed,
The Milky Way, the bird of Paradise,
Church bells beyond the stars heard, the soul's blood,
The land of spices; something understood.

JOHN DONNE
From *Holy Sonnets*

Batter my heart, three-personed God, for you
    As yet but knock, breathe, shine, and seek to mend;
    That I may rise and stand, o'erthrow me and bend
Your force to break, blow, burn and make me new.
I, like an usurped town to another due,   5
    Labour to admit you, but O, to no end.
    Reason your viceroy in me, me should defend,
But is captive'ed and proves weak or untrue,
Yet dearly I love you and would be loved fain,
    But am betrothed unto your enemy.   10
Divorce me, untie, or break that knot again,
    Take me to you, imprison me for I,
    Except you enthrall me, never shall be free,
    Nor ever chaste except you ravish me.

CHARLOTTE SMITH
From *Elegiac Sonnets,* SONNET I

The partial Muse has from my earliest hours
   Smiled on the rugged path I'm doomed to tread,
And still with sportive hand has snatch'd wild flowers,
   To weave fantastic garlands for my head:
But far, far happier is the lot of those   5
   Who never learn'd her dear delusive art;
Which, while it decks the head with many a rose,
   Reserves the thorn, to fester in the heart.
For still she bids soft Pity's melting eye
   Stream o'er the hills she knows not to remove,   10
Points every pang, and deepens every sigh
   Of mourning friendship, or unhappy love.
Ah! then, how dear the Muse's favours cost,
If those paint sorrow best—who feel it most!

SIR PHILIP SIDNEY
From *Astrophil and Stella*

Loving in truth, and fain in verse my love to show,
   That she, dear she, might take some pleasure of my pain,
   Pleasure might cause her read, reading might make her know,
   Knowledge might pity win, and pity grace obtain,—
I sought fit words to paint the blackest face of woe;   5
   Studying inventions fine, her wits to entertain,
   Oft turning others' leaves to see if thence would flow
   Some fresh and fruitful showers upon my sun-burned brain.
But words came halting forth, wanting invention's stay;
   Invention, nature's child, fled step-dame Study's blows,   10
   And others' feet still seemed but strangers in my way.
Thus, great with child to speak, and helpless in my throes,
   Biting my truant pen, beating myself for spite,
   Fool, said my muse to me, look in thy heart and write.

SIR PHILIP SIDNEY
From *Astrophil and Stella*

Who will in fairest book of Nature know,
How Virtue may best lodged in beauty be,

Let him but learn of love to read in thee,
Stella, whose fair lines, which true goodness show.
There shall he find all vices' overthrow,   5
Not by rude force, but sweetest sovereignty
Of reason, from whose light those night birds fly;
That inward sun in thine eyes shineth so.
And not content to be Perfection's heir
Thyself, dost strive all minds that way to move   10
Who mark in thee what is in thee most fair.
So while thy beauty draws the heart to love,
As fast thy Virtue bends that love to good:
"But ah," desire still cries, "give me some food."

SIR PHILIP SIDNEY
From *Astrophil and Stella*

With how sad steps, O moon, thou climb'st the skies!
   How silently, and with how wan a face!
   What! may it be that even in heavenly place
   That busy archer his sharp arrows tries?
Sure, if that long-with-love-acquainted eyes   5
   Can judge of love, thou feel'st a lover's case;
   I read it in thy looks,—thy languished grace
   To me, that feel the like, thy state descries.
Then, even of fellowship, O moon, tell me,
   Is constant love deemed there but want of wit?   10
   Are beauties there as proud as here they be?
Do they above love to be loved, and yet
   Those lovers scorn whom that love doth possess?
   Do they call virtue there ungratefulness?

SIR PHILIP SIDNEY
From *Astrophil and Stella*

Leave me, O love which reachest but to dust;
And thou, my mind, aspire to higher things;
Grow rich in that which never taketh rust,
Whatever fades but fading pleasure brings.
Draw in thy beams, and humble all thy might   5
To that sweet yoke where lasting freedoms be;

Which breaks the clouds and opens forth the light,
That doth both shine and give us sight to see.
O take fast hold; let that light be thy guide
In this small course which birth draws out to death,   10
And think how evil becometh him to slide,
Who seeketh heaven, and comes of heavenly breath.
    Then farewell, world; thy uttermost I see;
    Eternal Love, maintain thy life in me.

WILLIAM SHAKESPEARE

When in disgrace with fortune and men's eyes
I all alone beweep my outcast state,
And trouble deaf Heaven with my bootless cries,
And look upon myself and curse my fate,
Wishing me like to one more rich in hope,   5
Featured like him, like him with friends possessed,
Desiring this man's art and that man's scope,
With what I most enjoy contented least—
Yet in these thoughts myself almost despising,
Haply I think on thee, and then my state,   10
Like to the lark at break of day arising
From sullen earth, sings hymns at Heaven's gate.
    For thy sweet love remembered such wealth brings
    That then I scorn to change my state with kings.

WILLIAM SHAKESPEARE

My mistress' eyes are nothing like the sun,
Coral is far more red than her lips' red.
If snow be white, why then her breasts are dun,
If hairs be wires, black wires grow on her head.
I have seen roses damasked, red and white,   5
But no such roses see I in her cheeks.
And in some perfumes is there more delight
Than in the breath that from my mistress reeks.
I love to hear her speak, yet well I know
That music hath a far more pleasing sound.   10
I grant I never saw a goddess go,

My mistress, when she walks, treads on the ground.
  And yet, by Heaven, I think my loves as rare
  As any she belied with false compare.

JOHN MILTON
On the Late Massacre in Piedmont

Avenge, O Lord, thy slaughtered saints, whose bones
  Lie scattered on the Alpine mountains cold;
  Even them who kept thy truth so pure of old,
  When all our fathers worshipped stocks and stones,
Forget not: in thy book record their groans   5
  Who were thy sheep, and in their ancient fold
  Slain by the bloody Piedmontese, that rolled
  Mother with infant down the rocks. Their moans
The vales redoubled to the hills, and they
  To heaven. Their martyred blood and ashes sow   10
  O'er all the Italian fields, where still doth sway
The triple Tyrant; that from these may grow
  A hundred fold, who, having learnt thy way,
  Early may fly the Babylonian woe.

MARILYN NELSON WANIEK
Chopin

It's Sunday evening. Pomp holds the receipts
of all the colored families on the Hill
in his wide lap, and shows which white store cheats
these patrons, who can't read a weekly bill.
His parlor's full of men holding their hats   5
and women who admire his girls' good hair.
Pomp warns them not to vote for Democrats,
controlling half of Hickman from his chair.
The varying degrees of cheating seen,
he nods toward the piano. Slender, tall,   10
a Fisk girl passing-white, almost nineteen,
his Blanche folds the piano's paisley shawl
and plays Chopin. And blessed are the meek
who have to buy in white men's stores next week.

Percy Bysshe Shelley's "Ode to the West Wind" consists of five *terza rima* sonnets. Dante devised *terza rima* for the *Divine Comedy,* a poem that moves from hell to purgatory and, finally, heaven. *Terza rima's* three-part, forward moving structure echoes the pilgrim's journey as well as Christian numerology (namely, the Trinity). In the three-line stanza, the first and third lines rhyme and the middle rhyme sets the rhyme for the next stanza. The first stanza of Shelley's poem employs the endwords "being," "dead," and "fleeing"; the second stanza uses the middle endword, "dead," for the first and third lines' rhyme, "red," "Thou," and "bed."

PERCY BYSSHE SHELLEY
Ode to the West Wind

I
O wild West Wind, thou breath of Autumn's being,
Thou, from whose unseen presence the leaves dead
Are driven, like ghosts from an enchanter fleeing,

Yellow, and black, and pale, and hectic red,
Pestilence-stricken multitudes: O thou,   5
Who chariotest to their dark wintry bed

The winged seeds, where they lie cold and low,
Each like a corpse within its gave, until
Thine azure sister of the Spring shall blow

Her clarion o'er the dreaming earth, and fill   10
(Driving sweet buds like flocks to feed in air)
With living hues and odours plain and hill:

Wild Spirit, which art moving everywhere;
Destroyer and Preserver; hear, oh, hear!

II
Thou on whose stream, mid the steep sky's commotion,   15
Loose clouds like earth's decaying leaves are shed,
Shook from the tangled boughs of Heaven and Ocean,

Angels of rain and lightning: there are spread
On the blue surface of thine aëry surge,
Like the bright hair uplifted form the head   20

Of some fierce Maenad, even from the dim verge
Of the horizon to the zenith's height,
The locks of the approaching storm. Thou dirge

Of the dying year, to which this closing night
Will be the dome of a vast sepulchre,   25
Vaulted with all thy congregated might

Of vapours, from whose solid atmosphere
Black rain, and fire, and hail will burst: oh, hear!

III
Thou who didst waken from his summer dreams
The blue Mediterranean, where he lay,   30
Lulled by the coil of his chrystalline streams,

Beside a pumice isle in Baiae's bay,
And saw in sleep old palaces and towers
Quivering within the wave's intenser day,

All overgrown with azure moss and flowers   35
So sweet, the sense faints picturing them! Thou
For whose path the Atlantic's level powers

Cleave themselves into chasms, while far below
The sea-blooms and the oozy woods which wear
The sapless foliage of the ocean, know   40

Thy voice, and suddenly grow gray with fear,
And tremble and despoil themselves: oh, hear!

IV
If I were a dead leaf thou mightest bear;

If I were a swift cloud to fly with thee;
A wave to pant beneath thy power, and share   45

The impulse of thy strength, only less free
Than thou, O uncontrollable! If even
I were as in my boyhood, and could be

The comrade of thy wanderings over Heaven,
As then, when to outstrip thy skiey speed   50
Scarce seemed a vision; I would ne'er have striven

As thus with thee in prayer in my sore need.
Oh, lift me as a wave, a leaf, a cloud!
I fall upon the thorns of life! I bleed!

A heavy weight of hours has chained and bowed.   55
One too like thee: tameless, and swift, and proud.

Make me thy lyre, even as the forest is:
What if my leaves are falling like its own!
The tumult of thy mighty harmonies

Will take from both a deep, autumnal tone,   60
Sweet though in sadness. Be thou, Spirit fierce,
My spirit! Be thou me, impetuous one!

Drive my dead thoughts over the universe
Like withered leaves to quicken a new birth!
And, by the incantation of this verse,   65

Scatter, as from an unextinguished hearth
Ashes and sparks, my words among mankind!
Be through my lips to unawakened earth

The trumpet of prophecy! O, Wind,
If Winter comes, can Spring be far behind?   70

MORE WORKS IN THE *RONDEAU*

JOHN MCCRAE
In Flanders Fields

In Flanders fields the poppies blow
Between the crosses, row on row,
   That mark our place; and in the sky
   The larks, still bravely singing, fly
Scarce heard amid the guns below.   5

We are the dead. Short days ago
We lived, felt dawn, saw sunset glow,
   Loved, and were loved, and now we lie
     In Flanders fields.

Take up our quarrel with the foe: 10
To you from failing hands we throw
   The torch; be yours to hold it high.
   If ye break faith with us who die
We shall not sleep, though poppies grow
     In Flanders fields.   15

PAUL LAURENCE DUNBAR
We Wear the Mask

We wear the mask that grins and lies,
   It hides our cheeks and shades our eyes,—
This debt we pay to human guile;
With torn and bleeding hearts we smile,
And mouth with myriad subtleties.   5

Why should the world be over-wise,
In counting all our tears and sighs?
Nay, let them only see us, while
     We wear the mask.

We smile, but, O great Christ, our cries   10
To thee from tortured souls arise.
We sing, but oh the clay is vile
Beneath our feet, and long the mile;
But let the world dream otherwise,
    We wear the mask!   15

AN EXERCISE IN THE *SONNET*

Many of the sonnets we have read present a self in conflict, as the speaker faces
grave theological or emotional difficulties. Such sonnets are self-questioning;
their speakers question what they know. To imitate this dynamic, write a sonnet
whose speaker defends a person that he or she wishes to accuse, or accuses a person he or she wishes to defend. The person need not be a lover. Regardless, the
poem should pose at least one accusatory question that pivots into a justification.
As a model, you might consult Shakespeare's "When my love swears she is made
of truth," in which a pair of questions "But wherefore says she not she is unjust? /
And wherefore say not I that I am old?" that leads to a pronouncement that the
speaker only partially believes ("O loves best habit is in seeming trust").

5

COUPLETS

John Dryden called couplet verse "the most easy" of rhyming forms. According to Dryden, the form requires less work than quatrain verse, poetry in four-line stanzas. When a poet composes pairs of rhyming lines, "the work is sooner at end, every two lines concluding the labor of the poet." Dryden means that a writer of couplets thinks one line ahead whereas the writer of quatrains works in four-line units. Poets who write quatrains, Dryden maintained, "must bear along in his head the troublesome sense of four lines together." A writer of couplets attends to two lines; a writer of quatrains addresses "the troublesome sense" of four.

JOHN DRYDEN
To the Memory of Mr. Oldham

Farewell, too little and too lately known,
Whom I began to think and call my own:
For sure our souls were near allied, and thine
Cast in the same poetic mold with mine.
One common note on either lyre did strike,   5
And knaves and fools we both abhorred alike.

To the same goal did both our studies drive;
The last set out the soonest did arrive.
Thus Nisus fell upon the slippery place,
While his young friend performed and won the race.   10
O early ripe! To thy abundant store
What could advancing age have added more?
It might (what nature never gives the young)
Have taught the numbers of thy native tongue.
But satire needs not those, and wit will shine   15
Through the harsh cadence of a rugged line;
A noble error, and but seldom made,
When poets are by too much force betrayed.
Thy gen'rous fruits, though gathered ere their prime
Still showed a quickness; and maturing time   20
But mellows what we write to the dull sweets of rhyme.
Once more, hail and farewell; farewell, thou young,
But ah too short, Marcellus of our tongue;
Thy brows with ivy and with laurels bound;
But fate and gloomy night encompass thee around.   25

Background and Structure of the *Couplet*

Couplet verse might be easier to write competently than rhyming quatrains, but it may be harder to write *well*. Less complicated forms pose significant challenges. The rhyme's close proximity makes a bad rhyme
conspicuous, while a quatrain's third line can hide a less successful
rhyme. Couplet verse requires considerable skill to keep the poetry from
simply fulfilling the form's requirements. When a scholar laments "the
dull sameness of heroic couplets," he ignores successful examples. Attentive to the form's potential for "dull sameness," shrewd writers establish
variety within the couplet's seemingly rigid structure.

Dryden's own verse offers illuminating examples. Included in full at the
end of this chapter, "MacFlecknoe" relentlessly attacks Dryden's poetic
rival, the playwright Thomas Shadwell. Significantly, "dullness" constitutes
Shadwell's main fault, as when MacFlecknoe claims Shadwell as his heir:

Shadwell alone my perfect image bears,
Mature in dullness from his tender years:
Shadwell alone, of all my sons, is he
Who stands confirmed in full stupidity.

Each couplet offers what Dryden elsewhere calls "the jerk or sting of the epigram," a short, wounding insult. The rhyme adds a little sneer. This kind of couplet verse gains momentum as it progresses; it gives the impression that Dryden could continue forever, cataloguing Shadwell's faults. Such expansiveness marks much extended couplet verse, as the form relentlessly generates additional lines. This forward drive overtakes bad couplet verse, which seems unable to stop. Dryden, though, turns this dynamic to his advantage. The effortless movement from attack to attack enumerates Shadwell's faults. The repeated accusations convey the glee that Dryden feels when he ridicules his rival. In short, Dryden shows the great fun of attacking an easy target. The poem contrasts its cleverness with Shadwell's dullness, as when Dryden rhymes the one-syllable pronoun "he" with the multi syllabic noun "stupidity." Each prosodic flourish sharpens the comparison. "Thy inoffensive satires never bite," the poem later charges; the same cannot be said of Dryden's couplets.

"To the Memory of Mr. Oldham" uses the same form differently. A more somber, restrained poem, an elegy, not a satire, "To the Memory of Mr. Oldham" excuses a version of the defect that "MacFlecknoe" finds inexcusable: the lack of poetic skill.

> O early ripe! To thy abundant store
> What could advancing age have added more?
> It might (what nature gives the young)
> Have taught the numbers of thy native tongue.
> But Satire needs not these, and Wit will shine   5
> Through the harsh cadence of a rugged line.
> A noble error, and but seldom made,
> When poets are by too much force betrayed.

These rhymes are not flashy; with only a few exceptions, Dryden uncharacteristically sticks to rather plain, one-syllable rhymes. Instead of employing prosody to rebuke a rival's ineptitude, Dryden uses it to console. Couplet verse often works in rhetorical pairs, with thesis and antithesis, and parallelism. This passage builds a series of contrast— youth and old age, immature and mature poetry—but the couplets moderate these contrasts rather than set them into strict opposition. Instead of scorn, Dryden adds qualification upon qualification. For this strategy to work, the couplets cannot exist autonomously because the reader would pause over Oldham's poetic failure. They exist less as a series of epigrams, quotable, pithy statements, than as an extended meditation.

Consider, for instance, the characterization:

A noble error, and but seldom made,
When poets are by too much force betrayed.

These nicely balanced lines pivot around two mid-line pauses, the first falling after the fifth syllable and the second after the fourth. Readers who dislike couplet verse note how often its writers use adjectives to pad the line, to find enough syllables to fulfill the requirements. Such critics of the form might want to rearrange Dryden's couplet, removing an adjective from each line and, thus, one metrical foot:

An error, and but seldom made,
When poets are by force betrayed.

This change ruins the couplet. Dryden's lines emphasize the qualification, not the act: the adjectives "noble," not the noun it modifies, "error." They do so to direct attention away from Oldham's shortcomings and to emphasize his essential worth. "MacFlecknoe" cleanly separates the good poets from the bad; "To the Memory of Mr. Oldham" portrays a difference of degree, not kind.

Dryden wrote "heroic couplets," endstopped pairs of rhyming lines. The term derives from his translation of Virgil's Aeneid and Alexander Pope's translation of Homer's Iliad, which adapted those works' unrhymed hexameters into couplet verse. Pope admired Dryden's work. "I learned versification," he said, "wholly from Dryden's works." Yet Pope also claimed to improve Dryden's model, bringing it "to its perfection." The period from Dryden's birth in 1631 to Pope's death in 1744 witnessed the couplet's dramatic growth, when it achieved an unparalleled popularity and accomplishment. Poets such as Chaucer, Shakespeare, and Donne composed couplets before Dryden's birth; Byron, Keats, and, more recently, Robert Frost, Thom Gunn, and Marilyn Hacker wrote couplets after Pope's death. Later writers—most notably, Robert Browning—often worked to disguise the form, enjambing the lines to make the rhymes less prominent. Wilfred Owen uses off-rhymes, a strategy that the contemporary poet Jeredith Merrin pushes to an extreme. Achieving an odd, arresting music, Merrin's poem employs flamboyant rhymes, some full and some off, as well as varying the line lengths.

In the Augustan Age, though, virtually every noteworthy poet composed verse in this form, and the period's greatest poet, Pope, used it nearly exclusively, achieving a dazzling variety of effects. Dryden called rhyme "unnatural in a play." "No man," Dryden observed, "speaks in rhyme, neither ought he to do it on stage." Pope did not write plays; if he did, his characters would speak in couplets. Verse, he believed, requires a certain artificiality; an actor speaks differently when chatting to a stage-hand backstage than he does when performing to a paying audience. The couplet converts private thoughts into public utterance.

In Pope's work, each couplet stages a drama. At its best, it fulfills the reader's general expectations—Pope never violates the form—in surprising, inventive ways. A rigid form demands variety. Pope objected to rhymes repeated in near proximity as "tiresome to the Ear thro' their Monotony" and ridiculed poets who used "still expected rhymes":

Where-e'er you find *the cooling Western Breeze*,
In the Line, it *whispers thro' the Trees*;
If *Chrystal Streams with pleasing Murmurs creep*,
The Reader's threatened (not in vain) with *Sleep*.

Fulfilling this prophecy nearly two centuries later, Wallace Stevens chastised himself for the same mistake. "In the 'June Book,'" Stevens recalled, "I made 'breeze' rhyme with 'trees,' and have never forgiven myself." Verbal clichés inspire bad rhymes because they commit the same poetic sin; they bore the reader. (Stevens called his rhyme "unpardonably 'expected.'" Instead of the soporific "*Breeze* / *Trees*," "*creep* / *Sleep*," Pope's rhymes find unexpected relations, moving between languages ("true" and "*Billet-Doux*"), distant places ("the British Queen" and "a charming Indian Screen"), and incongruous states ("chaste" and "embrac'd). To keep versification from growing monotonous, the poet also varies the mid-line pause. Pope observed "that in any smooth English Verse of ten syllables, there is naturally a *Pause* at the fourth, fifth, or sixth syllable," "the judicious Change and Management of which depends the Variety of Versification."

The opening of Pope's "Epistle to Dr. Aburthnot" demonstrates these principles in action:

Shut, shut the door, good John! fatigued, I said.
Tie up the knocker! say I'm sick, I'm dead.
The dog-star rages! nay, 'tis past a doubt,
All Bedlam, or Parnassus, is let out:
Fire in each eye, and papers in each hand,   5
They rave, recite, and madden round the land . . . .

Just the mid-line pause shifts between the different positions, the meter achieves an impressive variety within a strict construction. Pope substitutes less frequently than any other major poet in English; his work shows the diversity that a seeming unvarying pattern can achieve. The first line, for instance, is perfectly regular iambic pentameter:

Shŭt, shút | thĕ doór, | goŏd Joh́n! | fătigúed, | Ĭ saíd,

The second "shut" receives more stress than the first, as the speaker, growing frantic, repeats his command. "Good" is swallowed in the clamor when the overwhelmed speaker shouts his servant's name, "John," appealing for his aid. Samuel Johnson praised Pope's verse as "always smooth, uniform, and gentle," "a velvet lawn, shaven by the scythe, and levelled by the roller." This passage, though, suggests the wildness that Pope's couplets achieve, while they stay within the form's strict parameters.

MORE WORKS IN *COUPLET VERSE*

Couplet verse rhymes in pairs; typically the meter is iambic pentameter, as in Ben Jonson's elegy, "On My First Son."

BEN JONSON
On My First Son

Farewell, thou child of my right hand, and joy;	a	
My sin was too much hope of thee, lov'd boy:	a	
Seven years thou wert lent to me, and I thee pay,	b	
Exacted by thy fate, on the just day.	b	
O could I lose all father now! For why	c	5
Will man lament the state he should envy,	c	
To have so soon 'scaped world's and flesh's rage,	d	
And if no other misery, yet age?	d	
Rest in soft peace, and, asked, say, "Here doth lie	e	
Ben Jonson his best piece of poetry."	e	10
For whose sake henceforth all his vows be such	f	
As what he loves may never like too much.	f	

ALEXANDER POPE
Epistle to Dr. Arbuthnot

P. Shut, shut the door, good John! fatigued, I said.
Tie up the knocker say I'm sick, I'm dead.
The dog-star rages! nay, 'tis past a doubt,
All Bedlam, or Parnassus, is let out:
Fire in each eye, and papers in each hand,   5
They rave, recite, and madden round the land.
What walls can guard me, or what shades can hide?
They pierce my thickets, through my grot they glide.
By land, by water, they renew the charge,
They stop the chariot, and they board the barge.   10
No place is sacred, not the church is free,
Ev'n Sunday shines no Sabbath-day to me:
Then from the Mint walks forth the man of rhyme,
Happy! to catch me just at dinner-time.
    Is there a parson, much bemused in beer,   15
A maudlin poetess, a rhyming peer,
A clerk, foredoomed his father's soul to cross,
Who pens a stanza when he should engross?
Is there, who, locked from ink and paper, scrawls
With desp'rate charcoal round his darkened walls?   20
All fly to Twit'nam, and in humble strain
Apply to me to keep them mad or vain.
Arthur, whose giddy son neglects the laws,
Imputes to me and my damned works the cause:
Poor Cornus sees his frantic wife elope,   25
And curses wit, and poetry, and Pope.
    Friend to my life! (which did not you prolong,
The world had wanted many an idle song)
What drop or nostrum can this plague remove?
Or which must end me, a fool's wrath or love?   30
A dire dilemma! either way I'm sped,
If foes, they write, if friends, they read me dead.
Seized and tied down to judge, how wretched I,
Who can't be silent, and who will not lie:
To laugh were want of goodness and of grace,   35
And to be grave exceeds all power of face.
I sit with sad civility, I read

With honest anguish and an aching head;
And drop at last, but in unwilling ears,
This saving counsel, "Keep your piece nine years."   40
  "Nine Years!" cries he who, high in Drury Lane,
Lulled by soft zephyrs through the broken pane,
Rhymes ere he wakes, and prints before Term ends,
Obliged by hunger and request of friends:
  "The piece, you think, is incorrect? why take it: 45
I'm all submission; what you'd have it, make it."
  Three things another's modest wishes bound:
My friendship, and a prologue, and ten pound.
  Pitholeon sends to me: "You know his Grace,
I want a patron; ask him for a place.   50
Pitholeon libeled me—"But here's a letter
Informs you, sir, 'Twas when he knew no better.
Dare you refuse him? Curll invites to dine;
He'll write a *Journal*, or he'll turn divine."
  Bless me! a packet.—"Tis a stranger sues,   55
A virgin tragedy, an orphan Muse."
If I dislike it, "Furies, death, and rage!"
If I approve, "Commend it to the stage."
There (thank my stars) my whole commission ends;
The players and I are, luckily, no friends.   60
Fired that the house reject him, " 'Sdeath, I'll print it,
And shame the fools—your int'rest, Sir, with Lintot."
"Lintot, dull rogue! will think your price too much!"
"Not, Sir, if you revise it, and retouch."
All my demurs but double his attacks;   65
At last he whispers, "Do; and we go snacks."
Glad of a quarrel, straight I clap the door:
"Sir, let me see your works and you no more."
  'Tis sung, when Midas' ears began to spring
(Midas, a sacred person and a king),   70
His very minister who spied them first
(Some say his queen) was forced to speak, or burst.
And is not mine, my friend, a sorer case,
When every coxcomb perks them in my face?
  A. Good friend, forbear! you deal in dang'rous things;   75
I'd never name queens, ministers, or kings.
Keep close to ears, and those let asses prick;
'Tis nothing—P. Nothing? if they bite and kick?

Out with it, *Dunciad!* let the secret pass,
That secret to each fool, that he's an ass.   80
The truth once told (and wherefore should we lie?),
The queen of Midas slept, and so may I.
   You think this cruel? take it for a rule,
No creature smarts so little as a fool.
Let peals of laughter, Codrus! round thee break,   85
Thou unconcerned canst hear the mighty crack:
Pit, box, and gall'ry in convulsions hurled,
Thou stand'st unshook amidst a bursting world.
Who shames a scribbler? break one cobweb through,
He spins the slight, self-pleasing thread anew: 90
Destroy his fib or sophistry, in vain,
The creature's at his dirty work again,
Throned in the center of his thin designs,
Proud of a vast extent of flimsy lines!
Whom have I hurt? has poet yet, or peer,   95
Lost the arched eyebrow, or Parnassian sneer?
And has not Colley still his lord, and whore?
His butchers Henley? his Freemasons Moore?
Does not one table Bavius still admit?
Still to one bishop Philips seem a wit?   100
Still Sappho—A. Hold! for God's sake—you'll offend,
No names—be calm—learn prudence of a friend.
I too could write, and I am twice as tall;
But foes like these—P. One flatter's worse than all.
Of all mad creatures, if the learned are right,   105
It is the slaver kills, and not the bite.
A fool quite angry is quite innocent:
Alas! 'tis ten times worse when they repent.
   One dedicates in high heroic prose,
And ridicules beyond a hundred foes;   110
One from all Grub Street will my fame defend,
And, more abusive, calls himself my friend.
This prints my letters, that expects a bribe,
And others roar aloud, "Subscribe, subscribe."
   There are, who to my person pay their court: 115
I cough like Horace, and, though lean, am short;
Ammon's great son one shoulder had too high,
Such Ovid's nose, and, "Sir! you have an eye:"
Go on, obliging creatures, make me see

All that disgraced my betters met in me.   120
Say for my comfort, languishing in bed,
"Just so immortal Maro held his head;"
And when I die, be sure you let me know
Great Homer died three thousand years ago.

    Why did I write? what sin to me unknown   125
Dipped me in ink, my parents', or my own?
As yet a child, nor yet a fool to fame,
I lisped in numbers, for the numbers came.
I left no calling for this idle trade,
No duty broke, no father disobeyed.   130
The Muse but served to ease some friend, not wife,
To help me through this long disease, my life;
To second, Arbuthnot! thy art and care,
And teach the being you preserved, to bear.
    But why then publish? Granville the polite,   135
And knowing Walsh, would tell me I could write;
Well-natured Garth inflamed with early praise;
And Congreve loved, and Swift endured my lays;
The courtly Talbot, Somers, Sheffield, read;
Ev'n mitered Rochester would nod the head,   140
And St. John's self (great Dryden's friends before)
With open arms received one poet more.
Happy my studies, when by these approved!
Happier their author, when by these beloved!
From these the world will judge of men and books,   145
Not from the Burnets, Oldmixons, and Cookes.
    Soft were my numbers; who could take offense,
While pure description held the place of sense?
Like gentle Fanny's was my flow'ry theme:
A painted mistress, or a purling stream.   150
Yet then did Gildon draw his venal quill;
I wished the man a dinner, and sate still.
Yet then did Dennis rave in furious fret;
I never answered—I was not in debt.
If want provoked, or madness made them print,   155
I waged no war with Bedlam or the Mint.
    Did some more sober critic come abroad?
If wrong, I smiled; if right, I kissed the rod.

Pains, reading, study are their just pretense,
And all they want is spirit, taste, and sense.   160
Commas and points they set exactly right,
And 'twere a sin to rob them of their mite.
Yet ne'er one sprig of laurel graced these ribalds,
From slashing Bentley down to piddling Tibbalds.
Each wight who reads not, and but scans and spells,   165
Each word-catcher that lives on syllables,
Ev'n such small critics some regard may claim,
Preserved in Milton's or in Shakespeare's name.
Pretty! in amber to observe the forms
Of hairs, or straws, or dirt, or grubs, or worms!   170
The things, we know, are neither rich nor rare,
But wonder how the devil they got there.
    Were others angry? I excused them too;
Well might they rage; I gave them but their due.
A man's true merit 'tis not hard to find;   175
But each man's secret standard in his mind,
That casting-weight pride adds to emptiness,
This, who can gratify? for who can guess?
The bard whom pilfered pastorals renown,
Who turns a Persian tale for half a crown,   180
Just writes to make his barrenness appear,
And strains from hard-bound brains eight lines a year;
He, who still wanting, though he lives on theft,
Steals much, spends little, yet has nothing left;
And he, who now to sense, now nonsense leaning,   185
Means not, but blunders round about a meaning;
And he, whose fustian's so sublimely bad,
It is not poetry, but prose run mad:
All these my modest satire bade translate,
And owned that nine such poets made a Tate.   190
How did they fume, and stamp, and roar, and chafe!
And swear, not Addison himself was safe.
    Peace to all such! But were there one whose fires
True genius kindles and fair fame inspires;
Blessed with each talent and each art to please,   195
And born to write, converse, and live with ease;
Should such a man, too fond to rule alone,
Bear, like the Turk, no brother near the throne;

View him with scornful, yet with jealous eyes,
And hate for arts that caused himself to rise;   200
Damn with faint praise, assent with civil leer,
And without sneering, teach the rest to sneer;
Willing to wound, and yet afraid to strike,
Just hint a fault, and hesitate dislike;
Alike reserved to blame or to commend,   205
A timor'us foe, and a suspicious friend;
Dreading ev'n fools, by flatterers besieged,
And so obliging, that he ne'er obliged;
Like Cato, give his little senate laws,
And sit attentive to his own applause;   210
While wits and Templars every sentence raise,
And wonder with a foolish face of praise—
Who but must laugh, if such a man there be?
Who would not weep, if Atticus were he?
    What though my name stood rubric on the walls,   215
Or plastered posts, with claps, in capitals?
Or smoking forth, a hundred hawkers' load,
On wings of winds came flying all abroad?
I sought no homage from the race that write;
I kept, like Asian monarchs, from their sight: 220
Poems I heeded (now be-rhymed so long)
No more than thou, great George! a birthday song,
I ne'er with wits or witlings passed my days
To spread about the itch of verse and praise;
Nor like a puppy daggled through the town,   225
To fetch and carry sing-song up and down;
Nor at rehearsals sweat, and mouthed, and cried,
With handkerchief and orange at my side;
But sick of fops, and poetry, and prate,
To Bufo left the whole Castalian state.   230
    Proud as Apollo on his forkèd hill
Sat full-blown Bufo, puffed by every quill;
Fed with soft dedication all day long,
Horace and he went hand in hand in song.
His library (where busts of poets dead   235
And a true Pindar stood without a head)
Received of wits an undistinguished race,
Who first his judgment asked, and then a place;

Much they extolled his pictures, much his seat,
And flattered every day, and some days eat: 240
Till grown more frugal in his riper days,
He paid some bards with port, and some with praise;
To some a dry rehearsal was assigned,
And others (harder still) be paid in kind.
Dryden alone (what wonder?) came not nigh,   245
Dryden alone escaped this judging eye;
But still the great have kindness in reserve,
He helped to bury whom he helped to starve.
  May some choice patron bless each grey-goose quill!
May every Bavius have his Bufo still!   250
So when a statesman wants a day's defense;
Or envy holds a whole week's war with sense,
Or simple pride for flattery makes demands,
May dunce by dunce be whistled off my hands!
Blessed be the great! for those they take away,   255
And those they left me; for they left me Gay;
Left me to see neglected genius bloom,
Neglected die, and tell it on his tomb:
Of all thy blameless life the sole return
My verse, and Queensberry weeping o'er thy urn!   260
  Oh, let me live my own, and die so too!
"To live and die is all I have to do."
Maintain a poet's dignity and ease,
And see what friends and read what books I please;
Above a patron, though I condescend   265
Sometimes to call a minister my friend.
I was not born for courts or great affairs;
I pay my debts, believe, and say my prayers;
Can sleep without a poem in my head,
Nor know if Dennis be alive or dead.   270
  Why am I asked what next shall see the light?
Heav'ns! was I born for nothing but to write?
Has life no joys for me? or (to be grave)
Have I no friend to serve, no soul to save?
"I found him close with Swift"—"Indeed? no doubt,"   275
Cries prating Balbus, "something will come out."
'Tis all in vain, deny it as I will:
"No, such a genius never can lie still";

And then for mine obligingly mistakes
The first lampoon Sir Will or Bubo makes.   280
Poor guiltless I! and can I choose but smile,
When every coxcomb knows me by my style?
   Cursed be the verse, how well soe'er it flow,
That tends to make one worthy man my foe,
Give virtue scandal, innocence a fear,   285
Or from the soft-eyed virgin steal a tear!
But he who hurts a harmless neighbor's peace,
Insults fall'n worth, or beauty in distress,
Who loves a lie, lame slander helps about
Who writes a libel, or who copies out;   290
That fop whose pride affects a patron's name,
Yet absent, wounds an author's honest fame;
Who can your merit selfishly approve,
And show the sense of it without the love;
Who has the vanity to call you friend,   295
Yet wants the honor, injured, to defend;
Who tells whate'er you think, whate'er you say,
And, if he lie not, must at least betray;
Who to the *dean* and *silver bell* can swear,
And sees at Cannons what was never there: 300
Who reads but with a lust to misapply,
Make satire a lampoon, and fiction lie.
A lash like mine no honest man shall dread,
But all such babbling blockheads in his stead.
   Let Sporus tremble—A. What? that thing of silk,   305
Sporus, that mere white curd of ass's milk?
Satire or sense, alas! can Sporus feel?
Who breaks a butterfly upon a wheel?
   P. Yet let me flap this bug with gilded wings,
This painted child of dirt, that stinks and stings;   310
Whose buzz the witty and the fair annoys,
Yet wit ne'er tastes, and beauty ne'er enjoys:
So well-bred spaniels civilly delight
In mumbling of the game they dare not bite.
Eternal smiles his emptiness betray,   315
As shallow streams run dimpling all the way.
Whether in florid impotence he speaks,
And, as the prompter breathes, the puppet squeaks;

Or at the ear of Eve, familiar toad,
Half froth, half venom, spits himself abroad,   320
In puns, or politics, or tales, or lies,
Or spite, or smut, or rhymes, or blasphemies;
His wit all see-saw, between that and this,
Now high, now low, now master up, now miss,
And he himself one vile antithesis.   325
Amphibious thing! that acting either part,
The trifling head or the corrupted heart,
Fop at the toilet, flatt'rer at the board,
Now trips a lady, and now struts a lord.
Eve's tempter thus the rabbins have expressed,   330
A cherub's face, a reptile all the rest.
Beauty that shocks you, parts that none will trust,
Wit that can creep, and pride that licks the dust.
    Not fortune's worshiper, nor fashion's fool,
Not lucre's madman, nor ambition's tool,   335
Not proud, nor servile, be one poet's praise,
That if he pleased, he pleased by manly ways:
That, flattery, even to kings, he held a shame;
And thought a lie in verse or prose the same
That not in fancy's maze he wandered long,   340
But stooped to truth and moralized his song;
That not for fame, but virtue's better end,
He stood the furious foe, the timid friend,
The damning critic, half-approving wit,
The coxcomb hit, or fearing to be hit;   345
Laughed at the loss of friends he never had,
The dull, the proud, the wicked, and the mad;
The distant threats of vengeance on his head,
The blow unfelt, the tear he never shed;
The tale revived, the lie so oft o'erthrown,   350
Th' imputed trash, and dullness not his own;
The morals blackened when the writings 'scape,
The libeled person, and the pictured shape;
Abuse, on all he loved, or loved him, spread,
A friend in exile, or a father dead;   355
The whisper that, to greatness still too near,
Perhaps yet vibrates on his sov'reign's ear—
Welcome for thee, fair Virtue! all the past

For thee, fair virtue! welcome even the last!
A. But why insult the poor, affront the great?   360
P. A knave's a knave to me, in every state;
Alike my scorn if he succeed or fail:
Sporus at court, or Japhet in a jail,
A hireling scribbler, or a hireling peer,
Knight of the post corrupt, or of the shire;   365
If on a pillory, or near a throne,
He gain his prince's ear, or lose his own.
    Yet soft by nature, more a dupe than wit,
Sappho can tell you how this man was bit;
This dreaded sat'rist Dennis will confess   370
Foe to his pride, but friend to his distress:
So humble he has knocked at Tibbald's door,
Has drunk with Cibber, nay, has rhymed for Moore.
Full ten years slandered, did he once reply?
Three thousand suns went down on Welsted's lie.   375
To please a mistress one aspersed his life;
He lashed him not, but let her be his wife.
Let Budgell charge low Grub Street on his quill,
And write whate'er he pleased, except his will.
Let the two Curlls of town and court abuse   380
His father, mother, body, soul, and Muse—
Yet why? that father held it for a rule,
It was a sin to call our neighbor fool;
That harmless mother thought no wife a whore:
Hear this, spare his family, James Moore!   385
Unspotted names, and memorable long!
If there be force in virtue, or in song.
    Of gentle blood (part shed in honor's cause,
While yet in Britain honor had applause)
Each parent sprung.—A. What fortune, pray?—P. Their own, 390
And better got, than Bestia's from the throne.
Born to no pride, inheriting no strife,
Nor marrying discord in a noble wife,
Stranger to civil and religious rage,
The good man walked innoxious through his age.   395
No courts he saw, no suits would ever try,
Nor dared an oath, nor hazarded a lie.
Unlearned, he knew no schoolman's subtle art,

No language but the language of the heart.
By nature honest, by experience wise,   400
Healthy by temp'rance, and by exercise;
His life, though long, to sickness passed unknown,
His death was instant, and without a groan.
O grant me thus to live, and thus to die!
Who sprung from kings shall know less joy than I.   405
    O Friend! may each domestic bliss be thine!
Be no unpleasing melancholy mine;
Me, let the tender office long engage
To rock the cradle of reposing age;
With lenient arts extend a mother's breath,   410
Make languor smile, and smooth the bed of death;
Explore the thought, explain the asking eye,
And keep awhile one parent from the sky!
On cares like these if length of days attend,
May heav'n, to bless those days, preserve my friend,   415
Preserve him social, cheerful, and serene,
And just as rich as when he served a queen!
    A. Whether that blessing be denied or giv'n,
Thus far was right, the rest belongs to heav'n.

JOHN DRYDEN
MacFlecknoe

All human things are subject to decay,
And when fate summons, monarchs must obey.
This Flecknoe found, who, like Augustus, young
Was called to empire, and had governed long;
In prose and verse was owned, without dispute,   5
Through all the realms of Nonsense, absolute.
This aged prince, now flourishing in peace,
And blessed with issue of a large increase;
Worn out with business, did at length debate
To settle the succession of the state;   10
And, pond'ring which of all his sons was fit
To reign, and wage immortal war with wit,
Cried: " 'Tis resolved; for nature pleads that he
Should only rule, who most resembles me.
Sh——— alone my perfect image bears,   15

Mature in dullness from his tender years:
Sh———— alone, of all my sons is he
Who stands confirmed in full stupidity.
The rest to some faint meaning make pretense,
But Sh———— never deviates into sense.   20
Some beams of wit on other souls may fall,
Strike through, and make a lucid interval;
But Sh————'s genuine night admits no ray,
His rising fogs prevail upon the day.
Besides, his goodly fabric fills the eye,   25
And seems designed for thoughtless majesty;
Thoughtless as monarch oaks that shade the plain,
And, spread in solemn state, supinely reign.
Heywood and Shirley were but types of thee,
Thou last great prophet of tautology.   30
Ev'n I, a dunce of more renown than they,
Was sent before but to prepare thy way;
And, coarsely clad in Norwich drugget, came
To teach the nations in thy greater name.
My warbling lute, the lute I whilom strung,   35
When to King John of Portugal I sung,
Was but the prelude to that glorious day,
When thou on silver Thames didst cut thy way,
With well-timed oars before the royal barge,
Swelled with the pride of thy celestial charge;   40
And big with hymn, commander of a host,
The like was ne'er in Epsom blankets tossed.
Methinks I see the new Arion sail,
The lute still trembling underneath thy nail.
At thy well-sharpened thumb from shore to shore   45
The treble squeaks for fear, the basses roar;
Echoes from Pissing Alley Sh———— call,
And Sh———— they resound from Aston Hall.
About thy boat the little fishes throng,
As at the morning toast that floats along.   50
Sometimes, as prince of thy harmonious band,
Thou wield'st thy papers in thy threshing hand,
St. André's feet ne'er kept more equal time,
Not ev'n the feet of thy own *Psyché's* rhyme;

Though they in number as in sense excel: 55
So just, so like tautology, they fell,
That, pale with envy, Singleton forswore
The lute and sword, which he in triumph bore,
And vowed he ne'er would act Villerius more."
Here stopped the good old sire, and wept for joy   60
In silent raptures of the hopeful boy.
All arguments, but most his plays, persuade
That for anointed dullness he was made.
   Close to the walls which fair Augusta bind
(The fair Augusta much to fears inclined),   65
An ancient fabric, raised t'inform the sight,
There stood of yore, and Barbican it hight:
A watchtower once; but now, so fate ordains,
Of all the pile an empty name remains.
From its old ruins brothel-houses rise,   70
Scenes of lewd loves, and of polluted joys;
Where their vast courts the mother-strumpets keep,
And, undisturbed by watch, in silence sleep.
Near these a Nursery erects its head,
Where queens are formed, and future heroes bred;   75
Where unfledged actors learn to laugh and cry,
Where infant punks their tender voices try,
And little Maximins the gods defy.
Great Fletcher never treads in buskins here,
Nor greater Jonson dares in socks appear;   80
But gentle Simkin just reception finds
Amidst this monument of vanished minds:
Pure clinches the suburbian Muse affords,
And Panton waging harmless war with words.
Here Flecknoe, as a place to fame well known,   85
Ambitiously designed his Sh————'s throne;
For ancient Dekker prophesied long since
That in this pile would reign a mighty prince,
Born for a scourge of wit, and flail of sense;
To whom true dullness should some *Psyches* owe,   90
But worlds of *Misers* from his pen should flow;
Humorists and *Hypocrites* it should produce,
Whole Raymond families, and tribes of Bruce.

Now Empress Fame had published the renown
Of Sh———'s coronation through the town.   95
Roused by report of Fame, the nations meet,
From near Bunhill, and distant Watling Street.
No Persian carpets spread th'imperial way,
But scattered limbs of mangled poets lay;
From dusty shops neglected authors come,   100
Martyrs of pies, and relics of the bum.
Much Heywood, Shirley, Ogilby there lay,
But loads of Sh——— almost choked the way.
Bilked stationers for yeomen stood prepared,
And Herringman was captain of the guard.   105
The hoary prince in majesty appeared,
High on a throne of his own labors reared.
At his right hand our young Ascanius sate,
Rome's other hope, and pillar of the state.
His brows thick fogs, instead of glories, grace,   110
And lambent dullness played around his face.
As Hannibal did to the altars come,
Sworn by his sire a mortal foe to Rome.
So Sh——— swore, nor should his vow be vain,
That he till death true dullness would maintain;   115
And, in his father's right, and realm's defense,
Ne'er to have peace with wit, nor truce with sense.
The king himself the sacred unction made,
As king by office, and as priest by trade.
In his sinister hand, instead of ball,   120
He placed a mighty mug of potent ale;
Love's Kingdom to his right he did convey,
At once his scepter, and his rule of sway;
Whose righteous lore the prince had practiced young,
And from whose loins recorded *Psyche* sprung.   125
His temples, last, with poppies were o'erspread,
That nodding seemed to consecrate his head.
Just at that point of time, if Fame not lie,
On his left hand twelve rev'rend owls did fly.
So Romulus, 'tis sung, by Tiber's brook,   130
Presage of sway from twice six vultures took.
Th'admiring throng loud acclamations make,

And omens of his future empire take.
The sire then shook the honors of his head,
And from his brows damps of oblivion shed   135
Full on the filial dullness: long he stood,
Repelling from his breast the raging god;
At length burst out in this prophetic mood:
    "Heav'ns bless my son, from Ireland let him reign
To far Barbados on the western main;   140
Of his dominion may no end be known,
And greater than his father's be his throne;
Beyond *Love's Kingdom* let him stretch his pen!"
He paused, and all the people cried, "Amen."
Then thus continued he: "My son, advance   145
Still in new impudence, new ignorance.
Success let others teach, learn thou from me
Pangs without birth, and fruitless industry.
Let *Virtuosos* in five years be writ;
Yet not one thought accuse thy toil of wit.   150
Let gentle George in triumph tread the stage,
Make Dorimant betray, and Loveit rage;
Let Cully, Cockwood, Fopling charm the pit,
And in their folly show the writer's wit.
Yet still thy fools shall stand in thy defense,   155
And justify their author's want of sense.
Let'em be all by thy own model made
Of dullness, and desire no foreign aid;
That they to future ages may be known,
Not copies drawn, but issue of thy own.   160
Nay, let thy men of wit too be the same,
All full of thee, and diff'ring but in name.
But let no alien Sedley interpose,
To lard with wit thy hungry *Epsom* prose.
And when false flowers of rhet'ric thou wouldst cull,   165
Trust nature, do not labor to be dull;
But write thy best, and top; and, in each line,
Sir Formal's oratory will be thine.
Sir Formal, though unsought, attends thy quill,
And does thy northern dedications fill.   170
Nor let false friends seduce thy mind to fame,

By arrogating Jonson's hostile name.
Let father Flecknoe fire thy mind with praise,
And uncle Ogleby thy envy raise.
Thou art my blood, where Jonson has no part: 175
What share have we in nature, or in art?
Where did his wit on learning fix a brand,
And rail at arts he did not understand?
Where made he love in Prince Nicander's vein,
Or swept the dust in *Psyche's* humble strain?   180
Where sold he bargains, "whip-stitch, kiss my arse,"
Promised a play and dwindled to a farce?
When did his Muse from Fletcher scenes purloin,
As thou whole Eth'rege dost transfuse to thine?
But so transfused as oil and water's flow,   185
His always floats above, thine sinks below.
This is thy province, this thy wondrous way,
New humors to invent for each new play:
This is that boasted bias of thy mind,
By which one way, to dullness, 'tis inclined;   190
Which makes thy writings lean on one side still,
And, in all changes, that way bends thy will.
Nor let thy mountain-belly make pretence
Of likeness; thine's a tympathy of sense.
A tun of man in thy large bulk is writ,   195
But sure thou'rt but a kilderkin of wit.
Like mine, thy gentle numbers feebly creep;
Thy tragic Muse gives smiles, thy comic sleep.
With whate'er gal thou sett'st thyself to write,
Thy inoffensive satires never bite.   200
In thy felonious heart though venom lies,
It does but touch thy Irish pen, and dies.
Thy genius calls thee not to purchase fame
In keen iambics, but mild anagram.
Leave writing plays, and choose for thy command   205
Some peaceful province in acrostic land.
There thou may'st wings display and altars raise,
And torture one poor word ten thousand ways.
Or, if thou wouldst thy different talents suit,
Set thy own songs, and sing them to thy lute."   210
    He said: but his last words were scarcely heard;

For Bruce and Longvil had a trap prepared,
And down they sent the yet declaiming bard.
Sinking he left his drugget robe behind,
Borne upwards by a subterranean wind.   215
The mantle fell to the young prophet's part,
With double portion of his father's art.

W. B. YEATS
Adam's Curse

We sat together at one summer's end,
That beautiful mild woman, your close friend,
And you and I, and talked of poetry.
I said: 'A line will take us hours maybe;
Yet if it does not seem a moment's thought,   5
Our stitching and unstitching has been naught.
Better go down upon your marrow-bones
And scrub a kitchen pavement, or break stones
Like an old pauper, in all kinds of weather;
For to articulate sweet sounds together   10
Is to work harder than all these, and yet
Be thought an idler by the noisy set
Of bankers, schoolmasters, and clergymen
The martyrs call the world.'

                    And thereupon   15
That beautiful mild woman for whose sake
There's many a one shall find out all heartache
On finding that her voice is sweet and low
Replied: 'To be born woman is to know—
Although they do not talk of it at school—   20
That we must labour to be beautiful.'

I said: 'It's certain there is no fine thing
Since Adam's fall but needs much labouring.
There have been lovers who thought love should be
So much compounded of high courtesy   25
That they would sigh and quote with learned looks
Precedents out of beautiful old books;
Yet now it seems an idle trade enough.'

We sat grown quiet at the name of love;
We saw the last embers of daylight die,   30
And in the trembling blue-green of the sky
A moon, worn as if it had been a shell
Washed by time's waters as they rose and fell
About the stars and broke in days and years.

I had a thought for no one's but your ears: 35
That you were beautiful, and that I strove
To love you in the old high way of love;
That it had all seemed happy, and yet we'd grown
As weary-hearted as that hollow moon.

ROBERT BROWNING
My Last Duchess

That's my last Duchess painted on the wall,
Looking as if she were alive. I call
That piece a wonder, now: Frà Pandolf's hands
Worked busily a day, and there she stands.
Will't please you sit and look at her? I said   5
"Frà Pandolf" by design, for never read
Strangers like you that pictured countenance,
The depth and passion of its earnest glance,
But to myself they turned (since none puts by
The curtain I have drawn for you, but I)   10
And seemed as they would ask me, if they durst,
How such a glance came there; so, not the first
Are you to turn and ask thus. Sir, 'twas not
Her husband's presence only, called that spot
Of joy into the Duchess' cheek: perhaps   15
Frà Pandolf chanced to say "Her mantle laps
Over my Lady's wrist too much," or "Paint
Must never hope to reproduce the faint
Half-flush that dies along her throat;" such stuff
Was courtesy, she thought, and cause enough   20
For calling up that spot of joy. She had
A heart—how shall I say?—too soon made glad,
Too easily impressed; she liked whate'er
She looked on, and her looks went everywhere.

Sir, 'twas all one! My favour at her breast,   25
The dropping of the daylight in the West,
The bough of cherries some officious fool
Broke in the orchard for her, the white mule
She rode with round the terrace—all and each
Would draw from her alike the approving speech,   30
Or blush, at least. She thanked men,—good! but thanked
Somehow—I know not how—as if she ranked
My gift of a nine-hundred-years-old name
With anybody's gift. Who'd stoop to blame
This sort of trifling? Even had you skill   35
In speech—(which I have not)—to make your will
Quite clear to such an one, and say, "Just this
Or that in you disgusts me; here you miss,
Or there exceed the mark"—and if she let
Herself be lessoned so, nor plainly set   40
Her wits to yours, forsooth, and made excuse,
—E'en then would be some stooping; and I choose
Never to stoop. Oh, sir, she smiled, no doubt,
Whene'er I passed her; but who passed without
Much the same smile? This grew; I gave commands;   45
Then all smiles stopped together. There she stands
As if alive. Will't please you rise? We'll meet
The company below, then. I repeat,
The Count your Master's known munificence
Is ample warrant that no just pretense   50
Of mine for dowry will be disallowed;
Though his fair daughter's self, as I avowed
At starting, is my object. Nay, we'll go
Together down, sir. Notice Neptune, though,
Taming a sea-horse, thought a rarity,   55
Which Claus of Innsbruck cast in bronze for me!

WILFRED OWEN
Strange Meeting

It seemed that out of battle I escaped
Down some profound dull tunnel, long since scooped
Through granites which titanic wars had groined.
Yet also there encumbered sleepers groaned,

Too fast in thought or death to be bestirred.   5
Then, as I probed them, one sprang up, and stared
With piteous recognition in fixed eyes,
Lifting distressful hands as if to bless.
And by his smile, I knew that sullen hall,
By his dead smile I knew we stood in Hell.   10
With a thousand pains that vision's face was grained;
Yet no blood reached there from the upper ground,
And no guns thumped, or down the flues made moan.
"Strange friend," I said, "here is no cause to mourn."
"None," said the other, "save the undone years,   15
The hopelessness. Whatever hope is yours,
Was my life also; I went hunting wild
After the wildest beauty in the world,
Which lies not calm in eyes, or braided hair,
But mocks the steady running of the hour,   20
And if it grieves, grieves richlier than here.
For of my glee might many men have laughed,
And my weeping something had been left,
Which must die now. I mead the truth untold,
The pity of war, the pity war distilled.   25
Now men will go content with what we spoiled,
Or, discontent, boil bloody, and be spilled.
They will be swift with swiftness of the tigress.
None will break ranks, though nations trek from progress.
Courage was mine, and I had mystery,   30
Wisdom was mine, and I had mastery:
To miss the march of this retreating world
Into vain citadels that are not walled.
Then, when much blood had clogged their chariot-wheels,
I would go up and wash them from sweet wells,   35
Even with truths that lie too deep for taint.
I would have poured my spirit without stint
But not through wounds; not on the cess of war.
Foreheads of men have bled where no wounds were.
I am the enemy you killed, my friend.   40
I knew you in this dark: for so you frowned
Yesterday through me as you jabbed and killed.
I parried; but my hands were loath and cold.
Let us sleep now. . . ."

JEREDITH MERRIN
Downtown Diner

Scuzzy Michael's Diner. Briefcase
and French loaf in tow, on my way to the office,

in need of the restroom and coffee.
Inside, flashback to San Jose and my greasy-

spoon, Welfare mornings in tattered   5
—not purposefully or artfully tattered—

jeans; the two-egg-and-hashbrown special
I ate then, with no one from that other, well-

dressed world to breeze in and deliver
a fresh sense of failure to us hunched-over   10

eaters. In Michael's, a woman looked up when
I walked in, then quickly down again.

And I may have spoiled her leisurely
breakfast—probably

the chief expense and pleasure of her day.   15
Fifteen years ago, in San Jose,

chic department stores could terrify:
the coolly assessing, arched eye-

brows of smartly dressed saleswomen
and consumers—who could beat them?   20

Even if you spend more of
the little you have,

it hurts less to shop at "cut-rate,"
unreproachful stores. Long-term poverty humiliates

like childhood: you might be judged wanting,   25
be laughed at any moment for something

not in your power to avoid. Only,
you can't outwait it like childhood. Maybe

that woman dipping toast into egg yolk had
less passion or ambition than I had;   30

maybe more. She should not have been
disturbed in that small consolation

of egg. Who possesses the wherewithal
for labor or love without small

consolations? Who can live?   35

AN EXERCISE IN *COUPLET VERSE*

On October 22, 1706, Alexander Pope sent William Walsh the following letter,
discussing his theories of versification:

> After the Thoughts I have already sent you on the subject of *English*
> Versification, you desire my opinion as to some farther particulars. There are
> 'indeed certain Niceties, which tho' not much observed even by correct Ver-
> sifiers, I cannot but think deserve to be better regarded.
>
> 1. It is not enough that nothing offends the Ear, but a good Poet will
> adapt the very Sounds, as well as Words, to the things he treats of. So that
> there is (if one may express it so) a Style of Sounds. As in describing a glid-
> ing Stream, the Numbers shou'd run easy and flowing; in describing a
> rough Torrent or Deluge, sonorous and swelling, and so of the rest. This is
> evident every where in *Homer* and *Virgil,* and no where else that I know of
> to any observable degree. . . .
> This, I think, is what very few observe in practice and is undoubtedly
> of wonderful force in imprinting the Image on the reader: We have one
> excellent Example of it in our Language, Mr. *Dryden's* Ode on St. *Caecilia's*
> Day, entitled, *Alexander's Feast.*
> 2. Every nice Ear, must (I believe) have observ'd, that in any smooth
> *English* Verse of ten syllables, there is naturally a *Pause* at the fourth, fifth,
> or sixth syllable. It is upon these the Ear rests, and upon the judicious
> Change and Management of which depends the Variety of Versification.
> For example,
>
> At the fifth.   *Where-e'er thy Navy* || *spreads her canvass Wings,*

At the fourth.   *Homage to thee* || *and Peace to all she brings*.

At the sixth.   *Like Tracts of Leverets* || *in the Morning Snow*.

Now I fancy, that to preserve an exact Harmony and Variety, the Pauses of the 4th or 6th shou'd not be continu'd above three lines together, without the Interposition of another; else it will be apt to weary the Ear with one continu'd Tone, as least it does mine: That at the 5th runs quicker, and carries not quite so dead a weight, so tires not so much tho' it be continued longer.

3. Another nicety is in relation to *Expletives*, whether Words or Syllables, which are made use of purely to supply a vacancy: *Do* before Verbs plural is absolutely such; and it is not improbable but future Refiners may explode *did* and *does* in the same manner, which are almost always used for the sake of Rhime. The same Cause has occasioned the promiscuous use of *You* and *Thou* to the same Person, which can never sound so graceful as either one or the other.

4. I would also object to the Irruption of *Alexandrine* Verses of twelve syllables, which I think should never be allow'd but when some remarkable Beauty or Propriety in them attones for the Liberty: Mr. *Dryden* has been too free to these, especially in his latter Works. I am of the same opinion as to *Triple Rhimes*.

5. I could equally object to the *Repetition* of the same Rhimes within four or six lines of each other, as tiresome to the Ear thro' their Monotony.

6. *Monosyllable-Lines*, unless very artfully managed, are stiff, or languishing: but may be beautiful to express Melancholy, Slowness, or Labour.

7. To come to the *Hiatus*, or Gap between two words which is caus'd by Two Vowels opening on each other (upon which you desire me to be particular) I think the rule in this case is either to use the *Caesura*, or admit the *Hiatus*, just as the Ear is least shock'd by either: For the *Caesura* sometimes offends the Ear more than the *Hiatus* itself, and our language is naturally overcharg'd with Consonants: As for example; If in this Verse,

The Old have Int'rest ever in their Eye,
we should say, to avoid the *Hiatus*,
But th' Old have Int'rest—

The *Hiatus* which has the worst effect, is when one word ends with the same Vowel that begins the following; and next to this, those Vowels whose sounds come nearest to each other are most to be avoided. O, A, or U, will bear a more full and graceful Sound than E, I, or Y. I know some people will think these Observations trivial, and therefore I am glad to corroborate them by some great Authorities, which I have met with in

Tully and *Quintilian*. . . . To conclude, I believe the Hiatus should be avoided with more care in Poetry than in Oratory; and I would constantly try to prevent it, unless where the cutting it off is more prejudicial to the Sound than the *Hiatus* itself. I am, &c.

Follow the principles that Pope outlines in his letter—but with one addition. Set the poem in a distinctly contemporary setting and use the language of our time.

6

SESTINA

The sculptor Henri Gaudier-Brezska told a friend that he admired Ezra Pound's poem "Altaforte: A Sestina" because it contains the word "piss." It doesn't; the poem exclaims, "Damn it all! all this our South stinks peace!" Gaudier-Brezska's mistake, though, is understandable. When Pound and other literati gathered to read their poetry, Pound performed so exuberantly that "the table shook and cutlery vibrated." Written in the voice of a medieval warrior, the poem needed (as its author admitted) a "54 inch chest" to read properly.

EZRA POUND
Altaforte: A Sestina

Loquitur: *En* Bertrans de Born. Dante Alighieri put this man in hell for that he was a stirrer-up of strife. Eccovi! Judge ye! Have I dug him up again? The scene is at his castle, Altaforte. "Papiols" is his jongleur. "The Leopard," the *device* of Richard (Coeur de Lion).

I

Damn it all! all this our South stinks peace.
You whoreson dog. Papiols, come! Let's to music!

119

I have no life save when the swords clash.
But ah! when I see the standards gold, vair, purple, opposing
And the broad fields beneath them turn crimson,   5
Then howl I my heart nigh mad with rejoicing.

II

In hot summer have I great rejoicing
When the tempests kill the earth's foul peace,
And the lightnings from black heav'n flash crimson,
And the fierce thunders roar me their music   10
And the winds shriek through the clouds mad, opposing,
And through all the riven skies of God's swords clash.

III

Hell grant soon we hear again the swords clash!
And the shrill neighs of destriers in battle rejoicing,
Spiked breast to spiked breast opposing!   15
Better one hour's stour than a year's peace
With fat boards, bawds, wine and frail music!
Bah! there's no wine like the blood's crimson!

IV

And I love to see the sun rise blood-crimson.
And I watch his spears through the dark clash   20
And it fills all my heart with rejoicing
And pries wide my mouth with fast music
When I see him so scorn and defy peace,
His lone might 'gainst all darkness opposing.

V

The man who fears war and squats opposing   25
My words for stour, hath no blood of crimson
But is fit only to rot in womanish peace
Far from where worth's won and the swords clash
For the death of such sluts I go rejoicing;
Yea, I fill all the air with my music.   30

VI

Papiols, Papiols, to the music!
There's no sound like to swords swords opposing,
No cry like the battle's rejoicing
When our elbows and swords drip the crimson
And our charges 'gainst "The Leopard's" rush clash.   35
May God damn for ever all who cry "Peace!"

VII

And let the music of the swords make them crimson!
Hell grant soon we hear again the swords clash!
Hell blot black for alway the thought "Peace!"

While Pound's blast introduced the sestina to modern poets, the form
quickly developed once poets pursued more subtle effects. Pound's poem
bellows and roars; Diane Thiel's "Love Letters" explores a quieter family
drama, where unspoken words are written and read.

DIANE THIEL
Love Letters

My mother wanted to learn some German
for my father and because her children
could already speak it a little.
She was tired of dusting the stacks of books
she couldn't read, tired of the letters   5
she always had to ask him to translate.

He was usually willing to translate
the cards his mother had written in German.
But sometimes there were other letters,
and when he read them to her and the children,   10
she had the same feeling she'd had with books
before she learned to read, when she was little.

She said it bothered her a little
that her own children would have to translate
for her, that they could pick up the same books   15
that were as Greek to her as they were German.

She started learning it from her children
and decided to leave my father letters.

She wrote my father daily love letters
and carefully placed them on the little   20
table where they put things for the children,
next to our favorite set of translations
of fairy tales we first heard in German.
She leaned one every day against his books,

the white paper stark beside the dark books.   25
But my father never answered her letters.
Instead he returned them with his German
corrections in the margin, his little
red marks—hieroglyphs for her to translate,
as if she were one of the children.   30

Maybe she was just one of the children
in that house surrounded by rows of books.
Maybe her whole life was a translation
of what she imagined in the letters.
The space between them made her that little   35
girl, wandering lost inside the German.

Because her own children were half-German,
she built her life around those little books
translating the lines of her own letters.

Background and Structure of the *Sestina*

"Love Letters" follows the sestina's usual pattern. It consists of six, six-line stanzas and a three-line envoy. The endwords repeat according to a prescribed pattern. In the first stanza, the endwords are (in this order) "German," "children," "little," "books," "letters," and "translate." As in all subsequent stanzas, the next stanza reshuffles the endwords into the following order, last, first, second-to-last, second, third-to-last, and third: "translate," "German," "letters," "children," "books," and "letters." The pattern can be sketched as:

1
2
3

4
5
6

6
1
5
2
4
3

3
6
4
1
2
5

5
3
2
6
1
4

4
5
1
3
6
2

2
4
6
5
3
1

Traditionally, the endwords also can repeat according to homonyms: "see," for instance, could repeat as "sea." Thiel gives her poem a little latitude, using "translations" and "translation" in the place of the word that the first stanza introduces, "translate." (Pound repeats the words more strictly, except when he confuses "rejoicing" and "music" in the fourth stanza, putting each in the other's place.) In the envoy, the three-line final stanza, the endwords repeat in one of the following two patterns (although some modern writers omit the envoy entirely): 5, 3, 1 or 1, 3, 5. All the other endwords repeat within the envoy's line, one within each line.

While all poetic forms involve repetitions, the sestina repeats endwords, not rhymes or lines. As consequence a sestina meditates on its six words, exploring their relation. One strategy is to choose words that have multiple meanings, introducing a linguistic amusement to offset the form's potential for monotony. Anthony Hecht's "Sestina d'Inverno" opens, "Here in this bleak city of Rochester." Surprising the reader with their inventiveness, subsequent stanzas mention "the earl of Rochester" and "the Rochester / Gas and Electric Co." The last example turns "Rochester" into an adjective, enjambing the line to change "Rochester" into a different part of speech. Such punning generally achieves comic effects.

"Love Letters" stays closer to the endword's meanings as introduced in the first stanza. In "Love Letters" the mother tries to learn German, her husband's first language. She wishes to remake her marriage and her relationship with her children, or, in the poem's terms, to translate them. The sestina exerts a psychological force as certain words encircle its subject. "German," "children," "little," "books," "letters," and "translate" suggest the fate the mother wishes to avoid but cannot, as a language and a life demeans her, making her like a "little girl, wandering lost inside the German." The form establishes a vocabulary that its main character cannot escape.

The transitions between a sestina's stanzas are especially tricky because the last line of the previous stanza and the first line of the next share the same endword. This close repetition poses a challenge; it risks banality if the word's meaning or inflection does not change. Turning this difficulty into an advantage, the poem uses one of the transitions to confront the mother's lowly status:

> But my father never answered her letters.
> Instead he returned them with his German
> corrections in the margin, his little
> red marks—hieroglyphs for her to translate,
> as if she were one of the children.   5
>
> Maybe she was just one of the children
> in that house surrounded by rows of books.

The repetition of "children" fixes the mother's place in the family. When the mother thinks of "her children," the language she uses insists on her control. The poem's saddest stanza lays bare the fact that her efforts to assert her dignity only inspire her husband's disrespect. When the poem suggests, "Maybe she was just one of the children," the politely hedging language confirms that the husband treats his wife "as if she were one of the children," not an adult, let alone the children's mother.

Before the twentieth century, the sestina was a minor form in English. Invented by Arnaut Daniel and made famous by Petrarch and Dante, it entered English literature during the sixteenth century, inspiring one masterpiece. Sir Philip Sidney's double sestina, "Ye goatherd gods," performs the form's formidable challenges twice. In a famous reading of the poem, William Empson described how "the poem beats, however rich its orchestration, with a wailing and immovable monotony, for ever upon the same doors in vain." The form continued to expand; after Barnabe Barnes's triple sestina, "Sestine 5," the form seemed to have little place to go and fell into neglect.

Prosodists generally hold the sestina in low regard; Paul Fussell and George Saintbury rank it as a minor form. From the twentieth century to the present, though, the sestina enjoyed a greater popularity than during any other period in the language's history. After W. H. Auden and Elizabeth Bishop wrote celebrated poems in the form, a generation of poets followed their examples. Many writers exploited the repetition's potential to evoke dark dramas of entrapment and obsession. Sestinas have explored the Holocaust, the Great Depression, and harrowing family dramas.

Why did the sestina address these grim subjects? To understand the form's success, we need to consider how its particular repetitions can seem menacing, as well as playful or comic. In an example generated from his own experience, Freud noted if a patron were handed a cloakroom ticket numbered "62," that number would seem unthreatening. If 62, however, appeared on the ticket, a cabin door, and several other places during a single day, the viewer might interpret it as an omen of the years he is destined to live. This repetition "surrounds what would otherwise be innocent enough with an uncanny atmosphere, and forces upon us the idea of something fateful and inescapable when otherwise we should have spoken only of 'chance.'"

Many darker sestinas achieve this "uncanny" effect, making their repetitions seem "fateful and inescapable." As we have seen, a sestina repeats its endwords according to a proscribed pattern, but the pattern is too complicated for readers to keep in mind as they proceed through a poem, unless they stop to consult a diagram. (In the one exception, the first line of a stanza repeats the previous line's endword.) The form inspires a particular form of anticipation and surprise; an attentive reader knows that certain words will repeat but cannot predict when, a dynamic that can make rather ordinary words—"German," "children," "little," "books," "letters," and "translate"—turn sinister.

MORE WORKS IN THE *SESTINA*

The sestina follows a particular repetition of endwords. The first stanza establishes the endwords. Elizabeth Bishop's "A Miracle for Breakfast" the endwords of the first stanza fall in the following order:

1. coffee
2. crumb
3. balcony
4. miracle
5. sun
6. river

Stanzas two and six, each of which consists of six lines, repeat the endwords according to a set order. The final, three-line stanza employs all the endwords at the end and the rough middle of each line.

ELIZABETH BISHOP
Miracle for Breakfast

At six o'clock we were waiting for coffee,	1	
waiting for coffee and the charitable crumb	2	
that was going to be served from a certain balcony,	3	
—like kings of old, or like a miracle.	4	
It was still dark. One foot of the sun	5	5
steadied itself on a long ripple in the river.	6	
The first ferry of the day had just crossed the river.	6	
It was so cold we hoped that the coffee	1	
would be very hot, seeing that the sun	5	
was not going to warm us; and that the crumb	2	10
would be a loaf each, buttered, by a miracle.	4	
At seven a man stepped out on the balcony.	3	

He stood for a minute alone on the balcony	3
looking over our heads toward the river.	6
A servant handed him the makings of a miracle,	4 15
consisting of one lone cup of coffee	1
and one roll, which he proceeded to crumb,	1
his head, so to speak, in the clouds—along with the sun.	5

Was the man crazy? What under the sun	5
was he trying to do, up there on his balcony!	3 20
Each man received one rather hard crumb,	2
which some flicked scornfully into the river,	6
and, in a cup, one drop of the coffee.	1
Some of us stood around, waiting for the miracle.	4

I can tell what I saw next; it was not a miracle.	4 25
A beautiful villa stood in the sun	5
and from its doors came the smell of hot coffee.	1
In front, a baroque white plaster balcony	3
added by birds, who nest along the river,	6
—I saw it with one eye close to the crumb—	2 30

and galleries and marble chambers. My crumb	2
my mansion, made for me by a miracle,	4
through ages, by insects, birds, and the river	6
working the stone. Every day, in the sun,	5
at breakfast time I sit on my balcony	3 35
with my feet up, and drink gallons of coffee.	1

We licked up the crumb and swallowed the coffee.	2	1
A window across the river caught the sun	6	5
as if the miracle were working, on the wrong balcony.	4	3

DANTE ALIGHIERI, TRANSLATED
BY DANTE GABRIEL ROSSETTI
Of the Lady Pietra degli Scrovigni

Author's note: I have translated this piece both on account of its great and peculiar beauty, and also because it affords an example of a form of composition which I have met with in no Italian writer before Dante's time, though it is not uncommon among the Provencal poets (see Dante, De Vulg. Eloq.). I have headed it with the name of a Paduan lady, to whom it is surmised by some

*to have been addressed during Dante's exile; but this must be looked upon as a
rather doubtful conjecture, and I have adopted the name chiefly to mark it at
once as not referring to Beatrice.*

To the dim light and the large circle of shade
I have clomb, and to the whitening of the hills,
There where we see no colour in the grass.
Natheless my longing loses not its green,
It has so taken root in the hard stone   5
Which talks and hears as though it were a lady.

Utterly frozen is this youthful lady,
Even as the snow that lies within the shade;
For she is no more moved than is the stone
By the sweet season which makes warm the hills   10
And alters them afresh from white to green,
Covering their sides again with flowers and grass.

When on her hair she sets a crown of grass
The thought has no more room for other lady,
Because she weaves the yellow with the green   15
So well that Love sits down there in the shade,—
Love who has shut me in among low hills
Faster than between walls of granite-stone.

She is more bright than is a precious stone;
The wound she gives may not be healed with grass: 20
I therefore have fled far o'er plains and hills
For refuge from so dangerous a lady;
But from her sunshine nothing can give shade,—
Not any hill, nor wall, nor summer-green.

A while ago, I saw her dressed in green,—   25
So fair, she might have wakened in a stone
This love which I do feel even for her shade;
And therefore, as one woos a graceful lady,
I wooed her in a field that was all grass
Girdled about with very lofty hills.   30

Yet shall the streams turn back and climb the hills
Before Love's flame in this damp wood and green
Burn, as it burns within a youthful lady,
For my sake, who would sleep away in stone
My life, or feed like beasts upon the grass,   35
Only to see her garments cast a shade.

How dark soe'er the hills throw out their shade,
Under her summer-green the beautiful lady
Covers it, like a stone cover'd in grass.

SIR PHILIP SIDNEY
"Ye goatherd gods . . ."

Strephon:

Ye goatherd gods, that love the grassy mountains,
Ye nymphs which haunt the springs in pleasant valleys,
Ye satyrs joyed with free and quiet forests,
Vouchsafe your silent ears to plaining music,
Which to my woes gives still an early morning,   5
And draws the dolor on till weary evening.

Klaius:

O Mercury, foregoer to the evening,
O heavenly huntress of the savage mountains,
O lovely star, entitled of the morning,
While that my voice doth fill these woeful valleys,   10
Vouchsafe you silent ears to plaining music,
Which oft hath Echo tired in secret forests.

Strephon:

I, that was once free burgess of the forests,
Where shade from sun, and sport I sought in evening,
I, that was once esteemed for pleasant music,   15
Am banished now among the monstrous mountains
Of huge despair, and foul affliction's valleys,
Am grown a screech owl to myself each morning.

Klaius:

I, that was once delighted every morning,
Hunting the wild inhabiters of forests,   20
I, that was once the music of these valleys,
So darkened am that all my day is evening,
Heartbroken so that molehills seem high mountains
And fill the vales with cries instead of music.

Strephon:

Long since, alas, my deadly swannish music   25
Hath made itself a crier of the morning,
And hath with wailing strength climbed highest mountains;
Long since my thoughts more desert be than forests,
Long since I see my joys come to their evening,
And state thrown down to overtrodden valleys.   30

Klaius:

Long since the happy dwellers of these valleys
Have prayed me leave my strange exclaiming music
Which troubles their day's work and joys of evening;
Long since I hate the night, more hate the morning;
Long since my thoughts chase me like beasts in forests   35
And make me wish myself laid under mountains.

Strephon:

Meseems I see the high and stately mountains
Transform themselves to low dejected valleys;
Meseems I hear in these ill-changed forests
The nightingales do learn of owls their music;   40
Meseems I feel the comfort of the morning
Turned to the mortal serene of an evening.

Klaius:

Meseems I see a filthy cloudy evening
As soon as sun begins to climb the mountains;
Meseems I feel a noisome scent, the morning   45

When I do smell the flowers of these valleys;
Meseems I hear, when I do hear sweet music,
The dreadful cries of murdered men in forests.

Strephon:

I wish to fire the trees of all these forests;
I give the sun a last farewell each evening;   50
I curse the fiddling finders-out of music;
With envy I do hate the lofty mountains
And with despite despise the humble valleys;
I do detest night, evening, day, and morning.

Klaius:

Curse to myself my prayer is, the morning;   55
My fire is more than can be made with forests,
My state more base than are the basest valleys.
I wish no evenings more to see, each evening;
Shaméd, I hate myself in sight of mountains
And stop mine ears, lest I grow mad with music.   60

Strephon:

For she whose parts maintained a perfect music,
Whose beauties shined more than the blushing morning,
Who much did pass in state the stately mountains,
In straightness passed the cedars of the forests,
Hath cast me, wretch, into eternal evening   65
By taking her two suns from these dark valleys.

Klaius:

For she, to whom compared, the Alps are valleys,
She, whose least word brings from the spheres their music,
At whose approach the sun rose in the evening,
Who where she went bare in her forehead morning,   70
Is gone, is gone, from these our spoiléd forests,
Turning to deserts our best pastured mountains.

Strephon:

These mountains witness shall, so shall these valleys.

Klaius:

These forests eke, made wretched by our music,
Our morning hymn is this, and song at evening.   75

AN EXERCISE IN THE *SESTINA*

The selection of end words constitutes a crucial moment in the composition of a sestina. In a letter, Elizabeth Bishop notes the option a writer faces:

> It seems to me there are two ways possible for a sestina—one is to use unusual words as terminations, in which case they would have to be used differently as often as possible—as you say, "change of scale." . . . That would make a very highly seasoned kind of poem. And the other way is to use as colorless words as possible—like Sydney, so that it becomes less of a trick and more of a natural theme and variations.

Writing of her own poem, "Sestina," Bishop observed, "I guess I have tried to do both at once." Consider Bishop's observations when you select end words for a sestina. Pick either "unusual" or "colorless" words, or a combination of each, considering the kind of sestina you wish to write: "a highly seasoned kind of poem" or "more of a natural theme and variations."

VILLANELLE

In 1894 Edward Arlington Robinson drafted "The House on the Hill"; two years later, he published a slightly revised version in his self-published debut, *The Torrent and The Night Before*. During this period, Robinson, a young man in his early twenties, experienced an agonizing homecoming. In 1892 his father died, his mother grew ill, and the prosperous family went bankrupt. Forced to drop out of Harvard, Robinson returned home to Maine, along with his brother, Dean, a morphine addict. A week after Robinson published "The House on the Hill," his mother died of what was called "black diphtheria"; afraid of contagion, the minister performed the funeral through a window and the brothers dug the grave and buried their mother because no one else would.

Though Robinson denied that "The House on the Hill" was autobiographical, it is hard not to hear his difficult family situation echoed in the poem he published:

EDWARD ARLINGTON ROBINSON
The House on the Hill

They are all gone away,
　The House is shut and still,
There is nothing more to say.

Through broken walls and gray
  The winds blow bleak and shrill: 5
They are all gone away.

Nor is there one to-day
  To speak them good or ill:
There is nothing more to say.

Why is it then we stray   10
  Around that sunken sill?
They are all gone away,

And our poor fancy-play
  For them is wasted skill:
There is nothing more to say.   15

There is ruin and decay
  In the House on the Hill:
They are all gone away,
There is nothing more to say.

Background and Structure
of the *Villanelle*

"The House on the Hill" is a villanelle. As such it consists of five three-line stanzas and one four-line stanza. The first stanza establishes a rhyme. The first and the third lines of the tercets rhyme: "away" rhymes with "say." The middle line sets a rhyme for all the middle lines of subsequent stanza, except the final one. "Still" rhymes with the middle line of the next stanzas' "ill," "will," and so on. The nineteen-line stanza, then, features two rhymes, which all the lines adhere to. In addition to this rhyme scheme, the villanelle features a distinctive repetition of lines. The first and third lines of the opening stanza—"They are all gone away" and "There is nothing more to say"—repeat in alternating fashion as the final lines of the following stanzas.

This intricate progression ends in the final, four-line stanza. This stanza's third line repeats the poem's opening, and the last line repeats the poem's third line. The final stanza's first, third, and fourth lines rhyme, and the second line rhymes with the middle lines of the previous stanzas. To diagram the first and last stanzas, I will assign numbers to the opening stanza's lines and letters to its rhyme scheme:

They are all gone away,	1	a
The House is shut and still,	2	b
There is nothing more to say.	3	a

This rhyme and line repetitions occur in the final stanza as:

There is ruin and decay		a
In the House on the Hill:		b
They are all gone away,	1	a
There is nothing more to say.	2	b

The villanelle form did not always have a set number of stanzas. Developing from popular Italian musical traditions, it has rather murky beginnings, which various scholars describe differently. Most however agree that Jean Passerat's sixteenth century poem, "J'ai perdu ma tourterelle," established the modern form. The poem opens (in George Wyndham's translation):

I have lost my turtle-dove;
Is not that her call to me?
To be with her were enough.

George Saintsbury called this poem "probably the most elegant specimen of a poetical trifle that the age produced." When the villanelle entered English in the nineteenth century, the members of the aesthetic movement also produced many elegant trifles, poems whose stock adjectives—"delicate," "golden," and "pale"—illustrate their poetic vision.

"The House on the Hill" transformed this rather genteel form, introducing what Robinson called "a more prosy combination than those generally admitted into the realm of meter." To accomplish this goal, Robinson shunned certain kinds of language, imagery, and rhythms. As in the other poems in *The Torrent and the Night Before*, he sought to avoid two, late nineteenth-century period styles—a poetic naturalism and clichéd Romanticism. "There is not a red-bellied robin in the collection," he bragged, nor any "nightingales and roses." "I have a weakness," he admitted with only nominal modesty, "for the suggestiveness of those artificial forms—that is when they treat of something besides bride-roses and ball-rooms. *Vers de société* pure and simple, has little charm for me."

Written within ten years of "The House on the Hill," two villanelles celebrated in their day highlight the kind of villanelle that Robinson did not want to write. Credited as the first villanelle published by "a 'known' or an 'established' American poet," James Whitcomb Riley's "The Best is Good Enough" opines,

> I quarrel not with destiny,
> But make the best of everything—
> The best is good enough for me.

Instead of trite moralizing, Ernest Dowson's preciously crafts language as dainty and silken as the mistress he describes:

> I took her dainty eyes, as well
> As silken tendrils of her hair:
> And so I made a Villanelle!

Both Dowson's and Riley's villanelles are self-congratulatory: every other stanza Dowson exclaims, "And so I made a Villanelle!" just as Riley's repetitions praise his modest expectations.

"The House on the Hill" presents a landscape notable for an utter want of human presence, with almost no evidence that people ever lived there. The poem never describes any furniture or distinctive architectural features, let alone an animating detail such as a child's swing or a well-worn pot. If a certain bird were to fly into Robinson's poem, it would be characterized as a bird, not "a red-bellied robin."

Exploiting an unrelentingly bleak verse style, Robinson's poem exemplifies one approach to the villanelle. Varied as little as possible, the repeated lines gain an arresting, incantatory power. Robinson does not transform the poem's declarations; he chooses not to revise the definite, unqualified statement, "There is nothing more to say." Another poet might have written:

> And our poor fancy-play
> would not be wasted skill
> if there were something more to say.

Or:

> Because our poor fancy-play
> For them is wasted skill,
> What else is there to say?

Robinson does not allow himself the latitude to make slight adjustments, to transform the refrain into a question or a conditional clause. Instead, the repeated lines remain self-contained; their new contexts barely change their meaning. Again and again the poem confronts the hard facts that the repeated lines present, dramatizing the speaker's helplessness, his inability to change the events or to offer any meaningful comment.

Robinson's villanelle regards the form fatalistically, as the structural requirements seem as unstoppable as the destruction that the poem describes. Neither can be avoided or even suspended. The poem goes so far as to suggest that the prosodic skill it displays might be literally useless:

> And our poor fancy-play
> For them is wasted skill:
> There is nothing more to say.

"The villanelle, even, can at its best achieve the closest intensity," Ezra Pound claimed, "when . . . the refrains are an emotional fact, which the intellect, in the various gyrations of the poem, tries in vain and in vain to escape." Consider the final stanza of Elizabeth Bishop's "One Art":

> —Even losing you (the joking voice, a gesture
> I love) I shan't have lied. It's evident
> The art of losing's not too hard to master
> Though it might look like (*Write it!*) like disaster.

Just after the poem's most formal language ("I shan't have lied" and "It's evident") surrounds its most intimate moment ("the joking voice, a gesture / I love"), the poem mixes what is desired and required. "*Write it!*" the speaker commands herself, unable to escape the final refrain. "The House on the Hill" pursues a more hopeless version of this approach; it never raises the possibility that it might resist the forces that crush it.

The other option is to play with villanelle's structural elements. Neither of the refrains that Marilyn Hacker's "Villanelle" employs, "Every day our bodies separate" and "Not understanding what we celebrate," form complete sentences. As a consequence, they present a number of grammatical possibilities; they can be used as dependent clauses or as subjects that have different objects. Also unlike Robinson, Hacker gives herself the freedom to revise the refrains. A change in punctuation alters "Every day our bodies separate" to "Every day our bodies' separate / routines are harder to perpetuate." Hacker shows a linguistic wit, a playfulness within the villanelle's foreboding restraints.

MORE WORKS IN THE *VILLANELLE*

A villanelle consists of five three-line stanzas and one four-line stanza. The first stanza establishes a rhyme. The first and the third lines of the tercets rhyme. The middle line sets a rhyme for all the middle lines of subsequent stanzas, except the final one. In addition to this rhyme scheme, the villanelle repeats lines. The first and third lines of the opening stanza alternatively repeat as the final lines of the following stanzas. The poem's first and second lines form the poem's last two lines. (Marilyn Nelson's "Daughters, 1900," varies this final element. The last line is its opening line, not its third line, and the penultimate rhymes with the opening line but does not repeat it.)

MARILYN HACKER
Villanelle
for D.G.B.

Every day our bodies separate,	*a*	*1*
exploded torn and dazed.	*b*	
Not understanding what we celebrate	*a*	*2*
we grope through languages and hesitate	*a*	
and touch each other, speechless and amazed;	*b*	5
and every day our bodies separate	*a*	*1*
us farther from our planned, deliberate	*a*	
ironic lives. I am afraid, disphased,	*b*	
not understanding what we celebrate	*a*	*2*
when our fused limbs and lips communicate	*a*	10
the unlettered power we have raised.	*b*	
Every day our bodies' separate	*a*	*1*
routines are harder to perpetuate.	*a*	
In wordless darkness we learn wordless praise,	*b*	
not understanding what we celebrate;	*a*	*2* 15
wake to ourselves, exhausted, in the late	*a*	
morning as the wind tears off the haze,	*b*	
not understanding how we celebrate	*a*	*1*
our bodies. Every day we separate.	*a*	*2*

OSCAR WILDE
Theocritus

O singer of Persephone!
  In the dim meadows desolate,
Dost thou remember Sicily?

Still through the ivy flits the bee
  Where Amaryllis lies in state;   5
O Singer of Persephone!

Simætha calls on Hecate,
  And hears the wild dogs at the gate;
Dost thou remember Sicily?

Still by the light and laughing sea   10
  Poor Polypheme bemoans his fate;
O Singer of Persephone!

And still in boyish rivalry
  Young Daphnis challenges his mate;
Dost thou remember Sicily?   15

Slim Lacon keeps a goat for thee;
  For thee the jocund shepherds wait;
O Singer of Persephone!
Dost thou remember Sicily?

ELIZABETH BISHOP
One Art

The art of losing isn't hard to master;
so many things seem filled with the intent
to be lost that their loss is no disaster.

Lose something every day. Accept the fluster
of lost door keys, the hour badly spent.   5
The art of losing isn't hard to master.

Then practice losing farther, losing faster:
places, and names, and where it was you meant
to travel. None of these will bring disaster.

I lost my mother's watch. And look! my last, or   10
next-to-last, of three loved houses went.
The art of losing isn't hard to master.

I lost two cities, lovely ones. And, vaster,
some realms I owned, two rivers, a continent.
I miss them, but it wasn't a disaster.   15

—Even losing you (the joking voice, a gesture
I love) I shan't have lied. It's evident
the art of losing's not too hard to master
through it may look like (*Write* it!) like disaster.

WELDON KEES
From *Five Villanelles*

The crack is moving down the wall.
Defective plaster isn't all the cause.
We must remain until the roof falls in.

It's mildly cheering to recall
That every building has its little flaws.   5
The crack is moving down the wall.

Here in the kitchen, drinking gin,
We can accept the damndest laws.
We must remain until the roof falls in.

And though there's no one here at all,   10
One searches every room because
The crack is moving down the wall.

Repairs? But how can one begin?
The lease has warnings buried in each clause.
We must remain until the roof falls in.   15

These nights one hears a creaking in the hall,
The sort of thing that gives one pause.
The crack is moving down the wall.
We must remain until the roof falls in.

MARILYN NELSON WANIEK
Daughters, 1900

Five daughters, in the slant light on the porch,
are bickering. The eldest has come home
with new truths she can hardly wait to teach.

She lectures them: the younger daughters search
the sky, elbow each others' ribs, and groan.   5
Five daughters, in the slant light on the porch

and blue-sprigged dresses, like a stand of birch
saplings whose leaves are going yellow-brown
with new truths. They can hardly wait to teach,

themselves, to be called "Ma'am," to march   10
high-heeled across the hanging bridge to town.
Five daughters. In the slant light on the porch

Pomp lowers his paper for a while, to watch
the beauties he's begotten with his Ann:
these new truths they can hardly wait to teach.   15

The eldest sniffs, "A lady doesn't scratch."
The third snorts back, "Knock, knock: nobody home."
The fourth concedes, "Well, maybe not in *church* . . ."
Five daughters in the slant light on the porch.

WILLIAM LOGAN
Macbeth's Daughter

A broken mirror is the soul's veneer,
though broken mirrors brought no luck to me.
I'm most impressive when I disappear.

I wander through this drowning atmosphere,
this city built upon a mirrored sea.   5
A broken mirror is the soul's veneer.

The mute voice is the loveliest, I hear;
But when I speak, there are no words for me.
I'm most persuasive when I disappear.

I took this dagger as a souvenir   10
and plunged it in the blown glass of the sea.
A broken mirror is the soul's veneer,

and plays are full of daughters—*Hamlet, Lear*—
though most have paid a death to silence me.
I'm most appealing when I disappear.   15

How could a daughter hope to interfere
against the tidal groaning of the sea?
A broken mirror is the soul's veneer.
I'm most unchanging when I disappear.

WILLIAM LOGAN
Macbeth's Daughter Drowned

I'm most unchanging when I disappear.
A broken mirror is the soul's veneer
against the tidal groaning of the sea.
How could a daughter hope to interfere?

I'm most appealing when I disappear,   5
though most have paid a death to silence me.
The plays are full of daughters—*Hamlet, Lear*—

but broken mirrors are the soul's veneer
plunged deep into the blown glass of the sea.
I took this dagger as a souvenir.   10

I'm most persuasive when I disappear,
yet when I speak, there are no words for me.
The mute voice is the loveliest, I hear.

A broken mirror is the soul's veneer,
a city built upon the mirrored sea.   15
I wander through its drowning atmosphere.

I'm most impressive when I disappear,
though broken mirrors brought no luck to me.
A broken mirror is the soul's veneer.

AN EXERCISE IN THE *VILLANELLE*

As we have seen, villanelles handle the repeated lines in one of two ways: they either keep the line (as in Robinson's "The House on the Hill") or see how different contexts might change the repeated words (as in Hacker's "Villanelle"). The first option pursues a formal steadfastness; the second introduces a linguistic playfulness. The first option risks monotony, the second, excessive frivolity. Both mark an attitude not only to the form but the ideas and emotion it explores. Pick one of these two strategies and write a villanelle.

8

OTHER FRENCH FORMS

J. K. STEPHEN
The Ballade of the Incompetent Ballade-Monger

I am not ambitious at all:
   I am not a poet, I know
(Though I do love to see a mere scrawl
   To order and symmetry grow).
   My muse is uncertain and slow,   5
I am not expert with my tools,
   I lack the poetic *argot*:
But I hope I have kept to the rules.

When your brain is undoubtedly small,
   'Tis hard, sir, to write in a row,   10
Some five or six rhymes to Nepaul,
   And more than a dozen to Joe:
   The meter is easier though,
Three rhymes are sufficient for ghouls,
   My lines are deficient in go,   15
But I hope I have kept to the rules.

Unable to fly let me crawl,
  Your patronage kindly bestow:
I am not the author of Saul,
  I am not Voltaire or Rousseau: 20
  I am not desirous, oh no!
To rise from the ranks of the fools,
  To shine with Gosse, Dobson, and Co.:
But I hope I have kept to the rules.

Dear Sir, though my language is low,   25
  Let me dip in Pierian pools:
My verses are only so so,
  But I hope I have kept to the rules.

"The Ballade of the Incompetent Ballad-Monger" follows what it calls "the rules." A ballade consists of three, eight-line stanzas, which rhyme according to the following pattern:

a
b
a
b
b
c
b
c

The final stanza, the envoy, consists of four lines, whose first line typically addresses a prince or another dignitary (as when Stephens begins "Dear Sir" in "The Ballade of the Incompetent Ballad-Monger"). The envoy rhymes:

b
c
b
c

The ballade presents a severe rhyming challenge. Each stanza typically shares the same rhymes: the first rhyme (labeled a), then, appears six times, the second rhyme (labeled b) appears fourteen times, and the third rhyme (labeled c) appears eight times. Finally, the poet must also manipulate the refrain, not only finding a new rhyme for it in each stanza but also avoiding the monotony that such repetitions can inspire.

Background and Structure of the *Ballade* and the *Triolet*

Edmund Gosse named 1876 as "the date of the reintroduction of the ballade into English literature." The medieval poets Chaucer and Lydgate wrote several poems in the form, but the ballade fell into a long neglect that stretched until a late nineteenth-century revival. When Oscar Wilde remembered his "undergraduate days at Oxford," he recalled "days of lyrical ardours and of studious sonnet-writing; days when one loved the exquisite intricacy and musical repetitions of the ballade, and the villanelle with its linked long-drawn echoes and completeness; days when one solemnly sought to discover the proper temper in which a triolet should be written; delightful days, in which I am glad to say, there was far more rhyme than reason." As Wilde's comments suggests, the form appealed to the poets associated with the aestheticism movement, who valued "more rhyme than reason." Many of the poets read and translated French verse, including ballades by Théodore de Banville and Banville's master, François Villon, a poet-thief. Published in 1849, the first complete edition of Villon's poetry attracted new readers in France as well as England. Nearly five centuries after his death, Villon's outrageous life and outlaw aesthetic increased the interest in his art, appealing to late nineteenth-century notion of the "dammed poet." "[O]ur sad bad glad mad brother," Swinburne called Villon. Expressing similar solidarity with the French *avant garde*, Austin Dobson, Swinburne, and Edmund Gosse translated Villon's verse; Dante Gabriel Rosetti's translation of "The Ballad of Dead Ladies" achieved particular fame (though it earned Gosse's censure because it varied the rhymes from stanza to stanza, instead of keeping them the same).

The ballade appealed to the English poets for contradictory reasons. Robert Louis Stevenson praised De Banville for demonstrating the form's relevance to modernity; the ballades, Stevenson wrote, "smack racily of modern life." De Banville's self-elegy, which Edmund Gosse translated, mentions a host of new characters: "the Impressionist, the Decedent, a score / Of other fresh fanatics." Such lines made the form seem relevant, capable of expressing modernity's latest developments and attitudes: "Fresh girt for service of the latter lyre" (in Swinburne's characterization). In France, the ballade contended with its considerable past, as when a character in Molière sneered "the ballade is nothing but a faded rose; it's completely out of date; it fairly reeks of the past." English poetry never produced such achievement in the form. As a consequence it lacked the burden of this weighty history. The ballade attracted the English poets because it seemed simultaneously modern, archaic, and new: current, largely untried in the language, and delicately faded.

It is significant that the most famous ballade in English remains Rosetti's translation, not a poem original to the language. Countless ballades, including Gwynn's "Ballade of the Yale Younger Poets of Yesteryear," attest to this fact when they echo Villon's *ubi sunt* questioning refrain. For readers interested in versification, Wilde's description of Oxford includes a suggestive detail. The student-poets tried the sonnet, a form that enjoys a distinguished history in English, and the villanelle, which would soon develop into a major form. The two other forms Wilde mentions—the ballade and the triolet—remain minor forms in the language, with a more limited accomplishment.

The triolet consists of eight lines. The first line repeats as fourth and seventh lines and rhymes with the third and fifth lines. The second line repeats as the final line, and rhymes with the sixth. The first rhyme is often masculine and the second rhyme feminine. In Robert Bridges's poem, I mark the rhymes alphabetically and the repeating lines with numbers:

When first we met we did not guess	*a*	*1*	
That Love would prove so hard a master;	*b*	*2*	
Of more than common friendliness	*a*		
When first we met we did not guess.	*a*	*1*	
Who could foretell this sore distress,	*a*		5
This irretrievable disaster	*b*		
When first we met?—We did not guessa	*a*	*1*	
That Love would prove so hard a master.	*b*	*2*	

Only three lines are not repeated; all lines rhyme. Poets in English use a number of line constructions, including lines of different lengths and meters. Bridges's poem sticks to iambic tetrameter, a longer line than some triolets employ but a foot shorter than iambic pentameter. As a consequence the rhymes arrive a little more quickly. Faced with such demands, Bridges uses dependent clauses as the repeated lines and modulates them a bit. The dependent clauses provide some syntactical flexibility as the poem shifts the same phrases into different sentences. A turning point typically occurs in a triolet's fifth and sixth lines, the only place where two successive lines do not include a repeated line. The fifth and sixth lines, then, prepare the poem for the final repetitions of each refrain while also shifting the context a bit. In Bridges's poem, the penultimate line splits the opening line into two sentences, varying the words' inflection as well as their meaning. This new arrangement adds intensity to the opening declaration, by stripping it of the dependent clause, "When first we met." It moves the phrase, "We did not guess," to the start of sentence, instead of the middle where it previously hid. This shift focuses attention on the unhappy lovers, making the circumstances of their meeting less important than their fate.

To call Bridges's triolet a good example of a minor form is not to diminish it. Poetic forms develop unpredictably; many forms declared dead have enjoyed amazing posthumous activity. (The sonnet, for instance, has done so many, many times.) A poem in a minor form may give greater pleasure than one that uses a major form, as it offers an interesting departure, an exploration of less familiar ground. Forms such as the triolet and ballade give occasions to consider what it means to master a complex rhyming form, a task that entails more than fulfilling the form's most visible requirements. As Stephen's ballade maintains, a poet who simply keeps to the prescribed metrical and rhyme scheme may write "incompetent" verse, even though he finds "Some five or six rhymes to Nepaul / And more than a dozen to Joe."

Accomplished verse disguises itself because the poet has learned to manipulate the appearance of control and submission. When a poet writes, the verse form and other aspects of the poem work together: a rhyme inspires an image, which in turn inspires the next rhyme. W. H. Auden, a master of nearly every form that this book discusses, observed that the finished poem must project to the reader a different dynamic than what actually occurs in composition. "In serious poetry," Auden maintained, "thought, emotion, event, must always appear to dictate the diction, meter, and rhyme in which they are embodied; vice versa, in comic poetry it is the words, meter, rhyme, which must appear to create the thoughts, emotions, and events they require." With very few exceptions— namely, the forms that the chapter on short comic forms discusses—a form does not dictate whether a writer composes a comic poem or a serious one. A ballade, for instance, has inspired serious and comic poetry. Instead, the writer's handling of form greatly influences the kind of poem he or she produces. If, as Stephen asserts, a difficult form may hide a lack of ambition, the skill necessary to write good comic verse often goes unnoticed. A comic writer of intricate forms plays the straight man, knowing he might be mistaken for a rube.

Swinburne pursued the opposite approach, introducing conspicuous formal obstacles to difficult forms. He wrote rhyming sestinas and stuffed his ballades with internal rhymes. "A Ballad of Dreamland" opens:

> I hid my heart in a nest of roses,
> Out of the sun's way, hidden apart;
> In a softer bed than the soft white snow's is,
> Under the roses I hid my heart.
> Why would it sleep not? why should it start,   5
> When never a leaf of the rose-tree stirred?
> What made sleep flutter his wings and part?
> Only the song of the secret bird.

As we have seen, the ballade's first rhyme appears the fewest times, six, as opposed to fourteen for the second rhyme, and eight for the third. The second rhyme, then, offers the sternest challenge; the first remains the easiest, perhaps too easy for Swinburne's taste. "Roses" may be a love poet's favorite flower, but it rarely appears as an end word in rhyming verse because so few rhymes for it exist (the singular "rose" has many more rhymes). In the first line, Swinburne introduces "roses" as the first rhyme word; in the fourth he rhymes it with "snow's is": "In a softer bed than the soft white snow's is." The line twists syntax and logic; except to meet the rhyme's demands, little reason exists for the line not to read "In a softer bed than the soft white snow."

When Edmund Gosse complimented Swinburne on the ballade, Swinburne described the difficulty that the form gave him: "the verse jibbed like horses new to harness, and wouldn't come up to the rhymes all right." After a night's sleep, he wrote the poem "exactly as it now stands," completing "the only lyric I couldn't do straight off the minute I wanted." Swinburne's repetitions achieve a hypnotic effect, foregrounding the poem's sounds. A sympathetic reader would say that he deliberately blurs comic and serious poetics modes and note that he does so in other poems.

In this poem, though, Swinburne never adequately solved the problem he introduced. In Auden's terms, the poem gives the wrong impression, proceeding like comic verse, with the form apparently driving the choices the poet makes.

Gwynn's ballade introduces another structural awkwardness to great effect. The poem considers the previous winners of the Yale Younger Poets series, the most prestigious first-book contest for poets under the age of 40. When the third stanza presents some wonderfully terrible rhymes, it acts like Swinburne's horses, jibbing against the harness:

> Where's Alfred Raymond Bellinger
> (If you'll allow me to exhale
> Him *avec un accent francais*)?
> Where's Faust (Henri) or Dorothy Belle
> Flanagan? Where is Paul Engle   5
> (To rhyme whose surname gave me trouble)?
> Hath tolled for all the passing bell?
> And where is Lindley Williams Hubbell?

Gwynn forces the first rhyme ("Bellinger / *francais*), a technique unskilled poets resort to when they cannot discover an appropriate rhyme word. But Gwynn does so self-consciously, with a clever aside and multilingual rhyme. Combining sophistication and an apparent awkwardness, he pretends that the form forces the rhyme. A few lines later he plays a similar game, distorting syntax to ask, "Where is Paul Engle / (To rhyme whose surname gave me trouble)?" In essence Gwynn cleverly imitates incompetence.

The envoy more quietly revises the ballade form. As we have seen, the a rhyme does not usually appear in the envoy; instead, this stanza rhymes b c b c. In Gwynn's poem, the envoy's first line should rhyme with "Yale" (the b rhyme), not "they" (the a rhyme). Gwynn, though, cannot resist the temptation of rhyming "Forché" a final time. One of America's most prominent contemporary poets, Forché hardly languishes in obscurity; the rhyme offers a bit of playful nonsense. To allow this flourish, Gwynn changes the envoy's traditional structure, substituting the a rhyme for the b. Some readers might fault Gwynn for this devia-tion, maintaining that a poet should keep to the chosen form. My opinion is that, since forms develop according to exigency, not edict, a deviation faces a subjective test: whether it gains more than it loses. In this case, the rhyme's pleasure outweighs the reservations it causes.

In his ballade, Stephen decries others' rudimentary skills. Unlike Swinburne, he picks flexible rhymes that offer many options: "all," "know," and "tools." The sensible rhymes allow him the opportunity to show off a bit, to introduce flashier rhymes, as when he pairs plainer language with words taken from French: "slow" and "argot," "bestow" and "Rousseau." The form, though, doesn't drive the poem so much as to provide the venue for Stephen to broadcast his views, to handle comic verse as if it were serious, making sure the form does not overtax his talent. Intricate French forms, Oscar Wilde noted, "have made our minor poets readable, and have not left us entirely at the mercy of geniuses."

MORE WORKS IN THE *BALLADE*

A ballade typically follows the following rhyme scheme for three stanzas, keeping the rhymes consistent from stanza to stanza: a b a b b c b c. The final line repeats as the final line of each stanza. The fourth stanza or envoy features the rhyme scheme, b c b c. The first line of the last stanza usually addresses a dignitary, often a prince (an aspect that Swinburne's "A Ballad of Dreamland" does not fulfill).

ALGERNON CHARLES SWINBURNE
A Ballad of Dreamland

I hid my heart in a nest of roses,	*a*
Out of the sun's way, hidden apart;	*b*
In a softer bed than the soft white snow's is,	*a*
Under the roses I hid my heart.	*b*
Why would it sleep not? why should it start,	*b* 5
When never a leaf of the rose-tree stirred?	*c*
What made sleep flutter his wings and part?	*b*
Only the song of a secret bird.	*c* *1*

Lie still, I said, for the wind's wing closes,	*a*
And mild leaves muffle the keen sun's dart;	*b* 10
Lie still, for the wind on the warm seas dozes,	*a*

And the wind is unquieter yet than thou art.   b
Does a thought in thee still as a thorn's wound smart? b
Does the fang still fret thee of hope deferred?   c
    What bids the lips of thy sleep dispart?   b   15
Only the song of a secret bird.   c   *1*

The green land's name that a charm encloses,   a
    It never was writ in the traveller's chart,   b
And sweet on its trees as the fruit that grows is,   a
    It never was sold in the merchant's mart.   b   20
    The swallows of dreams through its dim fields dart,   b
And sleep's are the tunes in its tree-tops heard;   c
    No hound's note wakens the wildwood hart,   b
Only the song of a secret bird.   c   *1*

Envoi

In the world of dreams I have chosen my part.   b
    To sleep for a season and hear no word   c
Of true love's truth or of light love's art,   b
    Only the song of a secret bird.   c   *1*

R. S. GWYNN
Ballade of the Yale Younger Poets of Yesteryear

Tell me where, oh, where are they,
Those Younger Poets of Old Yale
Whose laurels flourished for a day
But wither now beyond the pale?
Where *are* Chubb, Farrar, and Vinal   5
With fame as fragile as a bubble?
Where is the late Paul Tanaquil,
And where is Lindley Williams Hubbell?

Where's Banks? Where's Boyle? Where's Frances Flai-
Borne Mason? Where is T. H. Ferril?   10
Dorothy E. Reid or Margaret Ha-
Ley? Simmering in Bad Poets' Hell?
J. Ingalls' *Metaphysical*

Sword (hacking critics' weeds to stubble)?
Young Ashbery (that is, "John L.")?   15
And where is Lindley Williams Hubbell?

Where's Alfred Raymond Bellinger
(If you'll allow me to exhale
Him *avec un accent francais*)?
Where's Faust (Henri) or Dorothy Belle   20
Flanagan? Where is Paul Engle
(To rhyme whose surname gave me trouble)?
Hath tolled for all the passing bell?
And where is Lindley Williams Hubbell?

Prince of all poets, hear, I pray,   25
And raise them from their beds of rubble.
Where's Younger Carolyn Forché?
And where is Lindley Williams Hubbell?

G. K. CHESTERTON
A Ballad of Suicide

The gallows in my garden, people say,
Is new and neat and adequately tall.
I tie the noose on in a knowing way
As one that knots his necktie for a ball;
But just as all the neighbours—on the wall—   5
Are drawing a long breath to shout "Hurray!"
The strangest whim has seized me . . . . After all
I think I will not hang myself to-day.

To-morrow is the time I get my pay—
My uncle's sword is hanging in the hall—   10
I see a little cloud all pink and grey—
Perhaps the Rector's mother will *not* call—
I fancy that I heard from Mr. Gall
That mushrooms could be cooked another way—
I never read the works of Juvenal—   15
I think I will not hang myself to-day.
The world will have another washing day;

The decadents decay; the pedants pall;
And H. G. Wells has found that children play,
And Bernard Shaw discovered that they squall;   20
Rationalists are growing rational—
And through thick woods one finds a stream astray,
So secret that the very sky seems small—
I think I will not hang myself to-day.

Envoi

Prince, I can hear the trumpet of Germinal,   25
The tumbrils toiling up the terrible way;
Even to-day your royal head may fall—
I think I will not hang myself to-day.

FRANÇOIS VILLON, TRANSLATED BY DANTE GABRIEL
ROSSETTI
The Ballad of Dead Ladies

Tell me now in what hidden way is
    Lady Flora the lovely Roman?
Where's Hipparchia, and where is Thais,
    Neither of them the fairer woman?
    Where is Echo, beheld of no man,   5
Only heard on river and mere,—
    She whose beauty was more than human? . . .
But where are the snows of yester-year?

Where's Héloise, the learned nun,
    For whose sake Abeillard, I ween,   10
Lost manhood and put priesthood on?
    (From Love he won such dule and teen!)
    And where, I pray you, is the Queen
Who willed that Buridan should steer
    Sewed in a sack's mouth down the Seine? . . .   15
But where are the snows of yester-year?

White Queen Blanche, like a queen of lilies,
    With a voice like any mermaiden,—
Bertha Broadfoot, Beatrice, Alice,

And Ermengarde the lady of Maine,—   20
And that good Joan whom Englishmen
At Rouen doomed and burned her there,—
Mother of God, where are they then? . . .
But where are the snows of yester-year?

Nay, never ask this week, fair lord,   25
    Where they are gone, nor yet this year,
Except with thus much for an overword,—
    But where are the snows of yester-year?

DOROTHY PARKER
Ballade of a Great Weariness

There's little to have but the things I had,
    There's little to bear but the things I bore.
There's nothing to carry and naught to add,
    And glory to Heaven, I paid the score.
There's little to do but I did before,   5
    There's little to learn but the things I know;
And this is the sum of a lasting lore:
    Scratch a lover, and find a foe.

And couldn't it be I was young and mad
    If ever my heart on my sleeve I wore?   10
There's many to claw at a heart unclad,
    And little the wonder it ripped and tore.
There's one that'll join in their push and roar,
    With stories to jabber, and stones to throw;
He'll fetch you a lesson that costs you sore—   15
    Scratch a lover, and find a foe.

So little I'll offer to you, my lad;
    It's little in loving I set my store.
There's many a maid would be flushed and glad,
    And better you'll knock at a kindlier door.   20
I'll dig at my lettuce, and sweep my floor—
    Forever, forever I'm done with woe—
And happen I'll whistle about my chore,
    "Scratch a lover, and find a foe."

Oh, beggar or prince, no more, no morel   25
  Be off and away with your strut and show.
The sweeter the apple, the blacker the core—
  Scratch a lover, and find a foe!

AN EXERCISE IN THE *FRENCH FORMS*

Poetic forms provide opportunities for parody, especially when the form is closely associated with a particular poem. Forms also develop when writers dramatically depart from precedent. Write a ballade that parodies Rossetti's "Where Are the Snows of Yester-Year?" Exaggerate each element for comic effect. After you have finished a draft, make a list of the reproduced elements then write a second ballade that avoids all of them.

9

JAPANESE FORMS: TANKA AND *HAIKU*

Etheridge Knight composed a haiku sequence while incarcerated at Indiana State Prison for robbery. Gwendolyn Brooks visited Knight in prison, encouraging him to write haiku in order to rid his poetry of wordiness. The passage of time concerns few people more than prisoners. A jail sentence, after all, constitutes a problem of time, and prisoners have little to do except to observe the world around them, to consider the small developments that make physical and psychological survival possible. Knight's haiku count: the hour, the part of the day, month, and syllable. Note the exuberant exclamation of the final haiku in the sequence.

1
Eastern guard tower
glints in sunset; convicts rest
like lizards on rocks.

2
The piano man
is stingy at 3 A.M.
his songs drop like plum.

3
Morning sun slants cell.
Drunks stagger like cripple flies
on jailhouse floor.

4
To write a blues song
is to regiment riots
and pluck gems from graves.

5
A bare pecan tree
slips a pencil shadow down
a moonlit snow slope.

6
The falling snow flakes
Cannot blunt the hard aches nor
Match the steel stillness.

7
Under moon shadows
A tall boy flashes knife and
Slices star bright ice.

8
In the August grass
Struck by the last rays of sun
The cracked teacup screams.

9
Making jazz swing in
Seventeen syllables AIN'T
No square poet's job.

"To me writing haiku is a good exercise," Knight observed. "They draw pictures in very clean lines." The other haiku stay closer to the form's conventional imagery, recasting it in unfamiliar settings, as in the simile of the piano player, "his songs drop like plum." Mixing jazz and blues vernacular into the Japanese form, this section recasts the form's "very clean lines" into a very un-Zen-like boast. The second line is particularly flashing, wedding two three-syllables with a one-syllable proudly vernacular assertion "AIN'T."

Background and Structure of the *Japanese Forms*

Japanese metrical verse typically employs a distinct pattern, alternating lines of five and seven syllables. *Tanka* verse consists of five-line stanzas, which follows the pattern of 5 7 5 7, and 7 syllables per line. A syntactic or grammatical break after the third line often splits the poem into two parts: the "upper verses" and "lower verses." Exploiting this division, some poets composed verse whose two halves only distantly relate to each other. Renga verse follows the same syllable pattern as *tanka*, but one poet composes the first three lines and another poet composes the final two. In the thirteenth century, poets competed in highly regulated contests, with each poet writing a stanza in the form. The haiku developed from these traditions; in the nineteenth century a term described this new form, *haiku*, which combines the terms *haikai*, a form of linked verse, and *hokku*, the first stanza.

Typically haiku are seasonal poems. Exploiting the brevity that the form demands, many juxtapose fragmentary images in order to evoke the passing of time. The speaker remains impersonal; he or she reveals his inner life only through attention to the external world. "Is there any good in saying everything?" Basho once asked. Haiku work by exclusion and suggestion, as in his poem:

> On a withered bough
> A crow alone is perching;
> Autumn evening now.

Such elements attracted Imagists and other early free verse writers to the haiku. "We proposed," R. S. Flint remembered, "pure *vers libre*" and "Japanese *tanka* and *haiku*; we all wrote dozens of the latter as an amusement." As Flint's comments suggest, the haiku in English threatened to turn the form into free verse, as English and American poets used the form's characteristic imagery and manner of presentation, not its syllabic pattern.

Ezra Pound's work is often discussed in this manner, but he also subtly adopts the form, as in "Fan Piece for her Imperial Lord."

O fan of white silk,
    clear as frost on the grass-blade,
you are also laid aside.

Without significant difficulty, Pound might have kept to the haiku's 5 7 5 syllabic pattern; he simply needed to cut "also" or change "also" to "too" and remove one more syllable elsewhere in the line. Pound, though, preferred a 5 7 7 syllabic count, perhaps because it allowed the final line a little more flexibility. Many Japanese haiku employ fragmentary, end-stopped lines and quick syntactical juxtapositions. Just as Pound's silk fan and "frost on the grass-blade," recall imagery common to the Japanese haiku, the final line reproduces another familiar gesture, directly addressing an inanimate object. Working from a translation of a Chinese poem, "Fan Piece" achieves a certain impersonality even when expressing one of the most personal emotions: unrequited passion.

The haiku also offered Pound an example of how to represent a moment of intense perception and clarity, as in his most famous short lyric, "In the Station of the Metro":

The apparition of these faces in the crowd;
    Petals on a wet, black bough.

Pound called the poem a "*hokku*-like sentence." With a little more indirection, the poem alludes to the haiku form. The first line splits into two phrases, "The apparition" (five syllables) and "of these faces in the crowd" (seven syllables). The second line also comprises seven syllables. In essence, the poem submerges Pound's preferred 5 7 7 syllabic count. The grammatical structure, though, stays closer to the Japanese haiku. Though Pound called it a "sentence," the poem consists of a sentence fragment, with two noun phrases lacking a verb. In this respect, it resembles many Japanese haiku, which employ end-stopped lines that share fragmentary syntax. As it stands, a change in rhythm signals a change in perception, as the poem juxtaposes one line of iambic hexameter (six-foot verse) and one line of trochaic tetrameter (four-foot verse).

Most haiku in English fail because they do not achieve the right balance of humility and irreverence. A successful poem in a pre-existing form draws from the form's past as well as adds to it. Such forms often develop by synthesis, inspired by a seemingly unlikely influence. Some haiku writers obsequiously revere their Japanese models, producing Orientalist kitsch; others almost entirely ignore the form's advantages, composing short lyrics that lack technical precision. A recent haiku anthology includes brief excerpts from poets such as Keats, Hughes, and Marvell, which the editor crafted into three-line, one-sentence poems that follow no syllabic count. This literary vandalism forsakes the haiku's organizational structures, defining haiku simply as a "short epigrammatic nature poem."

The haiku form, though, balances spontaneity (the quickly observed detail or revelation) with discipline. Haikus need not remain solemn: the *haikai*, which the form developed from, means "humorous" because the poems offered subjects and themes lowlier than those that the courtly renga allowed. Issa, for instance, wrote several very funny poems about fleas.

Marilyn Hacker's haiku sequence explores the form gracefully. Addressing, like the Japanese poets, her "master," Hacker observes seasonal changes—but from inside a Parisian café. Some sentences wind through several haiku. Others use the traditional, fragmentary structure in surprising ways:

> Historical fog
> shrouds corporeal absence:
> a generation's.

This stanza converts seasonal images into an abstraction. Instead a frog jumping into a river or a plum falling from a tree, the final line considers historical amnesia. The first and third lines balance each other, as each consists of two words, one comprised of four syllables and a single syllable. In the first line, the four-syllable words precedes the one-syllable word; the third line reverses this pattern, creating, as befitting this form, a subtle mirroring effect.

MORE WORKS IN *HAIKU*

The haiku features a syllabic pattern of 5/7/5. To annotate this pattern, I have numbered each syllable.

Hashin (Daniel C. Buchanan, translator)

1   2   3   4   5

No sky and no earth

1   2   3 4 5   6   7

At all. Only the snowflakes

1   2   3   4 5

Fall incessantly.

Onitsura (Daniel C. Buchanan, translator)

Come! Come! Though I call
The fireflies are quite heedless
And go flitting by.

Letter to Munnsville, N.Y. from the Rue de Turenne

Hayden, my snow field
is this rain-slashed winter street,
worlds behind windows.

Robust old women
and men going to market   5
pull their wheeled caddies

along the pavement
Sunday morning, as nuns go
to break bread and pray.

Sometimes I'd like to   10
fade into the market crowd:
shawled, sack of soup greens.

Get rid of the "I"?
One more woman gets on line
at the bakery.   15

Open in an L-
shaped room with two tall windows,
a book of rich hours.

At midnight, full moon
over the rooftops, old friend   20
from other cities.

Healthy, at fifty
to be apprenticed to an
exigent master.

Where is the dog who   25
worked at the *Royal Turenne*
till four months ago?

Huge German shepherd,
thick patchy coat, wolf tail, a
frequent erection,   30

he sat, ears cocked, on
the street, always alert but
discreet with patrons

or lay under a
table, walked himself around   35
the block in off-hours.

He saw everything
and said nothing: the ground rules
for a café dog:

old dog whose old tricks   40
kept him faithful at his post
for a dozen years.

And it's a year since
Mme. Magin-Levacher,
ninety, went outside.   45

But the dog's not dead.
He stalks out to the curb, where
a blonde Lab sniffs trash—

a café dog would not
eat garbage! They circle, wag   50
tails, lope down the street.

The young Antillaise
from the Sécu runs upstairs
with my neighbor's mail.

Sixty years ago   55
knickered Jewish boys played ball
in the Place des Vosges,

sons of socialists
from Galicia, intent on
losing their accents.   60

Historical fog
shrouds corporeal absence:
a generation's.

Now black-bearded, black-
hatted men cause traffic jams   65
preaching in the street.

Barred from the chanting,
sweating behind an iron grille,
girls and women pray.

January rain   70
percussive on the panes; then
wind scours the sky blue.

Ice storms paralyze
Québec: winter will be long
across the ocean.   75

Fat drops glow on the
leaves of wet white primroses
in the window box

I've changed the sheets on
the bed I'll sleep in only   80
another six nights.

A month or six weeks,
three months or four, make a life
in miniature.

Each departure, as   85
it approaches, reminds me
of the final one.

So I leap ahead
to come back up the four flights
and unlock the door.   90

AN EXERCISE IN *HAIKU*

Poets in English struggle with the haiku because they approach the form either
too deferentially or too rudely. For this assignment, draw from the form's traditional seasonal imagery and manner of presentation (the quickly observed detail
set in a strict syllabic pattern) while extending the form by considering a landscape particular to the contemporary moment.

10

OTHER ASIAN FORMS

In 1859 Robert Fitzgerald published *Rubáiyat of Omar Khayyám*, a collection of lyrics attributed to a Persian astronomer who lived between 1048 and 1131. The book caused a sensation, generating several expanded editions circulated internationally. Admirers included Dante Gabriel Rossetti, Tennyson, Swinburne, and George Meredith. Thomas Hardy, a member of the London *"Omar Khayyám* club," asked that his favorite section be read to him on his deathbed. Fitzgerald did not translate literally; in some cases, he combined several stanzas into one. As if to address the detractors who noted the translation's inaccuracies, subsequent editions bore the subtitle "rendered into English verse," not "translated."

The poem adopts the rubáiyat stanza into English, using iambic pentameter while keeping the distinctive rhyme pattern, in which the first, second, and fourth lines rhyme.

> I sometimes think that never blows so red
> The Rose as where some buried Caesar bled;
>   That every Hyacinth the Garden wears
> Dropt in its Lap from some once lovely Head.

Emerson's translation of the same poem clarifies Fitzgerald's strategies:

166

Each spot where tulips prank their state
Has drunk the life-blood of the great;
The violets yon field which stain
Are moles of beauties Time has slain.

Emerson's four-foot iambic couplets proceed as emphatically as the argument they advance. Just as the assertion admits no exception, a clinching rhyme concludes each line and a hard stress nearly each metrical foot. Whereas Emerson's version strikes an impersonal tone, Fitzgerald's presents a sensuous, subjective perspective. "I sometimes think," the section opens, introducing an argument driven more by imagery than ratiocination or philosophical abstraction. In the *Rubáiyat* stanza, the third line admits a structural freedom, a temporary independence, which the fourth line removes. The couplet relaxes then contracts. The unvarying form coexists with the speaker's gloomy uncertainty, mixing fatalism, and Epicurean delight. The rhyme achieves a formal conclusion; the final image lingers over "some once lovely Head."

The *Rubáiyat* stanza inspired few original compositions in English, mainly tributes to Fitzgerald. Swinburne reportedly started "Laus Veneris" right after first encountering the *Rubáiyat*, but made one crucial change: the third line shares its rhyme with its counterpart in the next stanza. This strategy has two main effects; it links the stanzas, instead of keeping them autonomous, and makes the third line nearly as restricted as the others. Written in iambic tetrameter (four-foot lines), Robert Frost's "Stopping by Woods on a Snowy Evening" employs a similar form, as the third line sets the next stanza's rhyme. His "Desert Places" reproduces the *Rubáiyat* stanza but revises its customary themes:

They cannot scare me with their empty spaces
Between stars—on stars where no human race is.
I have it in me so much nearer home
To scare myself with my own desert places.

These lines introduce a new stance. Published the same year as Darwin's *On the Origin of Species*, Fitzgerald's Rubáiyat proposes an alternative, freely rendered from medieval Persian alternative, what Fitzgerald called "'Drink and make-merry' . . . saddest perhaps when most ostentatiously merry." Frost's "Desert Places" responds more grimly to the modern crisis of faith. Taking a form associated with Victorian sentimentality, the stanza projects fatalism unchecked by sensuality. The Rubáiyat stanza shares some basic similarities with the limerick, a short comic form discussed in the next chapter, whose first, second, and fourth lines also rhyme. In Frost's poem, delicate technique expresses a tough world view, with two-syllable triple rhymes common to comic verse, "spaces," "race is," and "places."

Because of cultural and linguistic reasons, the most popular forms in English largely arose from Romance language sources. Even some forms that originated outside Western Europe took European routes into English. Consisting of quatrains whose second and fourth lines repeat as the next stanza's first and third lines, the pantoum began in Malaysia, but it entered our language through French sources, when poets such as Baudelaire and Banville adopted the form. Following new patterns of immigration, travel, and education, different forms attract poets. While the *Rubáiyat* stanza never really advanced past Fitzgerald's wildly popular versions, the ghazal has enjoyed a surprising recent development, as poets of different aesthetic inclinations explore how it might offer more than an exotic gesture.

In 1968 several leading American poets translated Mirza Ghalib's ghazals. Because none knew Urdu, the original's language, they worked from literal translations. Inspired this experience, Adrienne Rich wrote two sequences, which she called ghazals. Both sequences featured unmetrical, logically autonomous couplet stanzas. Following Rich's example, other American poets wrote similarly constructed poems.

Starting in the early 1980s, Agha Shahid Ali started to argue for what he called "the real ghazal." "The *ghazal*," Ali observed, "is nothing if not about rules." Born in New Delhi, raised in Kashmir, and employed in the States, Ali chastised the poets for ignoring what he saw as the form's essence. "Western poets," he asserted, "were then aiming wildly at the exotic, so they wrote the poems they would have written anyway and just called them *ghazals*." In lectures, interviews, and essays, Ali promoted a stricter understanding of the form, defining it as metrically consistent verse arranged into end-stopped couplets, as his poem, "Of Fire":

AGHA SHAHID ALI
Of Fire

In a mansion once of love I lit a chandelier of fire . . .
I stood on a stair of water; I stood on a stair of fire.

When, to a new ghost, I recited, "Is That What You Are,"
at the windows in the knives he combed his hair of fire.

You have remained with me even in the missing of you.   5
Could a financier then ask me for a new share of fire?

I keep losing this letter to the gods of abandon.
Won't you tell me how you found it—in what hemisphere of fire?

Someone stirs, after decades, in a glass mountain's ruins.
Is Death a cry from an age that was a frozen year of fire?   10

I have brought my life here where it must have been once,
my wings, still hope and grief, but singed by a courtier of fire.

When the Husband of Water touched his Concubine of Snow,
he hardened to melt in their private affair of fire.

Don't lose me in the crowds of this world's cities,   15
or the Enemy may steal from me what gods revere of fire.

The way we move into a dream we won't ever remember,
statues will now move into wars for a career of fire.

What lights up the buildings? My being turned away! O,
     the injustice
as I step through a hoop of tears, all I can bare of fire.   20

Soldier: "The enemy can see you and that's how you die."
On the world's roof, breathless, he defends a glacier of fire.

I have come down to my boat to wish myself *Bon Voyage*.
If that's the true sound of brevity, what will reappear of fire?

A designer of horizons, I've come knocking at your door.   25
But my sunsets, please, for the Pacific's interior of fire.

I could not improve my skill to get ahead of storms though
I too enrolled in Doomsday to be a courier of fire.

"on the last day of one September" "one William was born"
Native of Water, Shahid's brought the Kashmir of fire.   30

(FOR W. S. MERWIN)

Ghazals follow a particular rhyming pattern. The first couplet uses only one end word or end phrase (in this case, "of fire"). Every subsequent couplet's final line repeats at its end that word or phrase, called the *radif*. In addition, the ghazal features an internal rhyme placed immediately before the radif, called the *qafia*. Ali uses "star" which rhymes with "hair," "share," and "hemisphere." The rhyme, then, sets up the repeated phrase, a technique suited for performance, as the audience anticipates the phrase. (Ghazals remain a popular musical form in Turkey, Iran, and India.) The end-stopped couplets remain syntactical complete and logically discrete. "Think of each couplet as a separate poem," Ali advised. Finally, the writer mentions his or her name or pseudonym in the final couplet.

Ali's advocacy found a receptive audience. A native speaker of Urdu, he described poetry composed in a language that many educated Americans do not know. His charisma and humor inspired friendships as well as poems. As a consequence, the ghazal reversed a form's usual development. As forms evolve, their restrictions typically relax. Once poets modify the form, the "variation" turns into the "rule." During the last two decades, though, American poets increasingly wrote ghazals that followed Ali's stricter definition. The anthology Ali organized, *Ravishing DisUnities: Real Ghazals in English*, offers the most visible sign of this development. Though it includes poems that do not include all of the elements outlined above, the poems incorporate far more than the previous generation of poets did, when they wrote what might be called free-verse ghazals.

To encounter a form is to behold a culture, a worldview, and a kind of wisdom. Ali's ghazals express nostalgia for Kashmir, the country of his childhood where he learned the form. As if all rhymes end there, Kashmir comprises the poem's final qafia, expressing an exile's dream of return. As in many other ghazals, the poem mixes earthly and mystical love; despite the number of apostrophes, the reader never learns whom the poem addresses. The poem, though, does not reproduce the intricate, quantitative meters that Urdu and Persian ghazals employ: no poems in English do. A poem, no matter how real, reproduces only certain aspects of its formal models. To address this challenge, Ali follows his own advice, constructing a metrically consistent line, consisting of six accents.

While the ghazal, like all popular forms, has inspired a great deal of bad poetry, two interesting responses have emerged. Some poets delight in the disharmonies that the form generates, as the repeated phrase generates puns and other wordplay. Language serves as their subject and vehicle, with language or a specific one comprising the radif. The form's unifying form inspires comprehensive wanderings, a nearly frantic exploration of material, postures, and tropes. Other poets convert the ghazal into a quieter, more meditative lyric structure. Presenting a unified progression of detail and scene, Grace Shulman's "Prayer" builds to a linguistic fact that echoes a political irony, "My name is Grace, Chana in Hebrew—and in Arabic."

MORE WORKS IN THE *RUBÁIYAT* AND THE *GHAZAL*

In the first couplet of a ghazal, the poem repeats the endword or end-phrase in both lines, the "radif," which e every subsequent couplet's final line repeats. The poem also features an internal rhyme placed immediately before the "radif," called the "qafia." In the following example, Rachel Wetzsteon's "Autumn," I have marked the rhyme ("qafia") as "a" and repeated word or phrase ("radif") as "1." The poem does not include the traditional mention of the poet's penname in the concluding couplet.

RACHEL WETZSTEON
Autumn

        a   1

I'm always in a good [mood] [on the first days of autumn,]

        a   1

unable to do much but [brood] [on the first days of autumn.]

Shivering trees lined the streets where I wandered,

        a   1

married to [solitude] [on the first days of autumn.]

All summer I swore I'd lost all hope—but there is no sight   5 a   1

sadder than a bitter [prude] [on the first days of autumn.]

The self I pieced together from a million *don'ts* and *cannots*

a   1

comes so wonderfully [unglued] [on the first days of autumn.]

All is fullness, ripeness, lushness. How badly I long to spill

a   1

the juices in which I [stewed] [on the first days of autumn!]   10

I will go down the path the fallen leaves make, a carpet

a   1

Inviting and crimson-[hued,] [on the first days of autumn.]

How fast my thoughts race on these gusty, raw evenings;

a   1

how fine to be [wooed] [on the first days of autumn.]

But for every new door the wind blows open,   15

a   1

an old fear is [renewed] [on the first day of autumn.]

Will the couples who fight through the long, hard winter

        a   1

be the same ones who billed and [cooed] [on the first days of autumn?]

Chilly hints of coming darkness—is it wrong

           a   1

not to feel somewhat [subdued] [on the first days of autumn?]   20

Mountains of snow will bury me soon enough;

          a   1

let no more cold blasts [intrude] [on the first days of autumn.]

Even in this wild city, where frowns make a good armor,

          a   1

we're all too thrilled to be [rude] [on the first days of autumn.]

GRACE SHULMAN
Prayer

Yom Kippur: wearing a bride's dress bought in Jerusalem,
I peer through swamp reeds, my thought in Jerusalem.

Velvet on grass. Odd, but I learned young to keep this day
just as I can, if not as I ought, in Jerusalem.

Like sleep or love, prayer may surprise the woman   5
who laughs by a stream, or the child distraught in Jerusalem.

My dress is Arabic: spangles, blue-green-yellow beads
the shades of mosaics hand-wrought in Jerusalem.

Jews, Muslims, prize, like the blue-yellow Dome of the Rock;
like strung beads-and-cloves said to ward off the drought in
   Jerusalem.   10

Both savor things that grow wild—coreopsis in April,
the rose that buds late, like an afterthought, in Jerusalem.

While car-bombs flared, an Arab poet translated
Hebrew verse whose flame caught in Jerusalem.

And you, Shahid, said Judah Halevi's sea as I,   15
on Ghalib's, course like an Argonaut in Jerusalem.

Stone lions pace the Sultan's gate while almonds bloom
into images, Hebrew and Arabic, wrought in Jerusalem.

No words, no metaphors, for guns that sear flesh
on streets where the people have fought in Jerusalem.   20

As this spider weaves a web in silence,
may Hebrew and Arabic be woven taut in Jerusalem.

Here at the bay, I see my face in the shallows
and plumb for the true self our Abraham sought in Jerusalem.

Open the gates to rainbow-colored words   25
of outlanders, their sounds untaught in Jerusalem.

My name is Grace, Chana in Hebrew—and in Arabic.
May its meaning, "God's love," at last be taught in Jerusalem.

from *Rubáiyat of Omar Khayyám*

(The *Rubáiyat* stanza rhymes its first, second, and fourth lines. The
third line is unrhymed.)

Ah, make the most of what we yet may spend,   A
Before we too into the Dust descend;   A
   Dust into Dust, and under Dust, to lie,
Sans Wine, sans Song, sans Singer, and—sans End!   A

Come, fill the Cup, and in the Fire of Spring   5
The Winter Garment of Repentance fling:

The Bird of Time has but a little way
To fly—and Lo! the Bird is on the Wing.

Lo! some we loved, the loveliest and the best
That Time and Fate of all their Vintage prest,   10
    Have drunk their Cup a Round or two before,
And one by one crept silently to Rest.

Alas, that Spring should vanish with the Rose!
That Youth's sweet-scented Manuscript should close!
    The Nightingale that in the Branches sang,   15
Ah, whence, and whither flown again, who knows!

AN EXERCISE IN THE *GHAZAL*

In classical ghazals the couplets are logically autonomous, meaning they explore different subjects, settings, attitudes, and imagery. This history presents two possibilities. Drawing from it, write a ghazal whose couplets differ as radically as possible; by doing so, you might see how much the form itself binds together these disparate elements. Conversely, write a ghazal that resists the form's history a bit. While keeping to the formal elements outlined in the chapter, move as smoothly as possible from each couplet to the next, seeing how the form might accommodate a different progression.

SHORT COMIC FORMS

As its title indicates, Wendy Cope's "Two Cures for Love" offers advice for the lovelorn:

1 Don't see him. Don't phone or write a letter.
2 The easy way: get to know him better.

Background and Structure of the *Epigram*

Cope's poem is an epigram, meaning a brief, aphoristic poem. Such poems are often, though not always, comic. *Epigram* comes from the Greek word for inscription; some early examples adorned tombstones. Dating from 60 B.C., *The Greek Anthology* includes poems that range from the whimsical to the weighty. As the examples included at the end of the chapter show, later masters of the epigram such as J. V. Cunningham, Dick Davis, and Ben Jonson have written in both styles, composing light verse as well as poetry that explores subjects as grave as mortality and life's most disquieting fears. Even when exploring such disparate phenomena, their poetry favors a plain style, achieving a chiseled quality as if the words were measured for marble.

"Two Cures for Love" describes love with wry cynicism; for the poem to succeed, the reader must not only recognize the situation but also share the speaker's suspicion that lovers inevitably disappoint. The reader must imagine him or herself as the speaker, not the object of desire. Like jokes, epigrams stay brief because they employ generalized types. Cope's poem does not particularize the speaker nor the beloved; unnamed, they remain everywoman, hopeful in love, and everyman, unworthy of this attention. Instead of detailing an individual conscious- ness (as much lyric poetry does), an epigram, like a good joke, discovers a common sensibility, a set of shared values.

But why does so much comic verse rhyme? To answer this question, let's turn to another short poem about desire's complications, A. R. Ammons's two-line "Their Sex Life":

One failure on
Top of another.

Ammons's poem rhymes less emphatically than Cope's. "Their Sex Life" employs an internal off rhyme, "failure / another," not a couplet end rhyme. Partly for this reason, Ammons's poem has a casual, offhand tone. In Cope's poem, the rhyme clinches the argument, adding a rhetorical force that underscores the rightness of the observation. In two lines Cope uses a host of conventions—namely, rhyme, meter, and listing—to pro- ject a pointed, knowing sense of control, a comic authority. Ammons largely eschews this authority, as well as the advantages it brings. Clever and amusing, his poem offers less complete satisfaction.

Just as jokes employ well-established formulas, this kind of comic verse plays variations on familiar knowledge. "I'd like to get to know you better," countless men have told perspective lovers. Cope's poem turns the phrase against its speaker, suggesting that knowledge will lead to dis- appointment, not arousal. In short, the poem keeps the seducer's words but changes their context and thus their meaning. Howard Nemerov's "The Common Wisdom" pursues a similar strategy:

Their marriage is a good one. In our eyes
What makes a marriage *good?* Well, that the tether
Fray but not break, and that they stay together.
One should be watching while the other dies.

Nemerov repeats a banality, "Their marriage is a good one." Like Cope's couplet, his quatrain does not invent new metaphors but inspects received language, interrogating the attitudes it disguises. Like much comic verse of this sort, it turns on a cliché; it disillusions rather than inspires. The poem's familiar form, a neatly rhyming quatrain, helps Nemerov to perform a rather tricky maneuver. He wants readers to chuckle in agreement, even though the poem ridicules a phrase that they most likely have uttered. To smooth this process, the form itself establishes a familiar context, a ground for reconciliation. Just as the poem proposes an alternative "Common Wisdom," the form restores a sense of the familiar. It performs a social, reconciliatory function.

MORE WORKS IN THE *EPIGRAM*

ALEXANDER POPE

Sir, I admit your gen'ral rule
That every poet is a fool:
But you yourself may serve to show it,
That every fool is not a poet.

ANONYMOUS

Here lies the body of Richard Hind,
Who was neither ingenious, sober, nor kind.

ANONYMOUS
On Sir John Guise

Here lies the body of Sir John Guise,
Nobody laughs and nobody cries;
Where his soul is, and how it fares,
Nobody knows, and nobody cares.

BEN JONSON
Of Death

He that fears death, or mourns it in the just,
Shows of the resurrection little trust.

BEN JONSON
To Fool or Knave

Thy praise or dispraise is to me alike;
One doth not stroke me, nor the other strike.

J.V. CUNNINGHAM

Lip was a man who used his head.
He used it when he went to bed.
With his friend's wife, and with his friend,
With either sex at either end.

J.V. CUNNINGHAM
Epitaph for Someone or Other

Naked I came, naked I leave the scene,
And naked was my pastime in between.

And what is love? Misunderstanding, pain,
Delusion, or retreat? It is in truth
Like an old brandy after a long rain,   5
Distinguished, and familiar, and aloof.

DOROTHY PARKER
Unfortunate Coincidence

By the time you swear you're his,
   Shivering and sighing,
And he vows his passion is
   Infinite, undying—
Lady, make a note of this: 5
   One of you is lying.

DOROTHY PARKER
De Profundis

Oh, is it, then, Utopian
To hope that I may meet a man
Who'll not relate, in accents suave,
The tales of girls he used to have?

DOROTHY PARKER
Comment

Oh, life is a glorious cycle of song,
A medley of extemporanea;
And love is a thing that can never go wrong;
And I am Marie of Roumania.

DICK DAVIS
Repentance

'I won't do that again' you say. We'll see.
Tomorrow is another day. Feel free.

DICK DAVIS
Desire

A myth that you believed in once, it's gone.
And you can't credit that you've been so stupid:
Damn the whole crew, you say, damn Venus, damn
Her sparrows, damn her little bastard Cupid.

DICK DAVIS
Fatherhood

O my children, whom I love,
Whom I snap at and reprove—
Bide your time and we shall see
Love and rage snap back at me.

JOHN CUNNINGHAM, AFTER THE GREEK OF SIMONIDES
On A Certain Alderman

That he was born it cannot be denied;
He ate, drank, slept, talk'd politics, and died.

SAMUEL TAYLOR COLERIDGE
On A Bad Singer

Swans sing before they die: 'twere no bad thing
Did certain persons die, before they sing.

SAMUEL TAYLOR COLERIDGE

What is an Epigram? A dwarfish whole,
Its body brevity, and wit its soul.

SAMUEL TAYLOR COLERIDGE

Truth I pursued, as Fancy sketched the way,
And wiser men than I went worse astray.

EDNA ST. VINCENT MILLAY
First Fig

My candle burns at both ends;
    It will not last the night;
But, ah, my foes, and oh, my friends—
    It gives a lovely light!

WALTER SAVAGE LANDOR
A Critic

With much ado you fail to tell
The requisites for writing well;
But what bad writing is, you quite
Have proved by every line you write.

Background and Structure of the *Limerick*

In some comic poems, rhyme expresses an anarchic spirit. This free-wheeling attitude does not arise from an absence of rules but their abundance:

There was an old man of Messina,	*a*
Whose daughter was named Opsibeena;	*a*
She wore a small wig, and rode out on a pig,	*b/b*
To the perfect delight of Messina.	A, with repeated end word/name

A limerick generally consists of five-line stanzas, whose first, second, and fifth lines rhyme, as well as the third and fourth lines. A limerick, then, has one triple rhyme and one rhyme pair. Edward Lear, the form's master as well as the author of this verse, sometimes combined the third and fourth lines into a single line whose first half rhymes with the second ("She wore a small *wig*, and rode out on a *pig* (my italics)). Limericks often have an anapestic base, with three feet in the first, second, and fifth lines, and two in the third and fourth. Though the form has many metrical variants, this example fits the pattern, with the final line scanned as:

Tŏ thĕ pér | fĕct dĕlíght | ŏf Mĕssínă.

Any child whose name rhymes with an insult knows the cruelty that rhymes can occasion. Lear was one such child, as his famous self-characterization explains:

> How pleasant to know Mr. Lear!
>   Who has written volumes of such stuff!
> Some think him ill-tempered and queer,
>   But a few think him pleasant enough.

Names play prominent roles in comic verse. In Lear's limericks, the first line ends with a name and repeats as the final line. Such verse shows a child-like appreciation of rhyme, a delight in its bizarre juxtapositions. Schoolyard wits turn such coincidences into judgments; a boy is derided as "queer" partly because his name rhymes with the insult. The rhyme seconds the self-mocking character judgment.

MORE WORKS IN THE *LIMERICK*

A limerick generally consists of five-line stanzas, whose first, second, and fifth lines rhyme, as well as the third and fourth lines. Rossetti combines the third and fourth lines into a single line. The last rhyme repeats the name introduced at the end of the first line

DANTE GABRIEL ROSSETTI
On Himself

There is a poor sneak called Rossetti;	*a*
As a painter with many kicks met he—	*a*

With more as a man—but sometimes he ran,   *b/b*
And that saved the rear of Rossetti.   *a*, with repeated
                                                                              end word/name

ALGERNON CHARLES SWINBURNE
On Arthur Hugh Clough

There was a bad poet named Clough
Whom his friends found it useless to puff;
    For the public, if dull,
    Has not quite such a skull
As belongs to believers in Clough.

EDWARD LEAR

There was a Young Lady whose chin,
Resembled the point of a pin;
So she had it made sharp, and purchased a harp,
And played several tunes with her chin.

EDWARD LEAR

There was an Old Man of the Isles,
Whose face was pervaded with smiles:
He sung high dum diddle, and played on the fiddle,
That amiable Man of the Isles.

EDWARD LEAR

There was an old Person whose habits,
Induced him to feed upon Rabbits;
When he'd eaten eighteen, he turned perfectly green,
Upon which he relinquished those habits.

EDWARD LEAR

There was an Old Man of Calcutta,
Who perpetually ate bread and butter;
Till a great bit of muffin, on which he was stuffing,
Choked that horrid old man of Calcutta.

Background and Structure of the *Clerihew*

As in the limerick, the first line of a clerihew contains a name. Named for its inventor, E. Clerihew Bentley, the form consists of a quatrain that rhymes in pairs:

Sir (then Mr.) Walter Beasant
Would never touch pheasant,
But Mr. James Rice
Thought it *so* nice.

Clerihew invented the form in 1890, as a 16-year-old student at St. Paul's; in 1905, he published *Biography for Beginners*, a collection illustrated by his classmate C. K. Chesterton. The clerihew typically inspires milder humor than limericks do, with in-jokes and public school facetiousness. Part of the reason is structural. The clerihew differs from the limerick, as the opening name disappears in the clerihew while it concludes the limerick. The limerick's more imposing form invites extravagant gestures, including forced rhymes and preposterous names. In Lear's poem, why is the "daughter" called "Opsibeena"? To rhyme with Messina, a nonsense solution to an otherwise impossible formal challenge. Ogden Nash expresses this idea even more directly, when he writes with feigned naiveté :

I was once slapped by a young lady named Miss Goringe,
And the only reason I was looking at her that way, she represented
   a rhyme for orange.

AN EXERCISE IN THE *SHORT COMIC FORMS*

These forms license a certain meanness and cynicism. Compose several poems in these forms to mock others' examples, then use the same form to deride exaggerated aspects of your own personality and/or appearance.

12

CLASSICAL IMITATIONS

Forms generally explain themselves. Regardless of whether readers know the appropriate terminology, close attention reveals the structures that define them. Sir Philip Sidney, though, realized his readers needed more help. Introducing this poem, he diagramed its meter and explained the metrical rules it employs, strategies that suggest the difficulty of approximating in English the forms that ancient Greek and Latin poets used. (To clarify how Sidney viewed this meter, I include his explanatory note in an appendix at the end of the chapter.)

If mine eyes can speak to do hearty errand,
Or mine eyes' language she do hap to judge of,
So that eyes' message be of her received,
    Hope, we do live yet.

But if eyes fail then, when I most do need them,   5
Or if eyes' language be not unto her known,
So that eyes' message do return rejected,
    Hope, we do both die.

Yet dying, and dead, do we sing her honour;
So become our tombs monuments of her praise;   10
So becomes our loss the triumph of her gain;
    Hers to be the glory.

If the senseless spheres do yet hold a music,
If the swan's sweet voice be not heard, but at death,
If the mute timber when it hath the life lost,   15
    Yieldeth a lute's tune,

Are then human minds privileged so meanly
As that hateful death can abridge them of power
With the voice of truth to record to all worlds
    That we be her spoils?   20

Thus not ending, ends the due praise of her praise;
Fleshly veil consumes, but a soul hath his life,
Which is held in love; love it is that hath joined
    Life to this our soul.

But if eyes can speak to do hearty errand,   25
Or mine eyes' message be of her received,
    Hope we do live yet.

While Sidney wrote, though, accentual syllabic had not emerged as the language's canonical meter. A number of options existed, including two systems that have since largely fallen out of use: Poulter's measure, couplets with lines of 12 and 14 syllables, and Skeltonics, short rhyming lines of two or three accents. Some English Renaissance poets composed poetry in Latin, Greek, and Italian, viewing these languages as more suitable than the language they spoke. Many saw English verse as artless and unformed. Even those who disagreed argued more for English verse's potential than for its accomplishment, as when George Puttenham pleaded, "There may be an art of our English poesie, as well as there is of the Latine and Greeke." Searching for formal models, many writers turned to the Greek and Latin verse that they studied in school and seemed most adequately measured. Trained to read and write poetry in classical languages, the poets used these systems when composing verse in their own language. For this reason, the most widely used terminology for form derives from classical sources. Following a familiar path for his well-born peers, Sidney learned Latin and Greek at the Shrewsbury School and Christ Church, Oxford, where he studied prosody as well as literature and philosophy. Showing the effects of this education, Sidney composed letters to his father in Latin and Greek. He also possessed extraordinary intelligence and curiosity, impressing classmates and teachers, and debating classical prosody with the leading experts of his day long after his schooldays ended.

Background and Structure
of the *Classical Imitations*

As we have seen, accentual-syllabic meter regulates the number of stressed and unstressed syllables included in each line. Classical meters work differently; the poems are regulated by quantity, by the duration it takes to pronounce a syllable. Instead of analyzing patterns of stress, such poems are scanned according to *short* and *long* syllables. A *long* syllable takes roughly twice as long to pronounce as a *short* one. When the Latin poets used Greek meters, they changed them. The Greek Sapphic stanza consists of four lines. The first three lines following the following pattern:

long, short, long, either short or long, long, short, short, long, short, long, long

The last line, the adonean, follows the following pattern:

long, short, short, long, long

Horace, a Latin poet, introduces two changes to uses the Sapphic stanza. The fourth syllable is long, not either short or long, and a caesura, a pause, follows the fifth or sixth syllable.

In his treatise *Apologie for Poetrie*, Sidney carefully weighs the benefits of "two sorts" "of versifying" "the one Auncient, the other Moderne." The *Auncient* system (quantity) seems more fit for music; indeed, classical poems were sung. The *Moderne* prosody offers "a certaine musicke to the ear"; it achieves a melody appropriate for silent reading. Sidney concludes that "there beeing in eyther sweetness, and wanting in neither majestie. Truly the English, before any other vulgar language I know, is fit for both sorts."

As these comments suggest, classical meters attracted Sidney at least partly because he wanted his poems to be sung. The poem's directions describe one character approaching another; she "took out of his hand the lute; and laying fast hold of Philoclea's face with her eyes, she sang these sapphics, speaking as it were to her own hope." Just as the invoked "lute" shows that how closely Sidney modeled himself after the poets of antiquity, Sidney calls his poems "sapphics" because they imitate the form made famous by the Greek poet Sappho. In his notes to the poem, Sidney scans the meter in the following manners, with the double marks on certain feet meaning that they can be scanned as either long or short:

Approximations of classical meters depend on fragmentary, corrupted texts. In Sidney's day as well as ours, controversies arise from issues such as pronunciation and pitch, inspiring scholarly disagreement that range from the thoughtful to the intensely pedantic. For our purposes, we should note that the approximations depend on how the author defines the Greek or Latin model. Sidney's scansion, for instance, differs from those I introduced, which rely on the contemporary classicist D. S. Raven's work. To adopt the quantitative meters to English, Sidney also faced the challenge on how to regulate syllable length. To do so, he constructed a series of rules (included in this chapter's appendix), many of which rely on classical precedent. With some exceptions, he counted a "consonant before consonant always long" and "single consonants commonly short."

One possible avenue around such difficulties is to compose classical imitations in accentual-syllabic verse. These poets transform the patterns of short and long syllables into a pattern of accented and unaccented syllables, producing an arresting odd effect, especially in the opening foot, a spondee, which contrasts with the line's otherwise iambic construction:

How the poor sailors stand amazed and tremble

While the hoarse thunder, like a bloody trumpet,

Roars a loud onset to the gaping waters,

　　Quick to devour them.

Robert Frost similarly adopts another classical form, hendecasyllab- ics, in "For Once, Then, Something." The poem takes the basic meter— trochee, dactyl, trochee, trochee, trochee—converting the pattern into accented and unaccented syllables:

Others taunt me with having knelt at well-curbs

Always wrong to the light, so never seeing

Deeper down in the well than where the water
Gives me back in a shining surface picture
Me myself in the summer heaven, godlike　　　　　　　5
Looking out of a wreath of fern and cloud puffs.
Once, when trying with chin against a well-curb,
I discerned, as I thought, beyond the picture,
Through the picture, a something white, uncertain,
Something more of the depths—and then I lost it.　　　10
Water came to rebuke the too clear water.
One drop fell from a fern, and lo, a ripple
Shook whatever it was lay there at bottom,
Blurred it, blotted it out. What was that whiteness?
Truth? A pebble of quartz? For once, then, something.　　　15

The poet Timothy Steele observed that poets who take Horace as their model typically employ this pattern of one trochee, followed by four iambic feet, the last foot with a feminine ending, while poets who follow

Sappho's model often stress odd syllables. If so, the writers depart from Horace's and Sappho's practices, changing the pattern of short and long syllables before fitting it to a pattern of stressed and unstressed syllables. The four-line stanza, with three lines of equal length followed by a shorter, indented line, provides a visual clue; the opening trochee adds a distinctive metrical gesture. I am not alone in finding many poems written in such forms hard to scan. Poets who write in such forms apparently pull against English's contours, using language as a point of resistance. Efforts at quantity rarely succeed as meters, achieving a measure that reader and poet similarly perceive. Yet poems that employ this pattern in accentual-syllabic form register an ingenious dissent. Organized according to linguistically foreign schemes, poems that approximate classical forms achieve a counter-music to more familiar strains, a pattern both orderly and difficult to measure.

MORE WORKS OF *CLASSICAL IMITATION*

TIMOTHY STEELE
Sapphics Against Anger
Angered, may I be near a glass of water;

May my first impulse be to think of Silence,

Its deities (who are they? do, in fact, they

    Exist? etc.).

May I recall what Aristotle says of   5
The subject: to give vent to rage is not to
Release it but to be increasingly prone
    To its incursions.

May I imagine being in the *Inferno*,
Hearing it asked: "Virgilio mio, who's   10
That sulking with Achilles there?" and hearing
    Virgil say: "Dante,

That fellow, at the slightest provocation,
Slammed phone receivers down, and waved his arms like
A madman. What Attilla did to Europe,   15
   What Genghis Khan did

To Asia, that poor dope did to his marriage."
May I, that is, put learning to good purpose,
Mindful that melancholy is a sin, though
   Stylish at present.   20

Better than rage is the post-dinner quiet,
The sink's warm turbulence, the streaming platters,
The suds rehearsing down the drain in spirals
   In the last rinsing.

For what is, after all, the good life save that   25
Conducted thoughtfully, and what is passion
If not the holiest of powers, sustaining
   Only if mastered.

ISAAC WATTS
The Day of Judgement

When the fierce North-wind with his airy forces
Rears up the Baltic to a foaming fury;
And the red lightning with a storm of hail comes
   Rushing amain down;

How the poor sailors stand amazed and tremble,   5
While the hoarse thunder, like a bloody trumpet,
Roars a loud onset to the gaping waters
   Quick to devour them.

Such shall the noise be, and the wild disorder
(If things eternal may be like these earthly),   10
Such the dire terror when the great Archangel
   Shakes the creation;

Tears the strong pillars of the vault of Heaven,
Breaks up old marble, the repose of princes,
Sees the graves open, and the bones arising,　　　　　15
　　　　Flames all around them.

Hark, the shrill outcries of the guilty wretches!
Lively bright horror and amazing anguish
Stare thro' their eyelids, while the living worm lies
　　　　Gnawing within them.　　　　　20

Thoughts, like old vultures, prey upon their heart-strings,
And the smart twinges, when their eye beholds the
Lofty Judge frowning, and a flood of vengeance
　　　　Rolling afore him.

Hopeless immortals! how they scream and shiver,　　　25
While devils push them to the pit wide-yawning
Hideous and gloomy, to receive them headlong
　　　　Down to the centre!

Stop here, my fancy: (all away, ye horrid
Doleful ideas!) Come, arise to Jesus,　　　　　30
How He sits God-like! And the saints around Him
　　　　Throned, yet adoring!

O may I sit there when He comes triumphant,
Dooming the nations! then ascend to glory,
While our Hosannas all along the passage　　　　　35
　　　　Shout the Redeemer!

WILLIAM COWPER
Hatred and Vengeance, My Eternal Portion

Hatred and vengeance, my eternal portion,
Scarce can endure delay of execution,
Wait, with impatient readiness, to seize my
　　　　Soul in a moment.

Damn'd below Judas: more abhorr'd than he was,   5
Who for a few pence sold his holy Master.
Twice betrayed, Jesus me, the last delinquent,
    Deems the profanest.

Man disavows, and Deity disowns me:
Hell might afford my miseries a shelter;   10
Therefore hell keeps her ever hungry mouths all
    Bolted against me.

Hard lot! encompass'd with a thousand dangers;
Weary, faint, trembling with a thousand terrors;
I'm called, if vanquish'd, to received a sentence   15
    Worse than Abiram's.

Him the vindictive rod of angry justice
Sent quick, and howling to the centre headlong;
I, fed with judgment, in a fleshly tomb, am
    Buried above ground.   20

APPENDIX

SIR PHILIP SIDNEY
Nota

The rules observed in these English measured verses be these:
    Consonant before consonant always long, except a mute and a liquid (as *rĕfrain*), such indifferent.
    Single consonants commonly short, but such as have a double sound (as *lăck, wĭll, tĭll*) or such as the vowel before doth produce long (as *hāte, debāte*).
    Vowel before vowel or diphthong before vowel always short, except such an exlamation as *ōh*; else the diphthongs always long and the single vowels short.
    Because our tongue being full of consonants and monosyllables, the vowel slides away quicklier than in Greek or Latin, which be full of vowels and long words. Yet are such vowels long as the pronunciation makes

long (as *glōry, lādy*), and such like as seem to have a diphthong sound (as *shōw, blōw, dīe, hīgh*).

Elisions, when one vowel meets with another, used indifferently as the advantage of the verse best serves; for so in our ordinary speech we do (for as well we say *thou art* as *th'art*), and like scope doth Petrarch take to himself sometimes to use apostrophe, sometimes not.

For the words derived out of Latin and other languages, they are measured as they are denizened in English and not as before they came over sea (for we say not *fortūnate* though the Latin say *fortūna*, nor *usūry* but *ūsury* in the first); so our language hath a special gift in altering them and making them our own.

Some words especially short.

Particles used now long, now short (as *bŭt, ŏr, nŏr, ŏn, tŏ*).

Some words, as the have diverse pronunciations, to be written diversely, (as some say *thōugh*, some pronounce it *thŏ*).

As for *mĕe, thĕe, shĕe*, though they may seem to be a double vowel by the wrong orthography, be here short, being indeed no other than the Greek iota; and the like of our *o*, which some write double in this word *dŏo*.

AN EXERCISE IN *CLASSICAL IMITATION*

Such forms inspire tour de force performances as poets grapple with a meter that seems literally to English. The challenge when writing in such meters is either to make the meter seem effortless or to present the effort as expressive. In the former case, the poem disguises its own art; a reader might not guess the meter until several readings. In the later case, a poem elevates the formal difficulty into a conspicuous, perhaps even oppressive element. Pick one of these strategies and make the meter as inconspicuous or conspicuous as productively possible.

13

FORMS OF FREE VERSE

Free verse has been the language's most popular form from the early twentieth century to the present day. For several reasons, though, the term can be misleading. Free verse poems do not lack patterns; they are not "free" in the sense that they lack all restrictions. (If so, they would not be poetry.) Rather, their patterns are not easily quantified.

The following poem by Anne Carson is written in free verse, meaning no countable metrical rhyming pattern governs it.

VII. But to Honor Truth Which Is Smooth Divine and Lives Among the Gods We Must (With Plato) Dance Lying Which Lives Down Below Amid the Mass of Men

All myth is an enriched pattern,
a two-faced proposition,
allowing its operator to say one thing and mean another,
   to lead a double life.
Hence the notion found early in ancient thought that all
   poets are liars.
And from the true lies of poetry   5
trickled out a question.

What really connects words and things?

Not much, decided my husband
and proceeded to use language
in the way that Homer says the gods do.   10
All human words are known to the gods but have for them
      entirely other meanings
alongside our meanings.
They flip the switch at will.

My husband lied about everything.

Money, meetings, mistresses,   15
the birthplace of his parents,
the store where he bought shirts, the spelling of his own name.
He lied when it was not necessary to lie.
He lied when it wasn't even convenient.
He lied when he knew they knew he was lying.   20

He lied when it broke their hearts.

My heart. Her heart. I often wonder what happened to her.

The first one.

There is something pure-edged and burning about the first
      infidelity in a marriage.
Taxis back and forth.   25

Tears.

Cracks in the wall where it gets hit.

Lights on late at night.

I cannot live without her.

Her, this word that explodes.   30

Lights still on in the morning.

Carson's poem exploits several possibilities that free verse provides. Without the support of rhyme or meter, other poetic elements gain importance. Irregular lines and stanzas embody an emotional development. The first six stanzas alternate between stanzas that consist of six lines and a single line. The final third of the poem employs one-line stanzas, which range from a single, one-syllable word ("Tears") to a line consisting of 14 words and 22 syllables. As in this kind of free verse, Carson's poem uses the page as a resource. The shift to one-line stanzas slows the poem's pacing. Instead of coolly professorial observations, the final lines offer shards of images, declarations, and language. The poem slows to torturous recollection.

George Oppen uses a related technique for different purposes in the following lines from his "Discrete Series":

      Thus
Hides the

Parts—the prudery
Of Frigadaire, of
Soda-jerking—   5

Thus

Above the

Plane of lunch, of wives
Removes itself
(As soda-jerking from   10
the private act

Of
Cracking eggs);

big-Business

Syntax plays a crucial role. Establishing a pattern, phrases synchronize with or run over the lines. In Carson's one-line stanzas, the grammatical unit follows lineation. She writes, "The first one" not "The first / one." Oppen's aggressive enjambments counterpoint grammar and syntax, introducing a hesitant rhythm: "Thus / Hides the // Parts." The white space emphasizes often-ignored words. Fittingly in a poem that explores hidden connections, "Thus" twice comprises an entire line while prepositions such as "above" and "of" gain prominence, dominating other lines. To express the pain that infidelity causes, Carson's poem shifts stanza form, introducing painful juxtapositions such as "My heart. Her heart." The pace evokes the obsessive self-reflection that such betrayals cause; she uses the form to control tempo. The relation of the parts to the whole concerns Oppen more than individual psychology; his poem explores the relation of grammatical parts to the sentence, as well as small economic exchanges to the larger system, "Big-Business."

The poem's arrangement hides its metrical base, which a rearrangement highlights:

> Thus hides the parts—the prudery
> of frigadaire, of soda-jerking—thus
> above the plane of lunch, of wives
> removes itself (as soda-jerking from
> the private act of cracking eggs); big-Business   5

In 1917 Eliot described "the ghost of some simple metre should lurk behind the arras in even the 'freest' verse; to advance menacingly as we doze, and withdraw as we rouse. Or, freedom is only truly freedom when it appears against the background of an artificial limitation." Eliot characterized not only his practice but Oppen's lines. The metrical base haunts the poem, a ghostly superstructure.

Both Carson and Oppen follow Modernist experimentation. In early manifestos, the Modernists argued that the free verse posed several advantages: it allowed a more complex, individualized, and musical rhythm, eliminated the rhetorical excesses that burdened metrical verse, and responded to contemporary speech's demands. Clarifying their practice, the poets argued that free verse constituted a new measure, not its absence. Amy Lowell defined free verse as "a verse form based on cadence"; Pound argued that it followed "the sequence of the musical phrase, not in sequence of the metronome." "I think the desire for vers libre," Pound observed, "is due to the sense of quantity reasserting itself after years of starvation." Ever modest, he cited his own poem, "Dance Figure," as proof of this "progress." The poem opens:

> Dark eyed,
> O woman of my dreams,
> Ivory sandaled,

> There is none like thee among the dancers,
> None with swift feet.   5

As we have seen, quantity is difficult, if not impossible, to regulate in English. Pound's attempts differ from Sidney's in that Pound does not want to establish rules to systematize his practice. A perceivable cadence, though, governs these end-stopped lines. (Each line ends with a comma or period.)

Perhaps because the term includes many different kinds of poetry, free verse strains most attempts at definition. It includes Whitman's long-line verse, with its oracular tones, anaphora, catalogues, and other echoes of the King James translation, Wallace Stevens's "Thirteen Ways of Looking at a Blackbird," whose sections cast, as in a cubist painting, multiple perspectives on a single object, and the prose poems I will consider in the next chapter. In a tellingly paradoxical phrase, William Carlos Williams claimed that free verse poems achieve "a persistent irregularity." "Whenever," he observed, "either by the agency of the eye or ear, a persistent irregularity of the metrical pattern is established in a poem, it can justly be called free verse." Some poets organize unmetrical lines into uniform stanzas; three- and four-line stanzas seem especially popular. These poems present "a persistent irregularity" to the ear, not eye.

Two examples clarify what "persistent irregularity" means in practice. As we have seen, forms require variation. Some poems suddenly change their stanzas or metrical base. No reader would predict the transformation that William Blake's "The Garden of Love" undergoes:

> I went to the Garden of Love,
> And saw what I never had seen:
> A Chapel was built in the midst,
> Where I used to play on the green.
>
> And the gates of this Chapel were shut,   5
> And Thou shalt not. writ over the door;
> So I turn'd to the Garden of Love,
> That so many sweet flowers bore,
>
> And I saw it was filled with graves,
> And tomb-stones where flowers should be: 10
> And Priests in black gowns, were walking their rounds,
> And binding with briars, my joys & desires.

For two stanzas, the poem proceeds with a bouncy, three-stress line, as in

Ĭ wént tŏ thĕ Gárdĕn ŏf Lóve

One exception occurs in the first two stanzas, when the second stanza admits an apparent metrical blemish, a line that some readers might force into the poem's three-stress structure, "And Thou shalt not. writ over the door." Quickly, though, the poem restores the three-stress base until the final lines shockingly reassert the apparent mistake:

And Priésts in black gówns, were wálking their róunds,

And bínding with bríars, my jóys & desíres.

Blake borrows this four-stress line, as wells as the briars, from Isaac Watts's "The Sluggard," one of the preacher-poet's "moral songs," using Watts's line to assault his sanctimoniousness.

"The Garden of Love" should not be classified as free verse. It establishes a sufficiently firm norm so the last two lines constitute variations. The poem lacks a "persistent irregularity"; its irregularity belongs to a countable pattern. It has a dominant meter and a departure, both of which can be scanned. H. D.'s "Grove of Academia" works differently:

That's it, I can sit here
on my rock-throne,
not moving,

or moving with everything,
like Cassiopea on her star-chair,   5
moving round the pole,

moving with the whole,
part of your giant-concept
of deserts, the earth entire

with water-fronts, sea-slopes,   10
storm, wind and thunder-crash;
I am perfectly supple and silent,

as I steal out (still lying here)
and integrate with the fan-weed,
the bubble-weed and the strings and straggle   15

of the long under-sea grass;
I do not compete with your vast concept,
the prick of pine-needles brings me back,

yet I am a part of it
as I am part of the spiked   20
or smooth or lacquered sea-grass.

This passage has some metrically similar lines but not a meter; it avoids a norm against which a reader might perceive variations. Instead, the sentence uses grammatical repetitions (four iterations of "moving," six of "I," and two of "part") to develop the rhythm. H. D., like Pound, organizes lines according to sound while retaining the flexibility to expand or contract them where she sees fit. Qualitative judgments guide such compositions as the free verse poet attends to her main resources: syntax, grammar, and sound.

MORE WORKS IN *FREE VERSE*

WILLIAM CARLOS WILLIAMS
The Young Housewife

At ten A.M. the young housewife
moves about in negligee behind
the wooden walls of her husband's house.
I pass solitary in my car.

Then again she comes to the curb
to call the ice-man, fish-man, and stands   5
shy, uncorseted, tucking in
stray ends of hair, and I compare her
to a fallen leaf.

The noiseless wheels of my car
rush with a crackling sound over   10
dried leaves as I bow and pass smiling.

T.S. ELIOT
The Waste Land

Nam Sibyllam quidem Curnis ego ipse oculis meis vidi in ampulla
pendere, et cum illi pueri dicerent: Σίβυλλα τί θέλεις, respondebát
illa: ἀποθανεῖν θέλω.
For Ezra Pound
Il Miglior Fabbro.

I. The Burial of the Dead
   April is the cruellest month, breeding
Lilacs out of the dead land, mixing
Memory and desire, stirring
Dull roots with spring rain.
Winter kept us warm, covering   5
Earth in forgetful snow, feeding
A little life with dried tubers.
Summer surprised us, coming over the Starnbergersee
With a shower of rain; we stopped in the colonnade,
And went on in sunlight, into the Hofgarten,   10
And drank coffee, and talked for an hour.
Bin gar keine Russin, stamm' aus Litauen, echt deutsch.
And when we were children, staying at the arch-duke's,
My cousin's, he took me out on a sled,
And I was frightened. He said, Marie,   15
Marie, hold on tight. And down we went.
In the mountains, there you feel free.
I read, much of the night, and go south in the winter.

   What are the roots that clutch, what branches grow
Out of this stony rubbish? Son of man,   20
You cannot say, or guess, for you know only
A heap of broken images, where the sun beats,
And the dead tree gives no shelter, the cricket no relief,
And the dry stone no sound of water. Only
There is shadow under this red rock,   25
(Come in under the shadow of this red rock),
And I will show you something different from either
Your shadow at morning striding behind you
Or your shadow at evening rising to meet you;

I will show you fear in a handful of dust.   30
     Frisch weht der Wind
     Der Heimat zu
     Mein Irisch Kind,
     Wo weilest du?
"You gave me hyacinths first a year ago;   35
"They called me the hyacinth girl."
—Yet when we came back, late, from the Hyacinth garden,
Your arms full, and your hair wet, I could not
Speak, and my eyes failed, I was neither
Living nor dead, and I knew nothing,   40
Looking into the heart of light, the silence.
Oed' und leer das Meer.

   Madame Sosostris, famous clairvoyante,
Had a bad cold, nevertheless
Is known to be the wisest woman in Europe,   45
With a wicked pack of cards. Here, said she,
Is your card, the drowned Phoenician Sailor,
(Those are pearls that were his eyes. Look!)
Here is Belladonna, the Lady of the Rocks,
The lady of situations.   50
Here is the man with three staves, and here the Wheel,
And here is the one-eyed merchant, and this card,
Which is blank, is something he carries on his back,
Which I am forbidden to see. I do not find
The Hanged Man. Fear death by water.   55
I see crowds of people, walking round in a ring.
Thank you. If you see dear Mrs. Equitone,
Tell her I bring the horoscope myself:
One must be so careful these days.

   Unreal City,   60
Under the brown fog of a winter dawn,
A crowd flowed over London Bridge, so many,
I had not thought death had undone so many.
Sighs, short and infrequent, were exhaled,
And each man fixed his eyes before his feet.   65
Flowed up the hill and down King William Street,
To where Saint Mary Woolnoth kept the hours

With a dead sound on the final stroke of nine.
There I saw one I knew, and stopped him, crying: "Stetson!"
"You who were with me in the ships at Mylae!   70
"That corpse you planted last year in your garden,
"Has it begun to sprout? Will it bloom this year?
"Or has the sudden frost disturbed its bed?
"Oh keep the Dog far hence, that's friend to men,
"Or with his nails he'll dig it up again!   75
"You! hypocrite lecteur!—mon semblable,—mon frère!"

II. A Game of Chess

The Chair she sat in, like a burnished throne,
Glowed on the marble, where the glass
Held up by standards wrought with fruited vines
From which a golden Cupidon peeped out   80
(Another hid his eyes behind his wing)
Doubled the flames of sevenbranched candelabra
Reflecting light upon the table as
The glitter of her jewels rose to meet it,
From satin cases poured in rich profusion;   85
In vials of ivory and coloured glass
Unstoppered, lurked her strange synthetic perfumes,
Unguent, powdered, or liquid—troubled, confused
And drowned the sense in odours; stirred by the air
That freshened from the window, these ascended   90
In fattening the prolonged candle-flames,
Flung their smoke into the laquearia,
Stirring the pattern on the coffered ceiling.
Huge sea-wood fed with copper
Burned green and orange, framed by the coloured stone,   95
In which sad light a carvéd dolphin swam.
Above the antique mantel was displayed
As though a window gave upon the sylvan scene
The change of Philomel, by the barbarous king
So rudely forced; yet there the nightingale   100
Filled all the desert with inviolable voice
And still she cried, and still the world pursues,
"Jug Jug" to dirty ears.

And other withered stumps of time
Were told upon the walls; staring forms   105
Leaned out, leaning, hushing the room enclosed.
Footsteps shuffled on the stair.
Under the firelight, under the brush, her hair
Spread out in fiery points
Glowed into words, then would be savagely still.   110

   "My nerves are bad to-night. Yes, bad. Stay with me.
"Speak to me. Why do you never speak. Speak.
   "What are you thinking of? What thinking? What?
"I never know what you are thinking. Think."

   I think we are in rats' alley   115
Where the dead men lost their bones.

   "What is that noise?"
                  The wind under the door.
"What is that noise now? What is the wind doing?"
                Nothing again nothing.   120
                      "Do
"You know nothing? Do you see nothing? Do you remember
"Nothing?"
   I remember
Those are pearls that were his eyes.   125
"Are you alive, or not? Is there nothing in your head?"

                             But
O O O O that Shakespeherian Rag—
It's so elegant
So intelligent   130
"What shall I do now? What shall I do?"
"I shall rush out as I am, and walk the street
"With my hair down, so. What shall we do tomorrow?
"What shall we ever do?"
                    The hot water at ten.   135
And if it rains, a closed car at four.
And we shall play a game of chess,
Pressing lidless eyes and waiting for a knock upon the door.

When Lil's husband got demobbed, I said—
I didn't mince my words, I said to her myself,   140
HURRY UP PLEASE ITS TIME
Now Albert's coming back, make yourself a bit smart.
He'll want to know what you done with that money he gave you
To get yourself some teeth. He did, I was there.
You have them all out, Lil, and get a nice set,   145
He said, I swear, I can't bear to look at you.
And no more can't I, I said, and think of poor Albert.
He's been in the army four years, he wants a good time,
And if you don't give it him, there's others will, I said.
Oh is there, she said. Something o' that, I said.   150
Then I'll know who to thank, she said, and give me a straight look.
HURRY UP PLEASE ITS TIME
If you don't like it you can get on with it, I said.
Others can pick and choose if you can't.
But if Albert makes off, it won't be for lack of telling.   155
You ought to be ashamed, I said, to look so antique.
(And her only thirty-one.)
I can't help it, she said, pulling a long face,
It's them pills I took, to bring it off, she said.
(She's had five already, and nearly died of young George.)   160
The chemist said it would be all right, but I've never been the same.
You *are* a proper fool, I said.
Well, if Albert won't leave you alone, there it is, I said,
What you get married for if you don't want children?
HURRY UP PLEASE ITS TIME   165
Well, that Sunday Albert was home, they had a hot gammon,
And they asked me in to dinner, to get the beauty of it hot—
HURRY UP PLEASE ITS TIME
HURRY UP PLEASE ITS TIME
Goonight Bill. Goonight Lou. Goonight May, Goonight.   170
Ta ta. Goonight. Goonight.
Good night, ladies, good night, sweet ladies, good night, good night.

III. The Fire Sermon

The river's tent is broken: the last fingers of leaf
Clutch and sink into the wet bank. The wind

Crosses the brown land, unheard. The nymphs are departed.   175
Sweet Thames, run softly, till I end my song.
The river bears no empty bottles, sandwich papers,
Silk handkerchiefs, cardboard boxes, cigarette ends
Or other testimony of summer nights. The nymphs are departed.
And their friends, the loitering heirs of city directors;   180
Departed, have left no addresses.
By the waters of Leman I sat down and wept . . .
Sweet Thames, run softly till I end my song,
Sweet Thames, run softly, for I speak not loud or long.
But at my back in a cold blast I hear   185
The rattle of the bones, and chuckle spread from ear to ear.
A rat crept softly through the vegetation
Dragging its slimy belly on the bank
While I was fishing in the dull canal
On a winter evening round behind the gashouse   190
Musing upon the king my brother's wreck
And on the king my father's death before him.
White bodies naked on the low damp ground
And bones cast in a little low dry garret,
Rattled by the rat's foot only, year to year.   195
But at my back from time to time I hear
The sound of horns and motors, which shall bring
Sweeney to Mrs. Porter in the spring.
O the moon shone bright on Mrs. Porter
And on her daughter   200
They wash their feet in soda water
Et O ces voix d'enfants, chantant dans la coupole!
Twit twit twit
Jug jug jug jug jug jug
So rudely forc'd.   205
Tereu

   Unreal City
Under the brown fog of a winter noon
Mr. Eugenides, the Smyrna merchant
Unshaven, with a pocket full of currants   210
C.i.f. London: documents at sight,
Asked me in demotic French

To luncheon at the Cannon Street Hotel
Followed by a weekend at the Metropole.

    At the violet hour, when the eyes and back   215
Turn upward from the desk, when the human engine waits
Like a taxi throbbing waiting,
I Tiresias, though blind, throbbing between two lives,
Old man with wrinkled female breasts, can see
At the violet hour, the evening hour that strives   220
Homeward, and brings the sailor home from sea,
The typist home at teatime, clears her breakfast, lights
Her stove, and lays out food in tins.
Out of the window perilously spread
Her drying combinations touched by the sun's last rays,   225
On the divan are piled (at night her bed)
Stockings, slippers, camisoles, and stays.
I Tiresias, old man with wrinkled dugs
Perceived the scene, and foretold the rest—
I too awaited the expected guest.   230
He, the young man carbuncular, arrives,
A small house agent's clerk, with one bold stare,
One of the low on whom assurance sits
As a silk hat on a Bradford millionaire.
The time is now propitious, as he guesses,   235
The meal is ended, she is bored and tired,
Endeavours to engage her in caresses
Which still are unreproved, if undesired.
Flushed and decided, he assaults at once;
Exploring hands encounter no defence;   240
His vanity requires no response,
And makes a welcome of indifference.
(And I Tiresias have foresuffered all
Enacted on this same divan or bed;
I who have sat by Thebes below the wall   245
And walked among the lowest of the dead.)
Bestows one final patronizing kiss,
And gropes his way, finding the stairs unlit . . .

    She turns and looks a moment in the glass,
Hardly aware of her departed lover;   250
Her brain allows one half-formed thought to pass:

"Well now that's done: and I'm glad it's over."
When lovely woman stoops to folly and
Paces about her room again, alone,
She smoothes her hair with automatic hand,   255
And puts a record on the gramophone.

   This music crept by me upon the waters
And along the Strand, up Queen Victoria Street.
O City city, I can sometimes hear
Beside a public bar in Lower Thames Street,   260
The pleasant whining of a mandolin
And a clatter and a chatter from within
Where fishmen lounge at noon: where the walls
Of Magnus Martyr hold
Inexplicable splendour of Ionian white and gold.   265

   The river sweats
   Oil and tar
   The barges drift
   With the turning tide
   Red sails   270
   Wide
   To leeward, swing on the heavy spar.
   The barges wash
   Drifting logs
   Down Greenwich reach   275
   Past the Isle of Dogs,
         Weialala leia
         Wallala leialala

   Elizabeth and Leicester
   Beating oars   280
   The stern was formed
   A gilded shell
   Red and gold
   The brisk swell
   Rippled both shores   285
   Southwest wind
   Carried down stream
   The peal of bells

White towers
> Weialala leia   290
> Wallala leialala

"Trams and dusty trees,
Highbury bore me. Richmond and Kew
Undid me. By Richmond I raised my knees
Supine on the floor of a narrow canoe."   295

"My feet are at Moorgate, and my heart
Under my feet. After the event
He wept. He promised 'a new start.'
I made no comment. What should I resent?"

"On Margate Sands.   300
I can connect
Nothing with nothing.
The broken fingernails of dirty hands.
My people humble people who expect
Nothing."   305
> la la

To Carthage then I came
Burning burning burning burning
O Lord Thou pluckest me out
O Lord Thou pluckest   310
burning

IV. Death by Water

Phlebas the Phoenician, a fortnight dead,
Forgot the cry of gulls, and the deep sea swell
And the profit and loss.
> A current under sea   315
Picked his bones in whispers. As he rose and fell
He passed the stages of his age and youth
Entering the whirlpool.
> Gentile or Jew
O you who turn the wheel and look to windward,   320
Consider Phlebas, who was once handsome and tall as you.

V. What the Thunder Said

After the torchlight red on sweaty faces
After the frosty silence in the gardens
After the agony in stony places
The shouting and the crying   325
Prison and palace and reverberation
Of thunder of spring over distant mountains
He who was living is now dead
We who were living are now dying
With a little patience   330

Here is no water but only rock
Rock and no water and the sandy road
The road winding above among the mountains
Which are mountains of rock without water
If there were water we should stop and drink   335
Amongst the rock one cannot stop or think
Sweat is dry and feet are in the sand

If there were only water amongst the rock
Dead mountain mouth of carious teeth that cannot spit
Here one can neither stand nor lie nor sit   340
There is not even silence in the mountains
But dry sterile thunder without rain
There is not even solitude in the mountains
But red sullen faces sneer and snarl
From doors of mudcracked houses   345
                              If there were water

    And no rock
    If there were rock
    And also water
    And water   350
    A spring
    A pool among the rock
    If there were the sound of water only
    Not the cicada
    And dry grass singing   355
    But sound of water over a rock
    Where the hermit-thrush sings in the pine trees
    Drip drop drip drop drop drop drop
    But there is no water

Who is the third who walks always beside you?   360
When I count, there are only you and I together
But when I look ahead up the white road
There is always another one walking beside you
Gliding wrapt in a brown mantle, hooded
I do not know whether a man or a woman   365
—But who is that on the other side of you?

What is that sound high in the air
Murmur of maternal lamentation
Who are those hooded hordes swarming
Over endless plains, stumbling in cracked earth   370
Ringed by the flat horizon only
What is the city over the mountains
Cracks and reforms and bursts in the violet air
Falling towers
Jerusalem Athens Alexandria   375
Vienna London
Unreal

A woman drew her long black hair out tight
And fiddled whisper music on those strings
And bats with baby faces in the violet light   380
Whistled, and beat their wings
And crawled head downward down a blackened wall
And upside down in air were towers
Tolling reminiscent bells, that kept the hours
And voices singing out of empty cisterns and exhausted wells.   385

In this decayed hole among the mountains
In the faint moonlight, the grass is singing
Over the tumbled graves, about the chapel
There is the empty chapel, only the wind's home.
It has no windows, and the door swings,   390
Dry bones can harm no one.
Only a cock stood on the rooftree
Co co rico co co rico
In a flash of lightning. Then a damp gust
Bringing rain   395

  Ganga was sunken, and the limp leaves
Waited for rain, while the black clouds
Gathered far distant, over Himavant.
The jungle crouched, humped in silence.
Then spoke the thunder   400
DA
Datta: what have we given?
My friend, blood shaking my heart
The awful daring of a moment's surrender
Which an age of prudence can never retract   405
By this, and this only, we have existed
Which is not to be found in our obituaries
Or in memories draped by the beneficent spider
Or under seals broken by the lean solicitor
In our empty rooms   410
DA
Dayadhvam: I have heard the key
Turn in the door once and turn once only
We think of the key, each in his prison
Thinking of the key, each confirms a prison   415
Only at nightfall, ethereal rumours
Revive for a moment a broken Coriolanus
DA
Damyata: The boat responded
Gaily, to the hand expert with sail and oar   420
The sea was calm, your heart would have responded
Gaily, when invited, beating obedient
To controlling hands

                      I sat upon the shore
Fishing, with the arid plain behind me   425
Shall I at least set my lands in order?
London Bridge is falling down falling down falling down
Poi s'ascose nel foco che gli affina
Quando fiam uti chelidon—O swallow swallow
Le Prince d'Aquitaine à la tour abolie   430
These fragments I have shored against my ruins
Why then Ile fit you. Hieronymo's mad againe.
Datta. Dayadhvam. Damyata.
            Shantih shantih shantih

WALT WHITMAN
from *Leaves of Grass (1855)*

I celebrate myself, and sing myself,
And what I assume you shall assume,
For every atom belonging to me as good belongs to you.

I loafe and invite my soul,
I lean and loafe at my ease observing a spear of summer grass.   5

My tongue, every atom of my blood, form'd from this soil, this air,
Born here of parents born here from parents the same, and their
    parents the same,
I, now thirty-seven years old in perfect health begin,
Hoping to cease not till death.

Creeds and schools in abeyance,   10
Retiring back a while sufficed at what they are, but never forgotten,
I harbor for good or bad, I permit to speak at every hazard,
Nature without check with original energy.

Houses and rooms are full of perfumes, the shelves are crowded
    with perfumes,
I breathe the fragrance myself, and know it and like it,   15
The distillation would intoxicate me also, but I shall not let it.

The atmosphere is not a perfume, it has no taste of the distillation,
    it is odorless,
It is for my mouth forever, I am in love with it,
I will go to the bank by the wood and become undisguised and naked,
I am mad for it to be in contact with me.   20

The smoke of my own breath,
Echos, ripples, buzz'd whispers, love-root, silk-thread, crotch and vine,
My respiration and inspiration, the beating of my heart, the passing
    of blood and air through my lungs,
The sniff of green leaves and dry leaves, and of the shore and
    dark-color'd sea-rocks, and of hay in the barn,
The sound of the belch'd words of my voice loos'd to the eddies
    of the wind,   25

A few light kisses, a few embraces, a reaching around of arms,
The play of shine and shade on the trees as the supple boughs wag,
The delight alone or in the rush of the streets, or along the
    fields and hill-sides,
The feeling of health, the full-noon trill, the song of me rising from
    bed and meeting the sun.

Have you reckon'd a thousand acres much? have you reckon'd the
    earth much?   30
Have you practis'd so long to learn to read?
Have you felt so proud to get at the meaning of poems?

Stop this day and night with me and you shall possess the origin
    of all poems,
You shall possess the good of the earth and sun, (there are millions
    of suns left,)
You shall no longer take things at second or third hand, nor look
    through the eyes of the dead, nor feed on the spectres
    in books,   35
You shall not look through my eyes either, nor take things from me
You shall listen to all sides and filter them from your self.

When Lilacs Last In the Dooryard Bloom'd

1
When lilacs last in the dooryard bloom'd,
And the great star early droop'd in the western sky in the night,
I mourn'd, and yet shall mourn with ever-returning spring.
Ever-returning spring, trinity sure to me you bring,
Lilac blooming perennial and drooping star in the west,   5
And thought of him I love.

2
O powerful western fallen star!
O shades of night—O moody, tearful night!
O great star disappear'd—O the black murk that hides the star!
O cruel hands that hold me powerless—O helpless soul of me!   10
O harsh surrounding cloud that will not free my soul.

3

In the dooryard fronting an old farm-house near the white-wash'd
    palings,
Stands the lilac-bush tall-growing with heart-shaped leaves of rich
    green,
With many a pointed blossom rising delicate, with the perfume
    strong I love,
With every leaf a miracle—and from this bush in the dooryard,   15
With delicate-color'd blossoms and heart-shaped leaves of rich
    green,
A sprig with its flower I break.

4

In the swamp in secluded recesses,
A shy and hidden bird is warbling a song.

Solitary the thrush,   20
The hermit withdrawn to himself, avoiding the settlements,
Sings by himself a song.
Song of the bleeding throat,
Death's outlet song of life, (for well dear brother I know,
If thou was not granted to sing thou would'st surely die.)   25

5

Over the breast of the spring, the land, amid cities,
Amid lanes and through old woods, where lately the violets peep'd
    from the ground, spotting the gray debris,
Amid the grass in the fields each side of the lanes, passing the
    endless grass,
Passing the yellow-spear'd wheat, every grain from its shroud
    in the dark-brown fields uprisen,
Passing the apple-tree blows of white and pink in the orchards,   30
Carrying a corpse to where it shall rest in the grave,
Night and day journeys a coffin.

6

Coffin that passes through lanes and streets,
Through day and night with the great cloud darkening the land,

With the pomp of the inloop'd flags with the cities draped
    in black,   35
With the show of the States themselves as of crape-veil'd women
    standing,
With processions long and winding and the flambeaus of the night,
With the countless torches lit, with the silent sea of faces
    and the unbared heads,
With the waiting depot, the arriving coffin, and the sombre faces,
With dirges through the night, with the thousand voices rising
    strong and solemn,   40
With all the mournful voices of the dirges pour'd around the
    coffin,
The dim-lit churches and the shuddering organs—where amid
    these you journey,
With the tolling tolling bells' perpetual clang
Here, coffin that slowly passes,
I give you my sprig of lilac.   45

7

(Nor for you, for one alone,
Blossoms and branches green to coffins all I bring,
For fresh as the morning, thus would I chant a song for you O sane
    and sacred death.
All over bouquets of roses,
O death, I cover you over with roses and early lilies,   50
But mostly and now the lilac that blooms the first,
Copious I break, I break the sprigs from the bushes,
With loaded arms I come, pouring for you,
For you and the coffins all of you O death.)

8

O western orb sailing the heaven,   55
Now I know what you must have meant as a month since
    I walk'd,
As I walk'd in silence the transparent shadowy night,
As I saw you had something to tell as you bent to me night
    after night,
As you droop'd from the sky low down as if to my side, (while
    the other stars all look'd on,)

As we wander'd together the solemn night, (for something
  I know not what kept me from sleep,)   60
As the night advanced, and I saw on the rim of the west how
  full you were of woe,
As I stood on the rising ground in the breeze in the cool
  transparent night,
As I watch'd where you pass'd and was lost in the netherward
  black of the night,
As my soul in its trouble dissatisfied sank, as where you sad orb,
Concluded, dropt in the night, and was gone.   65

9

Sing on there in the swamp,
O singer bashful and tender, I hear your notes, I hear your call,
I hear, I come presently, I understand you,
But a moment I linger, for the lustrous star has detain'd me,
The star my departing comrade holds and detains me.   70

10

O how shall I warble myself for the dead one there I loved?
And how shall I deck my song for the large sweet soul that
  has gone?
And what shall my perfume be for the grave of him I love?
Sea-winds blown from east and west,
Blown from the Eastern sea and blown from the Western sea,
  till there on the prairies meeting,   75
These and with these and the breath of my chant,
I'll perfume the grave of him I love.

11

O what shall I hang on the chamber walls?
And what shall the pictures be that I hang on the walls,
To adorn the burial-house of him I love?   80
Pictures of growing spring and farms and homes,
With the Fourth-month eve at sundown, and the gray smoke
  lucid and bright,
With floods of the yellow gold of the gorgeous, indolent,
  sinking sun, burning, expanding the air,

With the fresh sweet herbage under foot, and the pale green
leaves of the trees prolific,
In the distance the flowing glaze, the breast of the river, with a
wind-dapple here and there,   85
With ranging hills on the banks, with many a line against the
sky, and shadows,
And the city at hand with dwellings so dense, and stacks of
chimneys,
And all the scenes of life and the workshops, and the workmen
homeward returning.

12

Lo, body and soul—this land,
My own Manhattan with spires, and the sparkling and hurrying
tides, and the ships,
The varied and ample land, the South and the North in the   90
light, Ohio's shores and flashing Missouri,
And ever the far-spreading prairies cover'd with grass and corn.

Lo, the most excellent sun so calm and haughty,
The violet and purple morn with just-felt breezes,
The gentle soft-born measureless light,   95
The miracle spreading bathing all, the fulfill'd noon,
The coming eve delicious, the welcome night and the stars,
Over my cities shining all, enveloping man and land.

13

Sing on, sing on you gray-brown bird,
Sing from the swamps, the recesses, pour your chant
from the bushes,   100
Limitless out of the dusk, out of the cedars and pines.

Sing on dearest brother, warble your reedy song,
Loud human song, with voice of uttermost woe.

O liquid and free and tender!
O wild and loose to my soul—O wondrous singer!   105
You only I hear—yet the star holds me, (but will soon depart,)
Yet the lilac with mastering odor holds me.

14

Now while I sat in the day and look'd forth,
In the close of the day with its light and the fields of spring,
   and the farmers preparing their crops,
In the large unconscious scenery of my land with its lakes
   and forests,   110
In the heavenly aerial beauty, (after the perturb'd winds
   and the storms,)
Under the arching heavens of the afternoon swift passing,
   and the voices of children and women,
The many-moving sea-tides, and I saw the ships how they sail'd,
And the summer approaching with richness, and the fields
   all busy with labor,
And the infinite separate houses, how they all went on,
   each with its meals and minutia of daily usages,   115
And the streets how their throbbing throbb'd, and the
   cities pent—lo, then and there,
Falling upon them all and among them all, enveloping me
   with the rest,
Appear'd the cloud, appear'd the long black trail,
And I knew death, its thought, and the sacred knowledge
   of death.

Then with the knowledge of death as walking one side of me,   120
And the thought of death close-walking the other side of me,
And I in the middle as with companions, and as holding
   the hands of companions,
I fled forth to the hiding receiving night that talks not,
Down to the shores of the water, the path by the swamp
   in the dimness,
To the solemn shadowy cedars and ghostly pines so still.   125

And the singer so shy to the rest receiv'd me,
The gray-brown bird I know receiv'd us comrades three,
And he sang the carol of death, and a verse for him I love.

From deep secluded recesses,
From the fragrant cedars and the ghostly pines so still,   130
Came the carol of the bird.

And the charm of the carol rapt me,
As I held as if by their hands my comrades in the night,
And the voice of my spirit tallied the song of the bird.

Come lovely and soothing death,   135
Undulate round the world, serenely arriving, arriving,
In the day, in the night, to all, to each,
Sooner or later delicate death.

Prais'd be the fathomless universe,
For life and joy, and for objects and knowledge curious,   140
And for love, sweet love—but praise! praise! praise!
For the sure-enwinding arms of cool-enfolding death.

Dark mother always gliding near with soft feet,
Have none chanted for thee a chant of fullest welcome?
Then I chant it for thee, I glorify thee above all,   145
I bring thee a song that when thou must indeed come, come
    unfalteringly.

Approach strong deliveress,
When it is so, when thou hast taken them I joyously sing the dead,
Lost in the loving floating ocean of thee,
Laved in the flood of thy bliss O death.   150

From me to thee glad serenades,
Dances for thee I propose saluting thee, adornments and feastings
    for thee,
And the sights of the open landscape and the high-spread sky
    are fitting,
And life and the fields, and the huge and thoughtful night.

The night in silence under many a star,   155
The ocean shore and the husky whispering wave whose voice
    I know,
And the soul turning to thee O vast and well-veil'd death,
And the body gratefully nestling close to thee.

Over the tree-tops I float thee a song,
Over the rising and sinking waves, over the myriad fields
    and the prairies wide,   160

Over the dense-pack'd cities all and the teeming wharves and ways,
I float this carol with joy, with joy to thee O death.

15

To the tally of my soul,
Loud and strong kept up the gray-brown bird,
With pure deliberate notes spreading filling the night.   165

Loud in the pines and cedars dim,
Clear in the freshness moist and the swamp-perfume,
And I with my comrades there in the night.

While my sight that was bound in my eyes unclosed,
As to long panoramas of visions.   170

And I saw askant the armies,
I saw as in noiseless dreams hundreds of battle-flags,
Borne through the smoke of the battles and pierc'd with missiles
    I saw them,
And carried hither and yon through the smoke, and torn
    and bloody,
And at last but a few shreds left on the staffs, (and all in
    silence,)   175
And the staffs all splinter'd and broken.
I saw battle-corpses, myriads of them,
And the white skeletons of young men, I saw them,
I saw the debris and debris of all the slain soldiers of the war,
But I saw they were not as was thought,   180
They themselves were fully at rest, they suffer'd not,
The living remain'd and suffer'd, the mother suffer'd,
And the wife and the child and the musing comrade suffer'd,
And the armies that remain'd suffer'd.

16

Passing the visions, passing the night,   185
Passing, unloosing the hold of my comrades' hands,
Passing the song of the hermit bird and the tallying song of
    my soul,
Victorious song, death's outlet song, yet varying ever-altering song,

As low and wailing, yet clear the notes, rising and falling,
    flooding the night,
Sadly sinking and fainting, as warning and warning, and yet
    again bursting with joy,   190
Covering the earth and filling the spread of the heaven,
As that powerful psalm in the night I heard from recesses,
Passing, I leave thee lilac with heart-shaped leaves,
I leave thee there in the door-yard, blooming, returning with
    spring.

I cease from my song for thee,   195
From my gaze on thee in the west, fronting the west,
    communing with thee,
O comrade lustrous with silver face in the night.

Yet each to keep and all, retrievements out of the night,
The song, the wondrous chant of the gray-brown bird,
And the tallying chant, the echo arous'd in my soul,   200
With the lustrous and drooping star with the countenance
    full of woe,
With the holders holding my hand nearing the call of the bird,
Comrades mine and I in the midst, and their memory ever to
    keep, for the dead I loved so well,
For the sweetest, wisest soul of all my days and lands—and this
    for his dear sake,
Lilac and star and bird twined with the chant of my soul,   205
There in the fragrant pines and the cedars dusk and dim.

WALLACE STEVENS
Thirteen Ways of Looking at a Blackbird

I

Among twenty snowy mountains,
The only moving thing
Was the eye of the blackbird.

II

I was of three minds,
Like a tree   5
In which there are three blackbirds.

III

The blackbird whirled in the autumn winds.
It was a small part of the pantomime.

IV

A man and a woman
Are one.   10
A man and a woman and a blackbird
Are one.

V

I do not know which to prefer,
The beauty of inflections
Or the beauty of innuendoes,   15
The blackbird whistling
Or just after.

VI

Icicles filled the long window
With barbaric glass.
The shadow of the blackbird   20
Crossed it, to and fro.
The mood
Traced in the shadow
An indecipherable cause.

VII

O thin men of Haddam,   25
Why do you imagine golden birds?
Do you not see how the blackbird
Walks around the feet
Of the women about you?

VIII

I know noble accents   30
And lucid, inescapable rhythms;

But I know, too,
That the blackbird is involved
In what I know.

IX

When the blackbird flew out of sight,   35
It marked the edge
Of one of many circles.

X

At the sight of blackbirds
Flying in a green light,
Even the bawds of euphony   40
Would cry out sharply.

XI

He rode over Connecticut
In a glass coach.
Once, a fear pierced him,
In that he mistook   45
The shadow of his equipage
For blackbirds.

XII

The river is moving.
The blackbird must be flying.

XIII

It was evening all afternoon.   50
It was snowing
And it was going to snow.
The blackbird sat
In the cedar-limbs.

14

PROSE POETRY

The prose poem came of age in English during the early twentieth century, with Gertrude Stein's *Tender Buttons* (published in 1914) and William Carlos Williams's *Kora in Hell* (published 1920). While certain precedents existed in the language, French literature supplied the most celebrated models: notably, Charles Baudelaire's *Petits poèms en prose* and Arthur Rimbaud's *Illuminations*. Readers so associated the form with French literature that Williams, committed to an American idiom, protested that although "I was familiar with the typically French prose poem, its pace was not the same as my compositions."

The French writers developed prose poetry as an alternative to the alexandrine, the strictly organized twelve-syllable line that dominated French poetry. Rimbaud's first book included six hundred alexandrine lines, the structure that also inspired several of Baudelaire's most famous poems. When Baudelaire asked, "Which of us has not, on his ambitious days, dreamed up the miracle of a poetic prose, musical without rhythm or rhyme?" he imagined an escape from the alexandrine's characteristic rhythms and rhymes.

Because American literature lacks a single canonical form, the English-language prose poem did not develop as a point of resistance to an entrenched verse technique. Prose poetry advanced with free verse then

226

as a reaction to it. Early writers such as Oscar Wilde and Emma Lazarus drew from the King James translation. This kind of prose poem declined when poets favored less oracular models.

A prose poem consists of unlineated prose presented as poetry. This definition may seem unsatisfactory, except that presentation helps to define a number of genres. The stop sign at the end of my block functions as city planners intended: it warns drivers to stop before crossing the intersection. If I were to steal the sign and screw it to my hallway wall, no visitor would wonder how cars could squeeze through my doorways; they would recognize the sign as a decoration. The object would remain the same, but the presentation would change its function and, therefore, its classification. If someone were to spray paint "war" on the sign, the one-word alteration would produce a political statement.

Consider the following description of a violently angry dog:

> He needs that nether fury. He has big responsibilities—he sounds
> as though he guards the gates of hell. His lungs are fathomless, his
> hellhound rage is huge. He needs those lungs—for what? To keep
> them in, to keep them out.

This passage employs more conventional "poetic" techniques than some prose poems. In addition to a host of rhetorical devices, including parallelism, phrasal repetition, and alliteration, it has a recognizable iambic base and could easily be arranged to fit an iambic pentameter pattern (with only a single absent foot):

> He needs that nether fury. He has big
> responsibilities—he sounds as though
> he guards the gates of hell. His lungs
> are fathomless, his hellhound rage is huge.
> He needs those lungs—for what? To keep them in,   5
> to keep them out.

When building a scene to a climax, novelists employ such techniques; this passage ends a section of Martin Amis's *Money*, a moment of increasing intensity. Though it shares certain resemblance with poetry, readers have no trouble identifying *Money* as a novel because the book literally advertises itself as such. If I were to excerpt the passage and title it, "A Prose Poem about a Dog," the same words would be read differently.

No specific formal features clearly distinguish prose poems from other kinds of literary prose. Instead, we recognize prose poems by their genres. Robert Hass's "A Story About the Body," for example, illustrates one kind of prose poem: the short narrative. Such poems typically use plain, rhythmic language, offering, as Aristotle advised, a beginning, a middle, and an end, even when they depict a casual, inconspicuous act, a moment easily overlooked. While lyric poets generally eschewed narrative, the prose poem seemed to welcome highly compressed stories.

The prose poem's relatively loose structure also encourages severe self-imposed restraints. A prose poem might use only a single vowel (as in Christian Bök's sequence "Eunoia") or consist of a certain number of sentences governed by the author's age (as in Lyn Hejinian's *My Life*). Also, the poem might import structures from a nonliterary discourse such as *TV Guide* or literary scholarship. Such works make prose "poetic" by introducing flamboyant formal devices, by foregrounding technique, and express a weariness with free verse, a sense that the form lacks sufficient rigor.

Writers of the third major kind of prose poem draw techniques from fables, journal entries, and aphorisms. Leading models included Kafka and Borges, instead of Baudelaire and Rimbaud. In an entry from his series *20 Lines A Day,* Harry Matthews describes a young wife who cuts off the ends of a ham before she cooks the meat, a technique she learned from her mother. Intrigued, the husband asks his mother-in-law why she bakes this way; she in turn credits her mother, the wife's grandmother. When asked, the grandmother explains she cut off the ends because the entire ham would not fit in the pan she used years ago.

The prose poem consists of two paragraphs. The second comments on the first, beginning, "This fable, illustrating our inevitable ignorance about why things happen the way they do, was told to us on the first day of the More Time Course." The end of the sentence undercuts the conclusion that the dependant clause introduces: that custom, not reason, governs time-honored technique. Matthews's prose poem borrows a fable's conventions, but rejects its sanctimoniousness, the paternalistic moralism of the More Time Course, which teaches students how to "manage disagreeable emotions by scheduling them." Lost in a two-room funhouse, the poem offers a fable about a fable. Like many prose poems of its kind, it seems highly conscious and more than a little self-satisfied, less rejecting closure than adding a casual air to the closure it achieves.

In 1978 two judges for that year's Pulitzer Prize in poetry voted for Mark Strand's *The Monument*. The third judge and committee chair, Louis Simpson, vehemently objected because the book was composed primarily in prose. Another poet subsequently received the award. Thir-teen years later Charles Simic's prose poetry collection *The World Doesn't End* received the Pulitzer with little controversy, confirming that Simp-son defended a minority opinion. If the prose poem is a subversive form, it is subversive in a highly respectable fashion. No rapper or cowboy poet has won a Pulitzer Prize in poetry nor will any time soon. The most inter-esting prose poems are gluttonous; they feast on the language and devices that most lyric poems would find indigestible.

MORE WORKS IN *PROSE POETRY*

GERTRUDE STEIN
From *Tender Buttons*

A Carafe, that is a Blind Glass.

A kind in glass and a cousin, a spectacle and nothing strange a single hurt color and an arrangement in a system to pointing. All this and not ordinary, not unordered in not resembling. The difference is spreading.

A Chair

A widow in a wise veil and more garments shows that shadows are even. It addresses no more, it shadows the stage and learning. A reg-ular arrangement, the severest and the most preserved is that which has the arrangement not more than always authorised.

A suitable establishment, well housed, practical, patient and staring, a suitable bedding, very suitable and not more particularly than com-plaining, anything suitable is so necessary.

A fact is that when the direction is just like that, no more, longer, sudden and at the same time not any sofa, the main action is that without a blaming there is no custody.

Practice measurement, practice the sign that means that really means a necessary betrayal, in showing that there is wearing.

Hope, what is a spectacle, a spectacle is the resemblance between the circular side place and nothing else, nothing else.

To choose it is ended, it is actual and more than that it has it certainly has the same treat, and a seat all that is practiced and more easily much more easily ordinarily.

Pick a barn, a whole barn, and bend more slender accents than have ever been necessary, shine in the darkness necessarily.

Actually not aching, actually not aching, a stubborn bloom is so artificial and even more than that, it is a spectacle, it is a binding accident, it is animosity and accentuation.

If the chance to dirty diminishing is necessary, if it is why is there no complexion, why is there no rubbing, why is there no special protection.

Breakfast

A change, a final change includes potatoes. This is no authority for the abuse of cheese. What language can instruct any fellow.

A shining breakfast, a breakfast shining, no dispute, no practice, nothing, nothing at all.

A sudden slice changes the whole plate, it does so suddenly.

An imitation, more imitation, imitation succeed imitations.

Anything that is decent, anything that is present, a calm and a cook and more singularly still a shelter, all these show the need of clamor. What is the custom, the custom is in the centre.

What is a loving tongue and pepper and more fish than there is when tears many tears are necessary. The tongue and the salmon,

there is not salmon when brown is a color, there is salmon when
there is no meaning to an early morning being pleasanter. There
is no salmon, there are no tea-cups, there are the same kind of
mushes as are used as stomachers by the eating hopes that makes
eggs delicious. Drink is likely to stir a certain respect for an egg
cup and more water melon than was ever eaten yesterday. Beer is
neglected and cocoanut is famous. Coffee all coffee and a sample of
soup all soup these are the choice of a baker. A white cup means
a wedding. A wet cup means a vacation. A strong cup means an
especial regulation. A single cup means a capital arrangement
between the drawer and the place that is open.

Price a price is not in language, it is not in custom, it is not in praise.

A colored loss, why is there no leisure. If the persecution is so outrageous that nothing is solemn is there any occasion for persuasion.

A grey turn to a top and bottom, a silent pocketful of much heating,
all the pliable succession of surrendering makes an ingenious joy.

A breeze in a jar and even then silence, a special anticipation in a
rack, a gurgle a whole gurgle and more cheese than almost anything,
is this an astonishment, does this incline more than the original
division between a tray and a talking arrangement and even then a
calling into another room gently with some chicken in any way.

A bent way that is a way to declare that the best is all together, a
bent way shows no result, it shows a slight restraint, it shows a
necessity for retraction.

Suspect a single buttered flower, suspect it certainly, suspect it and
then glide, does that not alter a counting.

A hurt mended stick, a hurt mended cup, a hurt mended article of
exceptional relaxation and annoyance, a hurt mended, hurt and
mended is so necessary that no mistake is intended.

What is more likely than a roast, nothing really and yet it is never
disappointed singularly.

A steady cake, any steady cake is perfect and not plain, any steady cake has a mounting reason and more than that it has singular crusts. A season of more is a season that is instead. A season of many is not more a season than most.

Take no remedy lightly, take no urging intently, take no separation leniently, beware of no lake and no larder.

Burden the cracked wet soaking sack heavily, burden it so that it is an institution in fright and in climate and in the best plan that there can be.

An ordinary color, a color is that strange mixture which makes, which does make which does not make a ripe juice, which does not make a mat.

A work which is a winding a real winding of the cloaking of a relaxing rescue. This which is so cool is not dusting, it is not dirtying in smelling, it could use white water, it could use more extraordinarily and in no solitude altogether. This which is so not winsome and not widened and really not so dipped as dainty and really dainty, very dainty, ordinarily, dainty, a dainty, not in that dainty and dainty. If the time is determined, if it is determined and there is reunion there is reunion with that then outline, then there is in that a piercing shutter, all of a piercing shouter, all of a quite weather, all of a withered exterior, all of that in most violent likely.

An excuse is not dreariness, a single plate is not butter, a single weight is not excitement, a solitary crumbling is not only martial.

A mixed protection, very mixed with the same actual intentional unstrangeness and riding, a single action caused necessarily is not more a sign than a minister.

Seat a knife near a cage and very near a decision and more nearly a timely working cat and scissors. Do this temporarily and make no more mistake in standing. Spread it all and arrange the white place, does this show in the house, does it not show in the green that is not necessary for that color, does it not even show in the explanation and singularly not at all stationary.

LYN HEJINIAN
From *My Life*

So upright, twilit, quoted

This winter will not come again and no other will be like it. On the radio I heard the announcer introduce a Chopin nocturne as played by "one of the few immortals alive today." I wanted to carry my father up all those stairs. But the argument decays, the plot goes bit by bit. A doddering old man on the street stops to smile at toddlers. In the colors were shadows, the dark or aside, the dark of itself. The young women sat in front of the apartment building in the mornings, arranged on three levels of steps, like chorus boys on risers. A painting is a flat reflection. A fence is a belt, gives one confidence. When I say compulsion and characterize it as numb, I am thinking not of the satisfactions it invented for me as one compelled but of the impenetrable dutifulness of my will. When I learned to read, I had written my name in every one of his books. The bay tree grows beside water, is a sign of water in dry places, bends its growth over the wet underground. We never wanted more than something beginning worth continuing which remained unended. When one travels, one might "hit" a storm. I made it a point to be prompt, arriving for appointments on the dot. Save it for a rainy day. The night sways. Milk is spilled from the portrait bowl. I was puzzled—the future would never be revealed. *The New York Times* every day listed the times that satellites would pass over the state. Whatever was broken had to be taken somewhere, or someone had to be brought to it. But a married name won't guarantee access. From downstairs the grotesques—a Peruvian businessman who wore, or one might say "sported," beautiful pinstripe suits, his ancient invalided wife who suffered frequent and percussive epileptic seizures, and their very fat daughter who taught piano lessons every afternoon and every evening called up to ask if I'd been disturbed by the noise—invited me to tea and I had to accept. Acts are links, and likewise ideas. A comedy simply comes out o.k. by the end, in which someone gets married, so that life may be expected to go on. A canoe among ducks. The plow makes trough enough. The activity which in retrospect we can name "grieving" at the time like a surprise from without, a cousin jumping out from behind a door. Irritable, I was likely to stalk off. This latitude of my intuition of the world as bound. They are neither here nor there, those unrooted aquatic plants that float not at the surface of the pond but somewhat below, as if almost heavy or almost buoyant, hence floating with some qualification, midway without a term. We get around in cars so much they say we'll lose our baby toes. To give the proper term for an object or idea is to describe its end. The same holds for music, which also says nothing. Are all statements about unicorns necessarily metaphysical. Maybe many, window a light. In the dark we went out on the lawn to watch the satellite go by, now four years in the sky. It always gets darkest before it gets absolutely black. Good lot of groceries, and the baby on one hip reaching over, 50 years in between, but that might be a replacement, at least a comfort. All reflections have depth, are deep. It seemed that we had hardly begun and we were already there. He hangs his hands. Later Death seemed no more and no less imponderably peculiar to me than the pre-life of an individual, though the latter is never personified. In disguise? in resignation? in surprise? "How am I to choose between all the subjects I have remembered because they once seemed beautiful to me, now that I feel much the same about them all," he answered.

A pause, a rose, something on paper

A moment yellow, just as four years later, when my father returned home from the war, the moment of greeting him, as he stood at the bottom of the stairs, younger, thinner than when he had left, was purple—though moments are no longer so colored. Somewhere, in the background, rooms share a pattern of small roses. Pretty is as pretty does. In certain families, the meaning of necessity is at one with the sentiment of pre-necessity. The better things were gathered in a pen. The windows were narrowed by white gauze curtains which were never loosened. Here I refer to irrelevance, that rigidity which never intrudes. Hence, repetitions, free from all ambition. The shadow of the redwood trees, she said, was oppressive. The plush must be worn away. On her walks she stepped into people's gardens to pinch off cuttings from their geraniums and succulents. An occasional sunset is reflected on the windows. A little puddle is overcast. If only you could touch, or, even, catch those gray great creatures. I was afraid of my uncle with the wart on his nose, or of his jokes at our expense which were beyond me, and I was shy of my aunt's deafness who was his sister-in-law and who had years earlier fallen into the habit of nodding, agreeable. Wool station. See lightning, wait for thunder. Quite mistakenly, as it happened. Long time lines trail

behind every idea, object, person, pet, vehicle, and event. The afternoon happens, crowded and therefore endless. Thicker, she agreed.
It was a tic, she had the habit, and now she bobbed like my toy plas-
tic bird on the edge of its glass, dipping into and recoiling from the
water. But a word is a bottomless pit. It became magically pregnant
and one day split open, giving birth to a stone egg, about as big as a
football. In May when the lizards emerge from the stones, the stones
turn gray, from green. When daylight moves, we delight in distance.
The waves rolled over our stomachs, like spring rain over an orchard
slope. Rubber bumpers on rubber cars. The resistance on sleeping to
being asleep. In every country is a word which attempts the sound of
cats, to match an inisolable portrait in the clouds to a din in the air.
But the constant noise is not an omen of music to come. "Everything
is a question of sleep," says Cocteau, but he forgets the shark, which
does not. Anxiety is vigilant. Perhaps initially, even before one can
talk, restlessness is already conventional, establishing the incoherent
border which will later separate events from experience. Find a
drawer that's not filled up. That we sleep plunges our work into the
dark. The ball was lost in a bank of myrtle. I was in a room with the
particulars of which a later nostalgia might be formed, an indulged
childhood. They are sitting in wicker chairs, the legs of which have
sunk unevenly into the ground, so that each is sitting slightly tilted
and their postures make adjustment for that. The cows warm their
own barn. I look at them fast and it gives the illusion that they're
moving. An "oral history" on paper. *That* morning this morning. I
say it about the psyche because it is not optional. The overtones are
denser shadow in the room characterized by its habitual readiness, a
form of charged waiting, a perpetual attendance, of which I was
thinking when I began the paragraph, "So much of childhood is
spent in a manner of waiting."

ROBERT HASS
A Story About the Body

The young composer, working that summer at an artist's colony, had
watched her for a week. She was Japanese, a painter, almost sixty,
and he thought he was in love with her. He loved her work, and her
work was like the way she moved her body, used her hands, looked at
him directly when she made amused and considered answers to his
questions. One night, walking back from a concert, they came to her

door and she turned to him and said, "I think you would like to have me. I would like that too, but I must tell you that I have had a double mastectomy," and when he didn't understand, "I've lost both my breasts." The radiance that he had carried around in his belly and chest cavity—like music—withered very quickly, and he made himself look at her when he said, "I'm sorry. I don't think I could." He walked back to his own cabin through the pines, and in the morning he found a small blue bowl on the porch outside his door. It looked to be full of rose petals, but he found when he picked it up that the rose petals were on the top; the rest of the bowl—she must have swept them from the corners of her studio—was full of dead bees.

15

NEW FORMS AND OLD

Occasionally artists declare that they must invent new forms because the old ones are inadequate. "Poetry," Lyn Hejinian asserts, "requires an *invention of form*." "Various new ones [poetic devices] must be created constantly." According to this line of thinking, established poetic forms lose their power to disturb, to impede customary ways of thinking about language and the world. Poetry, Hejinian believes, de-familiarizes the familiar; it takes ordinary language and makes it strange. New forms are needed, then, to force reader and writer alike to encounter the unexpected.

Charles Bernstein's poem "From the Basque" demonstrates these ideas in practice:

Ears are poppin' everybody's dancin'
to the Andalusiana.
Ax, bat, delirious bobbing especially
establishes gulled surfeit.

This poem is a *homophonic translation*, meaning that Bernstein translated the sounds of a text written in another language (in this case,

Basque). Bernstein did not invent the form; he credits Louis and Celia Zukofsky's translation of the Latin poet Catullus as his inspiration. A half-decade old, the form is relatively new, especially when compared to more familiar structures such as the ballad or sonnet. Sound constitutes Bernstein's primary material; his translation expresses this aspect more than the original's imagery, voice, diction, or literal meaning. Like Bernstein's other poems, the homophonic translation radically departs from the conventions of spoken language. Filled with dissonance and discontinuities, it exists as a kind of sound experiment, a suggestive display of the poetic elements that Bernstein prizes and those he does not.

Ron Silliman describes homophonic translation as a "ghost dance of tongues," a description that nicely characterizes a certain tendency in contemporary poetry. Many writers organize poems around the language that the culture provides them, deforming these resources into arresting scraps and fragments. In some cases technology assists this process, as when poets use the google search engines to compose sestinas or sonnets out of the language floating through the internet. These poets use a new technology to write an old form; the writing procedure they employ inspires a certain style, the disjunctive, multivoiced rhetoric familiar to much contemporary poetry.

Exploring similar terrain from a different perspective, Edwin Morgan composed a series of poems that construct and deconstruct borrowed lines. "Manifesto" borrows from a famous proclamation from *The Communist Manifesto*, one translated into Russian from the original German. In English, the line urges, "Workers of the world unite." The rallying cry provides the letters and the spacing for Morgan's poem, a meditation upon the consequences of a German idea translated into Russian:

EDWIN MORGAN
Manifesto

```
   r     i  se
             st an    d
 pro      v e
             st a         y
       t r               y              5
   r  et r               y
     le ar           n
         r    e      a   d
         t r         a   in
```

```
            s     tra     in                        10
            v             i     e
      le a                d
          t     e   st
      r  et     e   st
   pro  t       e   st                               15
      ro   a          r
   p      r     e   s              s
   p      ri        s              e
   pr     i           n            t
      e                   di    t                    20
            s     a     y
   proletari      an s   in
      e    v e    r      y
      l           an   d
         a        r        e                         25
      o           n        e
   proletarii vsekh stran soedinyaites
```

This poem is a *visual poem*; typography, the arrangement on the page, constitutes its main structure. Unlike other visual poems such as Herbert's "Easter Wings" or "The Altar," "Manifesto" does not imitate an object's shape. Instead, the form allows Morgan to dramatize the process by which context transforms language. To the best of my knowledge, Morgan invented this form, which structures language into a reproducible pattern, as the poet Wendy Cope proved when she organized her own poems around other phrases.

Great poets do not necessarily devise new techniques. Ezra Pound once distinguished between two kinds of poets: the "inventors" and the "masters." Inventors discover a particular technique or method; masters "assimilate and co-ordinate a large number of preceding inventions." Surrey invented the English sonnet, which Shakespeare later borrowed toward the end of a sonnet craze. Few readers would prefer Surrey's poems to Shakespeare's, the work of the inventor to that of the master. A master such as Shakespeare synthesizes disparate elements; in Pound's phrase, he brings "the whole to a state of homogenous fullness."

Because poetic form, like language itself, exists in a perpetual state of flux, no clear line divides new and old artistic technique, the borrowed and the invented. One term for a poet, *troubadour* derives from *trobar*, which means to "find, compose, invent in verse." As the etymology suggests, poets both find and invent, sometimes in the same act. A technique might gain novelty when imported from another language, as when Eliot wrote a verse line influenced by the French poet Jules Laforgue or when Latin writers borrowed from Greek models. Such cross-cultural fertilizations inspire startling rearrangements of the unfamiliar and the established. Similarly, poets transform the forms they use, finding new uses and occasions. "We fill pre-existing forms and when we fill them we change and are changed," Frank Bidart observes.

Consider two poems that respond to the AIDS crisis. Starting with seven numbered lines, Joan Retallack's "AID/I/SAPPEARANCE" removes the letters "A," "I," "D," and "S" then "adjoining letters B H J C E R T, to F G K Q U, to L P V, to M O W, to N X, to Y." The form deconstructs the poem into a collection of letters and sounds until all only a section titled "Y" remains, consisting of seven, empty numbered lines:

for Stefan Fitterman
1. in contrast with the demand of continuity in the customary
    description
2. of nature the indivisibility of the quantum of action requires an
    essential
3. element of discontinuity especially apparent through the   5
    discussion of the
4. nature of light she said it's so odd to be dying and laughed still
    it's early
5. late the beauty of nature as the moon waxes turns to terror when
    it wanes   10
6. or during eclipse or when changing seasons change making
    certain things
7. disappear and there is no place to stand on and strangely we're
    glad

A I D S
for tefn Fttermn
1. n contrt wth the emn of contnuty n the cutomry ecrpton   15
2. of nture the nvblty of the quntum of cton requre n eentl
3. element of contnuty epeclly pprent through the cuon of the
4. nture of lght he t o o t be yng n lughe tll t erly
5. lte the beuty of nture the moon wxe turn to terror when t wne

6. or urng eclpe or when chngng eon chnge mkng certn thng   20
7. pper n there no plce to tn on n trngely we're gl

B H J C E R T

fo fn Fmn

1. n on w mn of onnuy n uomy pon
2. of nu nvly of qunum of on qu n nl
3. lmn of onnuy plly ppn oug uon of
4. nu of lg o o yng n lug ll ly   25
5. l uy of nu moon wx un o o wn wn
6. o ung lp o wn ngng on ng mkng n ng
7. pp n no pl o n on n ngly w gl

F G K Q U

o n mn

1. no n w m no on ny no my pon
2. o n nvly o nm o on n nl   30
3. lm no onny plly pp no on o
4. no l o o yn nl ll ly
5. l y o n moon wx no own wn
6. o n l pow n n no n n mn n n
7. pp n no pl o no n n nly w l   35

L P V

o n mn

1. no n w m no on ny no my on
2. o n ny o nm o on n n
3. m no onny y no on o
4. no o o y n n y
5. y o n moon wx no own wn   40
6. o now n n no n n mn n n
7. n no o no n n n y w

M O W

n

1. n n n n n y n y n
2. n n y n n n n

3. n n n y y n n   45
4. n y n n y
5. y n n x n n n
6. n n n n n n n n n
7. n n n n n n y

N X

1. y y   50
2. y
3. y y
4. y y
5. y
6.   55
7. y

Y

1.
2.
3.
4.   60
5.
6.
7.

"AID/I/SAPPEARANCE" uses a literary device to record devastation, to create a monument of erasure and loss. Mutating through the
poem, the form claims letters until only a skeletal structure remains. To
appreciate this poem, one must read it aloud, hearing its progress. After a
desperate keening-like sound, a seemingly inarticulate collection of letters, numbers, and sounds that articulate a terrible anguish, the poem
ends quietly with a simple count.

Thom Gunn's "The Beautician" uses more familiar poetic techniques
to address the AIDS crisis:

She, a beautician, came to see her friend
Inside the morgue, when she had had her cry.
She found the body dumped there all awry,
Not as she thought right for a person's end,
Left sideways like that on one arm and thigh.   5

In their familiarity with the dead
It was as if the men had not been kind
With her old friend, whose hair she was assigned
To fix and shape. She did not speak; instead
She gave her task a concentrated mind.   10

She did find in it some thin satisfaction
That she could use her tenderness as skill
To make her poor dead friend's hair beautiful
—As if she shaped an epitaph by her action,
She thought—being a beautician after all.   15

Composed in the language's most important meter, iambic pentameter, Gunn's poem consists of three, five-line stanzas whose first and fourth, and second, third, and fifth lines rhyme.

The poem contrasts the disorder that death imposes with the order that art establishes. The corpse is "dumped there all awry" "[l]eft sideways like that on one arm and thigh"; the beautician uses "tenderness as skill" "[t]o fix and shape." The poem's language compares the beautician to a poet. Considering the corpse, she works like an epitaph writer, creating a memorial to her friend. Accordingly, the poem can be read in two ways. It asserts either that art falsifies experience or performs necessary services; art makes an ugly situation almost pretty or honors the dead and comforts the living.

"AID/I/SAPPEARANCE" and "The Beautician" use strikingly different forms to consider a similar challenge: how to address the devastation that AIDS brought with a shapely work of art. In a telling rhyme, Gunn couples "skill" and "beautiful"; the poet's skill, like the beautician's, produces an aesthetically pleasing effect. Art and art-making create a kind of gratification, small and hard to define: "some thin satisfaction," in Gunn's phrase. The poem's obvious polish disguises its ambivalence. Reservations and qualifications fill the one-sentence final stanza.

While "The Beautician" employs familiar techniques, "AID/I/SAPPEARANCE" presents a seemingly bewildering form. The poem breaks language into smaller and smaller fragments, isolating an underlying order. The wordless final stanza offers a quiet moment of contemplation, a starkly simple invocation of loss. "AID/I/SAPPEARANCE" presents an elegant, cunning structure. The form achieves two contradictory effects; it echoes the devastation AIDS has wrought and creates an oddly compelling pattern, a terrible beauty.

Artists who create forms are often accused of gimmickry, just as those whose favor preexisting techniques are maligned as complacent. Forms, though, are nothing more than strategies; they are neither intrinsically good nor bad. Effective forms deepen the impulses that inspire a poem. They bring new knowledge to poets and readers alike. Gunn and Retallack craft forms that investigate the challenges they face as poets living in an age of AIDS. Their vastly different poems record and transform the suffering they witness.

NOTES

Like any study on poetic form or any poetic form, this work builds upon previous works, including many of those listed in the Recommended Additional Reading Appendix. In addition, I should like to note more specific debts.

My discussion of meter draws from George T. Wright, *Shakespeare's Metrical Art* (Berkeley: University of California Press, 1988), and the best account of iambic pentameter I know. On page 161 he offers the observation on extra-metrical ending that I quote.

For the histories of the ballad I discuss, see *The English and Scottish Popular Ballads* (Francis James Child, ed. Vol. 5 New York: The Folklore Press, 1956, p. 88–96), *Folk Songs of the South: Collected under the Auspices of the West Virginia Folk-Lore Society* (Cambridge: Harvard University Press, 1925, p. 154–158), and David Herd's, *Ancient and Modern Scottish Songs, Heroic Ballads, Etc., Vol. 2* (Edinburgh: John Wotherspoon, 1869, p. 172–5). Alan Bold's *The Ballad* (London: Methuen, 1979, p. 13–14) provides the source for the quote beginning, "There war never ane o' my sangs." I am indebted to the discussion of Keats's sonnets in Walter Jackson Bate's "Keats's Odes of May, 1819" in *Discussions of Poetry: Form and Structure* (Francis Murphy, ed. Boston: D. C. Heath and Company, 1964, p. 201–7). My source for Ezra Pound's performance of "Altaforte" is Humprey Carpenter's *A Serious Character: The Life of Ezra Pound* (Boston: Houghton Mifflin Company, 1988, p. 116, 217). My chapter on the villanelle draws from Ronald E. MacFarland, *The Villanelle: The Evolution of a Poetic Form* (Moscow, Idaho: The University of Idaho Press); on page 76, he offers the observation on James Whitcomb Riley's "The Best is Good Enough" that I quote. My information on Edwin Arlington Robinson derives from the following sources: William L. Anderson, *Edwin Arlington Robinson: A Critical Introduction* (New York: Houghton Mifflin, 1967, p. 74); *Untriangulated Stars: Letters of Edwin Arlington Robinson to Harry De Forest Smith 1890–1905* (Denham Sutcliffe, ed. Cambridge: Harvard University Press, 1947, p. 146). My discussion on the ballades draws from Helen Louise Cohen, *Lyric Forms from France: Their History and Their Use* (New York: Harcourt, Brace, and Company, 1922), whose anthology and introduction suggested many examples. D. S. Raven's scansion of Sapphic meter can be found in his *Latin Metre* (London: Bristol Classics, 1999, p. 143–4). Derek Attridge's *Well-Weighed Syllables: Elizabethan Verse in Classical Metres* (London, Cambridge University Press, 1974) helped me to negotiate the confusing terrain of approximations of classical meters. My discussion of Sidney is indebted to his elegant book.

RECOMMENDED ADDITIONAL READING

T. V. F. Brogan's *English Versification, 1570–1980: A Reference Guide with a Global Appendix* (Baltimore: Johns Hopkins University Press, 1981) is a monumental work of scholarship, with nearly 800 pages of annotated bibliographical material. Brogan's *Verseform: A Comparative Bibliography* (Baltimore: Johns Hopkins University Press, 1988) presents a more selective bibliography. Both are excellent.

The New Princeton Encyclopedia of Poetry and Poetics, Alex Preminger and T. V. F. Brogan, co-editors; Frank J. Warnke, O. B. Hardison, Jr., and Earl Miner, associate editors (Princeton: Princeton University Press, 1993) is the standard reference book, with uniformly excellent entries.

My study of contemporary metrical verse, *Questions of Possibility: Contemporary Poetry and Poetic Form* (New York: Oxford University Press, 2005) might interest readers who enjoyed this book.

Arranged according to this book's chapters, the following works introduce the wider field.

THEORIES OF FORM

Aristotle, *Poetics*, available in numerous translations.

Kenneth Burke, *The Philosophy of Literary Form: Studies in Symbolic Action* (Baton Rouge: Louisiana State University Press, 1941).

Charles Bernstein, *A Poetics* (Cambridge, MA: Harvard University Press, 1992).

Samuel Taylor Coleridge, *Biographia Literaria, or, Biographical Sketches of my Literary Life and Opinions* (London: Fenner, 1817) especially Chapters xiv and xviii.

G. W. F. Hegel, "Versification," *Aesthetics: Lectures on Fine Art*, Vol. II, T. M. Knox, trans. (Oxford: Clarendon Press, 1975) 1011–1034.

Samuel Johnson, *Selected Poetry and Prose*, Frank Brady and W. K. Wimsatt, eds. (Berkeley: University of California Press, 1977).

HISTORICAL STUDIES AND RESOURCES

Thomas Cable, *The Meter and Melody of Beowulf* (Urbana: University of Illinois Press, 1974).

Stuart Curran, *Poetic Form and British Romanticism* (New York: Oxford University Press, 1986).

246

Paul Fussell, Jr., *Theory of Prosody in Eighteenth-Century England* (Connecticut: Archon Books, 1966).

Robert Frank and Henry Sayre, eds., *The Line in Postmodern Poetry* (Urbana: University of Illinois Press, 1988).

Dana Gioia, David Mason, and Meg Schoerke, eds., with D. C. Stone, *Twentieth-Century American Poetics: Poets on the Art of Poetry* (Boston: McGraw-Hill, 2004).

Harvey Gross, ed., *The Structure of Verse: Modern Essays on Prosody* (New York : Ecco Press, 1979).

——— *Sound and Form in Modern Poetry: A Study of Prosody from Thomas Hardy to Robert Lowell* (Ann Arbor, University of Michigan Press, 1964).

C. B. McCully and J. J. Anderson, eds., *English Historical Metrics* (New York: Cambridge University Press, 1996).

Mark David Rasmussen, ed., *Renaissance Literature and its Formal Engagements* (New York: Palgrave, 2002).

George Saintsbury, *A History of English Prosody from the Twelfth Century to the Present Day*, 3 vols. (London: Macmillan, 1906–1910).

Brian Vickers, ed., *English Renaissance Literary Criticism* (New York: Oxford University Press, 1999).

W. K. Wimsatt, ed., *Versification: Major Language Types* (New York: New York University Press, 1972).

Susan J. Wolfson, *Formal Charges: The Shaping of Poetry in British Romanticism* (Stanford, CA: Stanford University Press, 1997).

METER

David Baker, ed., *Meter in English: A Critical Engagement* (Fayetteville: University of Arkansas Press, 1996).

Thomas Carper and Derek Attridge, *Meter and Meaning: An Introduction to Rhythm in Poetry* (New York: Routledge, 2003).

Richard D. Cureton, *Rhythmic Phrasing in English Verse* (New York: Longman, 1992).

Ezra Pound, "Treatise on Metre," *ABC of Reading* (New York: New Directions, 1934) 195–206.

Thomas A. Sebeok, ed., *Style in Language* (Cambridge, MA: MIT Press, 1960), especially "Metrics," with contributions from John Lotz, Seymour Chatman, Benjamin Hrushovski, John Hollander, W. K Wimsatt, Jr., and M. C. Beardsley.

Timothy Steele, *All the Fun's in How You Say a Thing: An Explanation of Meter and Versification* (Athens: Ohio University Press, 1999).

John Thompson, *The Founding of English Metre* (New York, Columbia University Press, 1961).

George T. Wright, *Shakespeare's Metrical Art* (Berkeley: University of California Press, 1988).

MUSICAL FORMS: BALLADS AND BLUES

Kevin Young, *Blues Poems* (New York: Everyman's Library, 2003).

Houston A. Baker, Jr., *Blues, Ideology, and Afro-American Literature: A Vernacular Theory* (Chicago: University of Chicago Press, 1984).

Hayden Carruth, "The Blues as Poetry," *Selected Essays and Reviews* (Port Townsend, Wash.: Cooper Canyon Press, 1996) 293–299.

Francis James Child, *The English and Scottish Popular Ballads*, in five volumes (Boston, New York: Houghton, Mifflin and Company, 1886–1998).

Thomas Percy, *Reliques of Ancient English Poetry: Consisting of Old Heroic Ballads, Songs, and Other Pieces of our Earlier Poets, (Chiefly of the Lyric kind.)* (London: J. Dodsley in Pall-Mall, 1765).

SONNET

John Fuller, ed., *The Oxford Book of Sonnets* (New York: Oxford University Press, 2000).

Phillis Levin, *The Penguin Book of the Sonnet: 500 Years of a Classic Tradition in English* (New York: Penguin Books, 2001).

Paul Oppenheimer, *The Birth of the Modern Mind: Self, Consciousness, and the Invention of the Sonnet* (New York: Oxford University Press, 1989).

Michael R. G. Spiller, *The Development of the Sonnet: An Introduction* (New York: Routledge, 1992).

―――― *The Sonnet Sequence: A Study of its Strategies* (New York: Twayne, 1977).

COUPLETS

Wallace Cable Brown, *The Triumph of Form; A Study of the Later Masters of the Heroic Couplet* (Chapel Hill: University of North Carolina Press, 1948).

Margaret Anne Doody, *The Daring Muse: Augustan Poetry Reconsidered* (New York: Cambridge University Press, 1985).

J. Paul Hunter, "Couplets and Conversation," *The Cambridge Companion to Eighteenth-Century, Poetry*, John Sitter, ed. (Cambridge University Press, 2001) 11–35.

William Bowman Piper, *The Heroic Couplet* (Cleveland, Case Western Reserve University, 1969).

David H. Richter, ed., *Ideology and Form in Eighteenth-Century Literature* (Lubbock, Texas: Texas Tech University Press, 1999), especially "Form as Meaning: Pope and the Ideology of the Couplet," by J. Paul Hunter, 147–162.

SESTINA

James Cummins, "Calliope Music: Notes on the Sestina," *Antioch Review* 55.2 (Spring 1997) 148–159.

Leslie A. Fielder, "Dante: Green Thoughts in a Green Shade," *No! In Thunder: Essays on Myth and Literature* (New York: Stein and Day, 1960) 23–45.

Anthony Hecht, "Sidney and the Sestina," *Green Thoughts, Green Shades: Essays by Contemporary Poets on the Early Modern Lyric*, Jonathan F. S. Post, ed. (Berkeley: University of California Press, 2002) 41–58.

John Frederick Nims, "The Sestina," *A Local Habitation: Essays on Poetry* (Ann Arbor: The University of Michigan Press, 1985) 269–306.

Marianne Shapiro, *Hieroglyph of Time: The Petrarchan Sestina* (Minneapolis: University of Minnesota Press, 1980).

VILLANELLE

Julie Kane, "The Myth of the Fixed-Form Villanelle," *Modern Language Quarterly* 64.4 (December 2003) 427–443.

Ronald E. McFarland, *The Villanelle: The Evolution of a Poetic Form* (Moscow, Idaho: University of Idaho Press, 1987).

OTHER FRENCH FORMS

Helen Louise Cohen, *Lyric Forms from France: Their History and Their Use* (New York: Harcourt, Brace, and Company, 1922).

Clive Scott, "The Nineteenth-Century Triolet: French and English Explorations of a Form," *Orbis Litterarum* 35 (1980) 357–372.

JAPANESE FORMS

Robert Hass, *The Essential Haiku: Versions of Basho, Buson, and Issa* (Hopewell, NJ: Ecco Press, 1994).

Earl Miner, *Japanese Linked Poetry: An Account with Translations of Renga and Haikai Sequences* (Princeton, N.J : Princeton University Press, 1979).

Kenneth Yasuda, *The Japanese Haiku: Its Essential Nature, History, and Possibilities in English* (Rutland, VT: Tuttle, 1957).

OTHER ASIAN FORMS

Ravishing DisUnities: Real Ghazals in English, Agha Shahid Ali, ed. (Hanover, New Hampshire: University Press of New England, 2000).

Agha Shahid Ali, "The Ghazal in America: May I?" *After New Formalism: Poets on Form, Narrative, and Tradition*, Annie Finch, ed. (Ashland, OR: Story Line Press, 1999) 123–132.

CLASSICAL IMITATIONS

Derek Attridge, *Well-Weighed Syllables: Elizabethan Verse in Classical Metres* (London, Cambridge University Press, 1974).

John Hollander, "Observations in the Art of English Quantity," *Vision and Resonance: Two Senses of Poetic Form* (New York: Oxford University Press, 1975) 59–70.

FORMS OF FREE VERSE

T. S. Eliot, "Reflections on Vers Libre," *To Criticize the Critic, and Other Writings* (London: Faber & Faber, 1965) 183–189.

Annie Finch, *The Ghost of Meter: Culture and Prosody in American Free Verse* (Ann Arbor: University of Michigan Press, 1993).

Charles O. Hartman, *Free Verse: An Essay on Prosody* (Princeton, NJ: Princeton University Press, 1980).

H. T. Kirby-Smith, *The Origins of Free Verse* (Ann Arbor: University of Michigan Press, 1996).

Timothy Steele, *Missing Measures: Modern Poetry and the Revolt against Meter* (Fayetteville: University of Arkansas Press, 1990).

PROSE POERTY

Mary Ann Caws and Hermine Riffaterre, eds., *The Prose Poem in France: Theory and Practice* (New York: Columbia University Press, 1983).

Michel Delville, *The American Prose Poem: Poetic Form and the Boundaries of Genre* (Gainesville: University Press of Florida, 1998).

N. Santilli, *Such Rare Citings: the Prose Poem in English literature* (Madison, NJ: Fairleigh Dickinson University Press; London; Cranbury, NJ: Associated University Presses, 2002).

David Lehman, ed., *Great American Prose Poems: from Poe to the Present* (New York: Scribner Poetry, 2003).

NEW FORMS AND OLD

Charles Bernstein, ed., *The Politics of Poetic Form: Poetry and Public Policy* (New York, NY: Roof, 1990).

Marjorie Perloff, *Radical Artifice: Writing Poetry in the Age of Media* (Chicago: University of Chicago Press, 1991).

———, *The Dance of the Intellect: Studies in the Poetry of the Pound Tradition* (New York: Cambridge University Press, 1985).

Rom Silliman, *The New Sentence* (New York: Roof, 1987).

ACKNOWLEDGMENTS

"Running the Deer Songs." From *Yaqui Deer Songs: Maso Bwikam* by Larry Evers and Felipe S. Molina. Copyright © 1987 by The Arizona Board of Regents. Reprinted by permission of the University of Arizona Press.

David Baker, "Works and Days" from *Changeable Thunder*. Copyright © 2001 by David Baker. Reprinted with the permission of the University of Arkansas Press, www.uapress.com.

"Countin' the Blues," Gertrude Rainey." From *Blues Legacies and Black Feminism* by Angela Y. Davis, copyright © 1998 by Angela Y. Davis. Used by permission of Pantheon Books, a division of Random House, Inc.

Three lines of lyrics from The Roots, "The Next Movement," *Things Fall Apart* (MCA, 1999). © 1999 Careers-BMG Music Publishing, Inc. (BMI)/ Grand Negaz Music/ Astral Body Music (BMI). Reprinted by permission.

"Refugee Blues," W. H. Auden. "Refugee Blues", copyright 1940 and renewed 1968 by W. H. Auden, from *Collected Poems* by W. H. Auden. Used by permission of Random House, Inc.

"Chopin," Marilyn Nelson Waniek. Reprinted by permission of Louisiana State University Press from *The Homeplace: Poems* by Marilyn Nelson Waniek. Copyright © 1990 by Marilyn Nelson Waniek.

"Downtown Diner," Jeredith Merrin, Bat Ode. Reprinted by permission.

"Love Letters," Diane Thiel. From *Echolocations*, Diane Thiel. Reprinted by permission of Story Line Press.

"A Miracle for Breakfast," Elizabeth Bishop. From *The Complete Poems 1927–1979*. Reprinted by Farrar, Straus and Giroux, LLC. Copyright © 1979, 1983 by Alice Helen Methfessel.

"Villanelle for D. G. B," Marilyn Hacker. In Presentation Piece "Villanelle". Copyright © 1974 by Marilyn Hacker, *Selected Poems: 1965–1990* by Marilyn Hacker. Used by permission of W. W. Norton & Company, Inc.

"One Art," Elizabeth Bishop. From *The Complete Poems 1927–1979*. Reprinted by Farrar, Straus and Giroux, LLC. Copyright © 1979, 1983 by Alice Helen Methfessel.

"The crack is moving down the wall . . ." from "Five Villanelles," Weldon Kees. Reprinted from *The Collected Poems of Weldon Kees*, edited by Donald Justice, by permission of the University of Nebraska Press. Copyright 1975, by the University of Nebraska Press. © renewed 2003 by the University of Nebraska Press.

"Daughters, 1900", Marilyn Nelson Waniek. Reprinted by permission of Louisiana State University Press from *The Homeplace: Poems* by Marilyn Nelson Waniek. Copyright © 1990 by Marilyn Nelson Waniek.

"Macbeth's Daughter," William Logan. From *Macbeth in Venice* by William Logan, copyright © 2003 by William Logan. Used by permission of Penguin, a division of Penguin Group (USA) Inc.

"Macbeth's Daughter Drowned," William Logan. From *Macbeth in Venice* by William Logan, copyright © 2003 by William Logan. Used by permission of Penguin, a division of Penguin Group (USA) Inc.

"Ballad of the Yale Younger Poets of Yesteryear," R. S. Gwynn. From *No Word of Farewell: Selected Poems 1970–2000*. Reprinted by permission of Story Line Press.

"Haiku," Etheridge Knight. From *Poems from Prison*. By permission of Broadside Press.

Haiku by Basho, translated by Kenneth Yasuda from *The Japanese Haiku: Its Essential Nature, History, and Possibility in English*. Copyright © 1957 by Charles E. Tuttle Co. Used by permission.

"No sky and no earth" by Hashin. From *One Hundred Famous Haiku*, translated by Daniel C. Buchanan, Japanese Publications 1973. Used by permission.

"Come! Come! Though I Call" by Onitsura. From *One Hundred Famous Haiku*, translated by Daniel C. Buchanan, Japanese Publications 1973. Used by permission.

"Letter to Munnsville, NY from Rue de Turenne," from *Squares and Courtyards* by Marilyn Hacker. Copyright © 2000 by Marilyn Hacker. Used by permission of W. W. Norton & Company, Inc.

"Of Fire," from *Call Me Ishmael Tonight: A Book of Ghazals* by Agha Shahid Ali. Copyright © 2003 by Asha Shahid Ali Literary Trust. Used by permission of W. W. Norton & Company, Inc.

"Autumn" by Rachel Wetzsteon. From *Ravishing DisUnities* (Wesleyan University Press, 2000). © 2000 by Rachel Wetzsteon and reprinted by permission of Wesleyan University Press.

"Prayer," by Grace Schulman. From *Ravishing Disunities: Real Ghazal in English* edited by Agha Shahid Ali. Copyright © 2000 by Wesleyan University Press. Used by permission.

"Two Cures for Love," by Wendy Cope. From *Serious Concerns*. Copyright by Wendy Cope. Reprinted by permission of Sll/Sterling Lord Literistic, Inc. and Faber and Faber.

"Their Sex Life," from *The Really Short Poems of A. R. Ammons* by A. R. Ammons. Copyright © 1990 by A. R. Ammons. Used by permission of W. W. Norton Company, Inc.

"The Common Wisdom," by Howard Nemerov, from *The Selected Poems of Howard Nemerov*, Swallow Press. Copyright © 2003 by Howard Nemerov. Used by permission.

"Lip was a man who used his head," "Epitaph for Someone or Other," and "And what is love?" from *Poems of J. V. Cunningham*, Copyright © 1997 Swallow Press. Used by permission.

"Repentance" is taken from *Touchwood* by Dick Davis, published by Anvil Press Poetry in 1996. Used by permission.

"Desire," by Dick Davis. From *Belonging*. Copyright © 2002 by Swallow Press. Used by permission.

"Fatherhood," by Dick Davis. From *A Kind of Love: Selected and New Poems*, University of Arkansas Press. Copyright © 1991 by Dick Davis. Used by permission of the author.

"Sapphics Against Anger," by Timothy Steele. From *Sapphics and Uncertainties: Poems 1970–1986*. Copyright © 1986, 1995 by Timothy Steele. Used by permission of the University of Arkansas Press, ww.uapress.com.

"VII. But to Honor Truth. . . . " From *The Beauty of the Husband* by Anne Carson, copyright © 2001 by Anne Carson. Used by permission of Alfred A. Knopf, a division of Random House, Inc.

"Discrete Series" by George Oppen. From *New Collected Poems*. Copyright © 2002 by New Directions Publishing Corporation. Used by permission.

"My Life," Lyn Hejinian. Excerpts from Lyn Hejinian's *My Life* (revised edition), Green Integer Books/Sun and Moon Press, selections 1 and 26, pages 7–8, 67–68. Copyright © 1987 by Lyn Hejinian. Reprinted with the permission of Green Integer Books, Los Angeles.

"A Story About the Body," Robert Hass. From *Human Wishes*. "A Story About the Body" by Robert Hass. Copyright © 1989 by Robert Hass. Reprinted by permission of HarperCollins Publishers Inc.

"Manifesto," Edwin Morgan. From *Collected Poems of Edwin Morgan*. Reprinted by permission.

"AID/I/SAPPEARANCE" Joan Retallack. From *How to Do Things With Words*, Green Integer Books/Sun and Moon Press. Copyright © 1998 by Joan Retallack. Reprinted with the permission of Green Integer Books, Los Angeles.

"The Beautician," Thom Gunn. From *Collected Poems* by Thom Gunn. Reprinted by Farrar, Straus and Giroux. Copyright © 1994 by Thom Gunn. From *Collected Poems* by Thom Gunn. Reprinted by Faber & Faber. Copyright © 1994 by Thom Gunn.

INDEX